OFFICIAL
BLUE BOOK OF UNITED STATES COINS ®

1993
HANDBOOK
OF
UNITED STATES
COINS

With Premium List

By R. S. YEOMAN

★

FIFTIETH EDITION

Edited by Kenneth Bressett

Containing mint records and prices paid by dealers for all U.S. coins from 1616 to the present time, including Colonials, Regular Issues, Commemoratives, Territorials, Gold, Proof Sets, and Mint Sets. Information on collecting coins—how coins are produced—mints and mint marks—grading of coins—location of mint marks—preserving and cleaning coins—starting a collection—history of mints and interesting descriptions of all U.S. copper, nickel, silver and gold coins. Fully illustrated.

Whitman Coin Products

WESTERN PUBLISHING COMPANY, INC.
RACINE, WISCONSIN 53404

9050-93 **ISBN: 0-307-19897-9** **Printed in U.S.A.**

Important Notice

THIS BOOK IS *NOT A RETAIL PRICE LIST*

Premium prices are the average amount dealers will pay for coins (according to condition) if required for their stock.

IF YOU HAVE COINS TO SELL

The publisher of this book is not in the rare coin business; however, the chances are that the dealer from whom you purchased this book is engaged in the buying and selling of rare coins—contact him first. In the event that you purchased this book from a source other than a numismatic establishment, consult your local telephone directory for the names of coin dealers (they will be found sometimes under the heading of "Stamp and Coin Dealers"). If you live in a city or town that does not have any coin dealers, it is suggested that you obtain a copy of one of the trade publications in order to obtain the names and addresses of many of the country's leading dealers.

The following numismatic magazines are obtainable by subscription. They are published monthly or as indicated below. Information or sample copies may be obtained by writing to the individual publisher.

COINage Magazine
2660 E. Main St.
Ventura, California 93003

Coins Magazine
700 E. State Street
Iola, Wisconsin 54990

Numismatic News (Weekly)
700 E. State Street
Iola, Wisconsin 54990

Coin World (Weekly)
P.O. Box 150
Sidney, Ohio 45367

The Numismatist
818 North Cascade Ave.
Colorado Springs, Colorado 80903
(Published monthly by American Numismatic Assn.)

Current *retail* valuations of all U.S. coins are listed in Whitman's A GUIDE BOOK OF UNITED STATES COINS by R. S. Yeoman, Western Publishing Company, Inc., Racine, Wisconsin. ($9.95 Hard Cover; $6.95 Soft Cover)

Brief guides to grading are placed before each major coin type in this book. For those readers who desire more detailed descriptions of all coin grades, we recommend OFFICIAL A.N.A. GRADING STANDARDS FOR UNITED STATES COINS, Western Publishing Company, Inc., Racine, Wisconsin ($10.95).

Foreword

Since 1941, annually revised editions of this Handbook have aided thousands of people who have coins to sell or are actively engaged in collecting United States coins. The popular coin folder method of collecting by date has created ever-changing premium values, based on the supply and demand of each date and mint. Through its panel of contributors the Handbook has, over the years, reported these changing values. It also serves as a source of general numismatic information to all levels of interest in the hobby.

The premium list gives representative prices paid by dealers for various United States coins. These are averages of prices assembled from many widely separated sources. On some issues slight differences in price among dealers may result from proximity to the various mints or heavily populated centers. Other factors, such as local supply and demand or dealers' stock conditions, may also tend to cause deviations from the prices listed. While many coins bring no premium when circulated, they usually bring premium prices in Uncirculated and Proof condition.

The publisher of this book does not deal in coins; therefore, the values shown here are not offers to purchase (or sell) but are included only as general information.

CONTRIBUTORS

Lee F. Hewitt, the former editor and publisher of the NUMISMATIC SCRAPBOOK MAGAZINE, was an early contributor, having supplied many of the historical references and explanations which appear throughout this book.

Charles E. Green gave valuable counsel when the first edition of the HANDBOOK was undertaken. He supplied most of the original mint data and was a regular contributor to each revised edition until his death in 1955.

CONTRIBUTORS TO THE FIFTIETH EDITION

Kerry Emmrich — *Project Coordinator*

Gary Adkins
Professional Numismatic Services
14760 Pennock Avenue
Apple Valley, MN 55124

Tony Adkins

Robert F. Batchelder
Robert F. Batchelder Company
1 West Butler Avenue
Ambler, PA 19002

Gerald L. Bauman
New York Rare Coin Corp.
2420 Ralph Ave., Suite 119
Brooklyn, NY 11234

Philip E. Benedetti

George H. Blenker
Rice Lake, WI 54868

Phil Bressett
2722 16th Street
Racine, WI 53405

Hy Brown
P.O. Box 1269
Mentor, OH 44061-1269

Bill Causey
American Gold & Silver Corp.
780 East Foothill Blvd.
Suite D-7
Upland, CA 91786

J. H. Cline
P.O. Box 68
Palm Harbor, FL 34682

Tom Culhane
The Elusive Spondulix
954 A Stuyvesant Avenue
Union, NJ 07083

Marc A. Dixon
Hindsight Financial
907 South A. Street
Arkansas City, KS 67005

Henry G. Garrett
P.O. Box 4334
Valley Village Station
No. Hollywood, CA 91607-0334

William G. Gay

Dorothy Gershenson

Ira M. Goldberg

Lawrence S. Goldberg

Kenneth M. Goldman
P.O. Box 404
Needham, MA 02192

Paul H. Grosz

James L. Halperin
Heritage Rare Coin Galleries
Heritage Plaza
Highland Park Village
Dallas, Texas 75205-3500

Gene L. Henry

John W. Highfill
Oklahoma Federated Gold &
Numismatics, Inc.
P.O. Box 25
Broken Arrow, OK 74013-0025

Karl D. Hirtzinger

Jesse Iskowitz
Numismatic Investments
Chattanooga, TN

Robert H. Jacobs
c/o Jakes Marketplace, Inc.
2955 N. Central Avenue
Chicago, IL 60634

Floyd O. Janney

A.M. Kagin
Kagin's Numismatic Investment Corp.
910 Insurance Exchange Building
Des Moines, IA 50309

Donald H. Kagin
Marin Numismatics
98 Main Street #201
Triburon, CA 94920

Paul S. Kagin
Des Moines, IA

Bradley S. Karoleff
Coins +
2092 Mall Road
Florence, KY 41042

Stanley Kesselman

Jerry Kimmell
P.O. Box 45
Avon Lake, OH 44012

Mike Kliman

Abner Kreisberg

Denis W. Loring

Virg Marshall III, Inc.
116 West D
Wymore, NE 68466

Robert T. McIntire
McIntire Rare Coins, Inc.
27 Crestview Plaza
Jacksonville, AR 72076-0546

Glenn Miller
P.O. Box 1106
Boston, MA 02103

Michael C. Moline
Advance Coin
Beverly Hills, CA 90210

Sylvia Novack
San Bernardino, CA

Sidney L. Nusbaum
Arch City Supply Company
P.O. Box 13490
St. Louis, MO 63138

William S. Panitch
855 Central Avenue, Suite 103
Albany, NY 12206

Robert M. Paul
315 South Street
Philadelphia, PA 19147

William P. Paul

Joel D. Rettew
P.O. Box 8604
Newport Beach, CA 92658

Leonard R. Saunders

Gerald R. Scherer, Jr.
Silvertowne

J.S. Schreiber
Omaha, NE

Robert R. Shaw

James A. Simek

Thomas J. Smith
Chicago, IL

William J. Spencer
American Coin & Stamp Supply, Inc.
2724 Sixteenth Street
Racine, WI 53405

Maurice A. Storck
P.O. Box 644
Portland, ME 04104-0644

Charles Surasky
Gold & Silver Emporium
15760 Ventura Blvd., #110
Encino, CA 91436

COLLECTING COINS

Numismatics or coin collecting is one of the world's oldest hobbies, dating back several centuries. Coin collecting in America did not develop to any extent until about 1840, as our pioneer forefathers were too busy carving a country out of wilderness to afford the luxury of a hobby. The discontinuance of the large-sized cent in 1857 caused many persons to attempt to accumulate a complete set of the pieces while they were still in circulation. One of the first groups of collectors to band together for the study of numismatics was the Numismatic and Antiquarian Society of Philadelphia, organized on January 1, 1858. Lack of an economical method to house a collection held the number of devotees of coin collecting to a few thousand until the Whitman Publishing Company and other manufacturers placed the low-priced coin boards and folders on the market some years ago. Since that time the number of Americans collecting coins has increased many-fold.

The Production of Coins

To collect coins intelligently it is necessary to have some knowledge of the manner in which our coins are produced. They are made in factories called "mints." The Mint of the United States was established at Philadelphia by a resolution of Congress dated April 2, 1792. The Act also provided for the coinage of gold eagles ($10), half-eagles and quarter-eagles, the silver dollar, half-dollar, quarter-dollar, dime (originally spelled "disme") and the half-disme or half-dime; the copper cent and half cent. According to the Treasury Department, the first coins struck were one-cent and half-cent pieces, in March of 1793 on a hand-operated press. Most numismatic authorities consider the half-disme of 1792 as the first United States coinage, quoting the words of George Washington as their authority. Washington, in his annual address, November 6, 1792, having said, "There has been a small beginning in the coining of the Half-Dimes, the want of small coins in circulation calling the first attention to them." In the new Philadelphia Mint are exhibited a number of implements, etc., from the original mint, and some coins discovered when the old building was wrecked. These coins included half-dismes, and the placard identifying them states that Washington furnished the silver and gave the coined pieces to his friends as souvenirs.

Prior to the adoption of the Constitution, the Continental Congress arranged for the issuance of copper coins under private contract. These are known as the "Fugio cents" from the design of the piece, which shows a sundial and the Latin word "fugio"—"I Fly" or, in connection with the sundial, "Time Flies." The ever appropriate motto, "Mind Your Business," is also on the coin.

In the manufacture of a given coin the first step is the cutting of the "die." Prior to the latter part of the nineteenth century dies for United States coins were "cut by hand." Briefly this method is as follows: The design having been determined, a drawing the exact size of the coin is made. A tracing is made from this drawing. A piece of steel is smoothed and coated with transfer wax, and the tracing impressed into the wax. The engraver then tools out the steel where the relief or raised effect is required. If the design is such that it can all be produced by cutting away steel, the die is hardened and ready for use. Some dies are not brought to a finished state, as some part of the design can perhaps be done better in relief. In that case, when all that can be accomplished to advantage in the die is completed, it is hardened, a soft-steel impression is taken from it, and the unfinished parts are then completed. This piece of steel is in turn hardened and, by a press, driven into another piece of soft-steel, thus making a die which, when hardened, is ready for the making of coins.

This hand method of cutting dies accounts for the many die varieties of early United States coins. Where the amount of coinage of a given year was large enough to wear out several dies, each new die placed in the coining press created another die variety of that year. The dies being cut by hand, no two were exactly alike in every detail, even though some of the major elements (head, wreath, etc.) were sunk into the die by individual master punches. Of the cents dated 1794, over sixty different die varieties have been discovered.

Hundreds of dies are now used by the mints of the United States each year, but they are all made from one master die, which is produced in the following manner:

After the design is settled upon, the plaster of paris or wax model is prepared several times the actual size of the coin. When this model is finished an electrotype (an exact duplicate in metal) is made and prepared for the reducing lathe. The reducing lathe is a machine, working on the principle of the pantograph, only in this case the one point traces or follows the form of the model while another and much smaller point in the form of a drill cuts away the steel and produces a reduced size die of the model. The die is finished and details are sharpened or worked over by an engraver with chisel and graver. The master die is used to make duplicates in soft-steel which are then hardened and ready for the coining press. To harden dies, they are placed in cast-iron boxes packed with carbon to exclude the air, and when heated to a bright red are cooled suddenly with water.

In the coinage operations the first step is to prepare the metal. Alloys that have been used are: silver coins, 90% silver and 10% copper; five-cent pieces, 75% copper and 25% nickel; one-cent pieces, 95% copper and 5% zinc. (The 1943 cent consists of steel coated with zinc; and the five-cent piece 1942-1945 contains 35% silver, 56% copper and 9% manganese.) Under the Coinage Act of 1965, the composition of dimes, quarters and half dollars was changed to eliminate or reduce the silver content of these coins. The copper-nickel "clad" dimes, quarters, halves and dollars are composed of an outer layer of copper-nickel (75% copper and 25% nickel) bonded to an inner core of pure copper. The silver clad half dollar and dollar have an outer layer of 80% silver bonded to an inner core of 21% silver, with a total content of 40% silver. Current cents are made from a core of 99.2% zinc, 0.8% copper, with a plating of pure copper.

Alloys are melted in crucibles and poured into molds to form ingots. The ingots are in the form of thin bars and vary in size according to the denomination of the coin. The width is sufficient to allow three or more coins to be cut from the strips.

The ingots are next put through rolling mills to reduce the thickness to required limits. The strips are then fed into cutting presses which cut circular blanks (planchets) of the approximate size of the finished coin. The blanks are run through annealing furnaces to soften them; next through tumbling barrels, rotating cylinders containing cleaning solutions which clean and burnish the metal, and finally into centrifugal drying machines.

The blanks are next fed into a milling machine which produces the raised or upset rim. The blank is now ready for the coining press.

The blank is held firmly by a collar, as it is struck under heavy pressure varying from 40 tons for the one-cent pieces and dimes to 170 tons for silver dollars. Upper and lower dies impress the design on both sides of the coin. The pressure is sufficient to produce a raised surface level with that of the milled rim. The collar holding the blank for silver or clad coins is grooved. The pressure forces the metal into the grooves of the collar, producing the "reeding" on the finished coin.

How a Proof Coin Is Made

Selected dies are inspected for perfection and are highly polished and cleaned. They are again wiped clean or polished after every 15 to 25 impressions and are replaced frequently to avoid imperfections from worn dies. Coinage blanks are polished and cleaned to assure high quality in striking. They are then hand fed into the coinage press one at a time, each blank receiving two blows from the dies to bring up sharp, high relief details. The coinage operation is done at slow speed with extra pressure. Finished proofs are individually inspected and are handled by gloves or tongs. They also receive a final inspection by packers before being sonically sealed in special plastic cases.

Certain coins, including Lincoln cents, Buffalo nickels, Quarter Eagles, Half Eagles, Eagles and Double Eagles, between the years 1908 and 1916 were made with a matte or sandblast surface. Matte proofs have a dull frosted surface which was either applied to the dies, or produced by special treatment after striking.

Mints and Mint Marks

In addition to the Philadelphia Mint, the U.S. Government has from time to time established branch mints in various parts of the country. At the present time a branch mint operates in Denver. Starting in 1968, proof sets and some of the regular coins are produced at the San Francisco Assay Office. The Denver Mint has operated since 1906. A mint was operated at New Orleans from 1838 to 1861 and again from 1879 to 1909. Mints were also in service at Carson City, Nevada, from 1870 to 1893; at Charlotte, North Carolina, from 1838 to 1861; at Dahlonega, Georgia, from 1838 to 1861; and at San Francisco since 1854.

Coins struck at Philadelphia before 1979 (except 1942 to 1945 five-cent pieces) do not carry a mint mark. The mint mark is found only on coins struck at the branch mints. It is a small letter, usually found on the reverse side. The Lincoln cent is one exception to the rule. All coins minted after 1967 have the mint mark on the obverse. The letters to signify the various mints are as follows:

"C" for Charlotte, North Carolina (on gold coins only).
"CC" for Carson City, Nevada.
"D" for Dahlonega, Georgia (gold coins only, 1838 to 1861).
"D" For Denver, Colorado (from 1906 to date).
"O" for New Orleans, Louisiana.
"P" for Philadelphia, Pennsylvania.
"S" for San Francisco, California.
"W" for West Point, New York.

The mint mark is of utmost importance to collectors due to the fact that the coinage at the branch mints has usually been much smaller than at Philadelphia and many of the early branch mint pieces are very scarce.

DISTINGUISHING MARKS

The illustrations and explanations in this section will help the collector to identify certain well-known varieties.

HALF CENTS OF
1795-1796
SHOWING LOCATION OF
POLE TO CAP

The end of the staff or pole lies parallel with the line of the bust, which is pointed. The die-maker, probably through error, omitted the pole on some of the dies of 1795 and 1796.

Pole to Cap

No Pole to Cap

STEMLESS WREATH VARIETY OF HALF CENTS AND LARGE CENTS

Observe the reverse side for this variety. Illustrations at left show both stemless and stems to wreath types for each comparison—stemless wreath found on 1804, 1805, 1806, Half cents. 1797, 1802, 1803 Large cents.

Stemless Wreath

Stems to Wreath

1804 HALF CENT PROTRUDING TONGUE OR SPIKED CHIN VARIETY

DISTINGUISHING MARKS

Details showing differences in 1804 plain 4 and crosslet 4. Note serif on horizontal bar of figure 4 as shown at right.

Plain 4

Crosslet 4

THE 1856 FLYING EAGLE CENT

Collectors are advised to inspect any 1856 Flying Eagle cent carefully.

A few tests will aid in establishing genuineness of this cent, as follows:

THE DATE

The 6 in the date should be as illustrated. If the lower half is thick, it is probably an altered 1858. A magnifying glass will often reveal poor workmanship.

The figure 5 slants slightly to the right on a genuine 1856. The vertical bar points to the center of the ball just beneath. On the 1858, this bar points *outside* the ball. (Compare the two illustrations.)

THE LEGEND

The center of the O in OF is crude and almost squared on the genuine 1856, but on the large letter 1858 it is rounded.

The letters A and M in America are joined in both the 1856 and large letter 1858, but they join at a slight angle on the 1856, while the bottom of the letters form a smooth curve on the 1858 large letter cent.

1858 FLYING EAGLE CENT

Large Letters

Letters A and M in the word AMERICA are joined on the LARGE LETTER variety. They are separated on the SMALL LETTER variety.

Small Letters

1864 BRONZE INDIAN HEAD CENT WITH "L" ON RIBBON

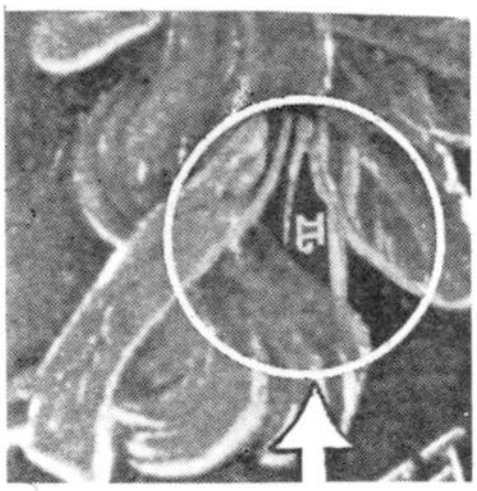

A small "L," the initial of the designer Longacre, was added to the Indian design late in 1864 and was continued through 1909. For coins in less than fine condition, this small letter will often be worn away. The point of the bust is rounded on the 1864 variety without "L"; pointed on the variety with "L." The initial must be visible, however, for the 1864 variety to bring the higher premium. If the coin is turned slightly so that the Indian faces the observer, the highlighted details will usually appear to better advantage.

DISTINGUISHING MARKS

During 1909 initials appeared on reverse. Starting in 1918 they appear below the shoulder.

1918-S Quarter
8 Over 7
A variety of this kind is rarely found in coinage of the twentieth century.

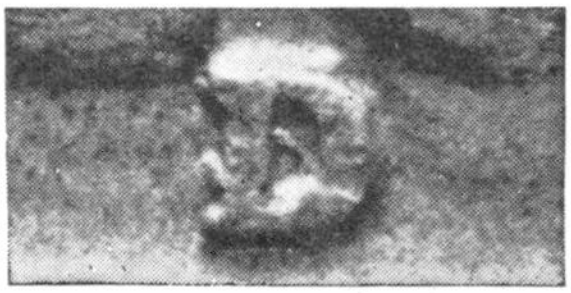

1938D over S Nickel Variety

1942 Dime with 2 over 1

1955 Cent Error
"Doubled Die" Obverse

Large Date Cent
1960

Small Date Cent
1960

Large Date Cent
1982

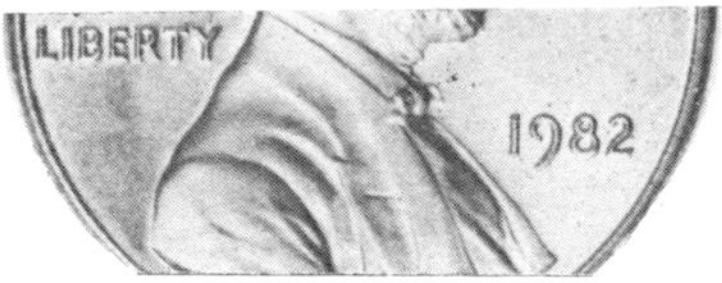

Small Date Cent
1982

CONDITION OF COINS

Essential elements of the A.N.A. grading system

PROOF — A specially made coin distinguished by sharpness of detail and usually with a brilliant mirrorlike surface. Proof refers to the method of manufacture and is not a condition, but normally the term implies perfect mint state unless otherwise noted and graded as below. See page 40 for details.

MINT STATE — The terms Mint State (MS) and Uncirculated (Unc.) are interchangeably used to describe coins showing no trace of wear. Such coins may vary to some degree because of blemishes, toning or slight imperfections as described in the following subdivisions.

UNCIRCULATED (MS-70) — Perfect new condition, showing no trace of wear. The finest quality possible, with no evidence of scratches, handling or contact with other coins. Very few regular issue coins are ever found in this condition.

UNCIRCULATED (MS-65) — An above average Uncirculated coin which may be brilliant or lightly toned and has very few contact marks on the surface or rim. MS-67 or MS-63 indicates a slightly higher or lower grade of preservation.

UNCIRCULATED (MS-60) — Has no trace of wear but may show a number of contact marks, and surface may be spotted or lack some luster.

CHOICE ABOUT UNCIRCULATED (AU-55) — Barest evidence of light wear on only the highest points of the design. Most of the mint luster remains.

ABOUT UNCIRCULATED (AU-50) — Has traces of light wear on many of the high points. At least half of the mint luster is still present.

CHOICE EXTREMELY FINE (EF-45) — Light overall wear shows on highest points. All design details are very sharp. Some of the mint luster is evident.

EXTREMELY FINE (EF-40) — Design is lightly worn throughout, but all features are sharp and well-defined. Traces of luster may show.

CHOICE VERY FINE (VF-30) — Light even wear on the surface and highest parts of the design. All lettering and major features are sharp.

VERY FINE (VF-20) — Shows moderate wear on high points of design. All major details are clear.

FINE (F-12) — Moderate to considerable even wear. Entire design is bold with overall pleasing appearance.

VERY GOOD (VG-8) — Well worn with main features clear and bold although rather flat.

GOOD (G-4) — Heavily worn with design visible but faint in areas. Many details are flat.

ABOUT GOOD (AG-3) — Very heavily worn with portions of lettering, date and legends worn smooth. The date may be barely readable.

IMPORTANT: Damaged coins, such as those which are bent, corroded, scratched, holed, nicked, stained, or mutilated, are worth less than those without defects. *Flawless uncirculated coins are generally worth more than values quoted in this book.* Slightly worn coins ("sliders") which have been cleaned and conditioned ("whizzed") to simulate uncirculated luster are worth considerably less than perfect pieces.

Unlike damage inflicted after striking, manufacturing defects do not always lessen values. Examples are: Colonial coins with planchet flaws and weakly struck designs; early silver and gold with weight adjustment "file marks" (parallel cuts made prior to striking); and pieces with "lint marks" (dust or other foreign matter which may mar the surface during striking).

Brief guides to grading are placed before each major coin type in this book. For those readers who desire more detailed descriptions of all coin grades, we recommend OFFICIAL A.N.A. GRADING STANDARDS FOR UNITED STATES COINS, by the American Numismatic Association.

Preserving and Cleaning Coins

Most numismatists will tell you to "never clean a coin" and it is good advice! Cleaning coins will almost always reduce their value.

Some effort should be made to keep uncirculated and proof coins bright so they won't need cleaning. Tarnish on a coin is purely a chemical process caused by oxygen in the air acting on the metal or by chemicals with which the coin comes in contact. One of the commonest chemicals causing tarnish is sulphur; most paper, with the exception of specially manufactured "sulphur-free" kinds, contains sulphur due to the sulphuric acid that is used in paper manufacture. Therefore do not wrap coins in ordinary paper; also keep uncirculated and proof coins away from rubber bands (a rubber band placed on a silver coin for a few days will produce a black stripe on the coin where the band touched). The utmost in protection is obtained by storing the coin in an airtight box.

Many coins become marred by careless handling. Always hold the coin by the edge. The accompanying illustration shows the right and wrong way to handle numismatic specimens. It is a breach of numismatic etiquette to handle another collector's coin except by the edge, even if it is not an uncirculated or proof piece.

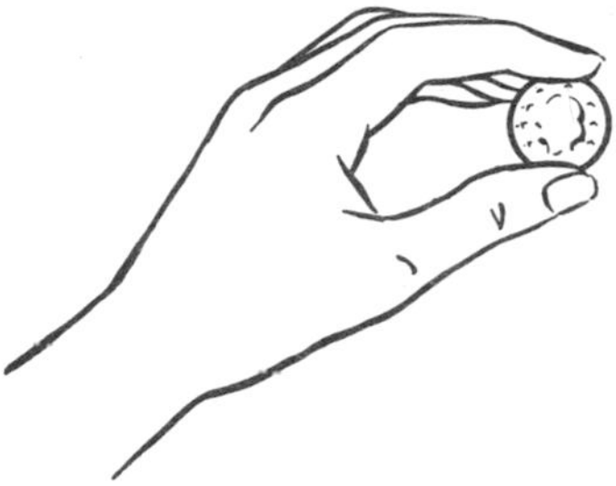

RIGHT

WRONG

Starting a Collection

One may start a collection of United States coins with very little expense by systematically assembling the various dates and mint marks of all the types and denominations that are now in general circulation. Whitman's coin folders make this possible.

With the exception of the price paid for the coin folder, collecting coins received in everyday business transactions entails no expense whatever; a Jefferson nickel taken out of circulation, for example, can always be spent for 5 cents if the occasion arises. Filling an album or two out of circulation is probably the best method of determining whether coin collecting appeals to you. Not everyone can be a successful coin collector. It requires patience, intelligence of a high order, and a certain desire to know the meaning behind a lot of things that at first glance and to the ordinary person appear meaningless. You may not be cut out to be a collector but you'll never know until you look further into the subject, and if by the time an album or two of coins are collected you have no burning desire to acquire many more different coins, you will probably never be a collector. However, the chances are that you will be, because if you have read this far in this book it shows that you are interested in the subject.

Perfection is the goal of every endeavor and coin collecting is no exception. After an album has been filled with circulated specimens, the next step will be to replace them with coins in uncirculated condition, or perhaps to start collecting an obsolete series; in either case, it will be necessary to purchase some coins from dealers or other collectors. The most logical way to keep abreast with the market, or obtain the addresses of the country's leading dealers, is to subscribe to one or more of the trade publications (see page 2 for list of the coin publications). These magazines carry advertisements of various dealers listing coins for sale. Moreover, through this source the beginner may obtain price lists and catalogs from the dealers.

There are several good reference books available at reasonable prices which will be helpful to the collector who wishes to know more about U. S. coins and paper money. R. S. Yeoman's A GUIDE BOOK OF UNITED STATES COINS (Red Book) is an expanded version of THE HANDBOOK. It lists retail values of all regular U. S. coins and also lists all coins of the U. S. Colonial period and private and territorial gold coins.

Most coin, book and hobby dealers can supply the following titles:

A Guide Book of U.S. Coins — Yeoman
Let's Collect Coins — Bressett
Official Grading Standards for U.S. Coins — A.N.A.
Common Sense Coin Investment — Bowers
Basics of Coin Grading — Bressett
Coins, Questions and Answers — Mishler
United States Coin Price Trends — Bressett and Bowers

Join a Coin Club

A beginner should join a "coin club" if he is fortunate enough to live in a city which has one. The association with more experienced collectors will be of great benefit. Practically all the larger cities have one or more clubs and they are being rapidly organized in the smaller towns. The publications mentioned on page 2 carry information about coin clubs and special events such as coin shows and conventions.

UNITED STATES PAPER MONEY

Paper money issued by the United States government is collected widely in this country. The first issue of "greenbacks" was made in 1861; paper money was not issued by our government for circulation prior to that date. Collectors of U.S. notes prefer them in crisp, new condition; but the old style large-sized notes even in worn condition are usually worth more than face value.

Before the issuance of the first U.S. government paper money, many banks throughout the country issued their own currency. These issues are commonly referred to as "broken bank notes" although that is somewhat of a misnomer as many of the banks did not "go broke" (a few are still in existence) and redeemed their paper money issues. There are thousands of varieties of these notes in existence, most of which are very common and worth from $2.00 to $5.00 each. Before and during the American Revolution the various individual states and the Continental Congress issued paper money. The common varieties of these Colonial notes are worth from $3.00 to $10.00; a few are quite rare.

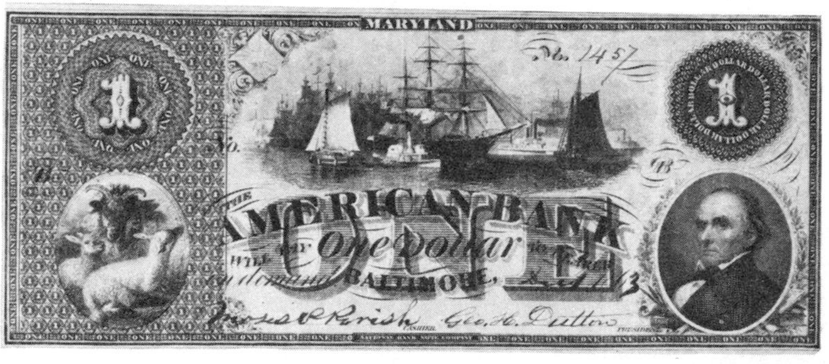

"Broken Bank" note of 1863

I. THE BRITISH COLONIES IN AMERICA

SOMMER ISLANDS (Bermuda)

This coinage, the first struck for the English colonies in America, was issued about 1616. The coins were known as "Hogge Money" or "Hoggies."

The pieces were made of copper lightly silvered, in four denominations: shilling, sixpence, threepence and twopence, indicated by Roman numerals. The hog is the main device and appears on the obverse side of each. SOMMER ISLANDS is inscribed within beaded circles. The reverse shows a full-rigged galleon with the flag of St. George on each of four masts.

Shilling

	Good	V. Good	Fine	V. Fine
Twopence	$950.00	$1,600	$2,600	$4,500
Threepence (V. Rare)	——	——	——	——
Sixpence	750.00	1,200	1,900	2,750
Shilling	950.00	1,400	2,300	4,000

MASSACHUSETTS

"NEW ENGLAND" COINAGE (1652)

In 1652 the General Court of Massachusetts ordered the first metallic currency to be struck in the English Americas, the New England silver threepence, sixpence, and shilling. These coins were made from silver bullion procured principally from the West Indies. Joseph Jenks made the punches for the first coins at his Iron Works in Saugus, Massachusetts, close to Boston where the mint was located. John Hull was appointed mintmaster; his assistant was Robert Sanderson.

Note: Early American coins are rare in conditions better than listed and valued much higher.

NE Shilling (1652)

	V. Good	Fine	V. Fine
NE Threepence *(2 known)*	——	——	——
NE Sixpence *(7 known)*	——	——	$30,000
NE Shilling	$2,750	$6,000	13,000

MASSACHUSETTS

WILLOW TREE COINAGE (1653-1660)

The simplicity of the design on the N.E. coins invited counterfeiting and clipping of the edges. Therefore, they were soon replaced by the Willow, Oak and Pine Tree series. The Willow Tree coins were struck from 1653 to 1660, the Oak Trees 1660 to 1667, and the Pine Trees 1667 to 1682. All of them (with the exception of the Oak Tree twopence) bore the date 1652.

Many varieties of all of these coins exist. Values shown are for the most common types.

Sixpence

	Fair	Good	Fine
Willow Tree Threepence 1652 *(3 known)*.	—	—	—
Willow Tree Sixpence 1652	—	—	—
Willow Tree Shilling 1652	$1,700	$3,500	$8,000

OAK TREE COINAGE (1660-1667)

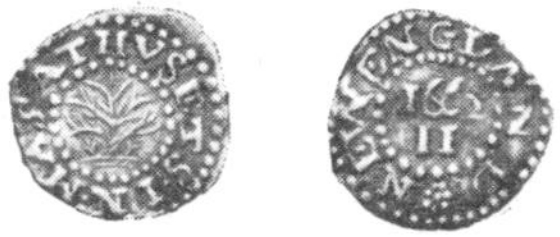

Twopence

Threepence

	Good	V. Good	Fine	V. Fine
Oak Tree Twopence 1662...............	$125.00	$225.00	$500.00	$1,000
Oak Tree Threepence 1652	145.00	350.00	600.00	1,550
Oak Tree Sixpence 1652...............	140.00	300.00	600.00	1,550
Oak Tree Shilling 1652................	140.00	300.00	600.00	1,600

PINE TREE COINAGE (1667-1682)

The first pine tree coins were minted on the same size planchets as the Oak Tree pieces. Subsequent issues of the shilling were narrower and thicker to conform to the size of English coins.

Shilling,
Large Planchet
(1667-1674)

MASSACHUSETTS
PINE TREE COINAGE (1667-1682)

Shilling,
Small Planchet
(1675-1682)

	Good	*V. Good*	*Fine*	*V. Fine*
Pine Tree Threepence 1652	$100.00	$215.00	$350.00	$750.00
Pine Tree Sixpence 1652	125.00	225.00	375.00	850.00
Pine Tree Shilling, large planchet 1652	175.00	300.00	475.00	1,000
Pine Tree Shilling, small planchet 1652	150.00	250.00	425.00	900.00

MARYLAND

In 1658 Cecil Calvert, the "Lord Proprietor of Maryland," had coinage struck in England for use in Maryland.

There were four denominations: shillings, sixpence, and fourpence (groat) in silver, and a copper penny (denarium). The silver coins have the bust of Lord Baltimore on the obverse, and the Baltimore family Arms with the denomination in Roman numerals on the reverse.

Lord Baltimore Shilling

Fourpence (groat)

	Good	*V. Good*	*Fine*	*V. Fine*
Penny (Copper) (Ex. Rare)	—	—	—	—
Fourpence	$450.00	$800.00	$2,000	$3,750
Sixpence	425.00	600.00	1,500	2,200
Shilling	500.00	900.00	2,000	3,750

NEW JERSEY
ST. PATRICK OR MARK NEWBY COINAGE

Mark Newby, who came to America from Dublin, Ireland, in November 1681, brought copper pieces believed by numismatists to have been struck in England c. 1670-1675. These are called St. Patrick coppers.

The coin received wide currency in the New Jersey Province, having been authorized to pass as legal tender by the General Assembly in May 1682.

The smaller piece, known as a farthing, was never specifically authorized for circulation in the Colonies.

NEW JERSEY

St. Patrick Farthing

	V. Good	Fine	V. Fine
St. Patrick "Farthing"	$40.00	$75.00	$250.00
St. Patrick "Halfpenny"	60.00	100.00	285.00

II. COINAGE AUTHORIZED BY ROYAL PATENT

AMERICAN PLANTATIONS TOKEN

These tokens struck in nearly pure tin were the first authorized coinage for the British colonies in America. They were made under a franchise granted in 1688 to Richard Holt. Restrikes were made c. 1828 from original dies. These are valued at about half as much as the originals.

	Fine	E. Fine	Unc.
(1688) James II Plantation Token farthing, 1/24 PART REAL — Tin	$135.00	$250.00	$800.00

COINAGE OF WILLIAM WOOD

ROSA AMERICANA COINS

William Wood, an Englishman, obtained a patent from George I to make tokens for Ireland and the American Colonies.

The Rosa Americana pieces were issued in three denominations, halfpenny, penny and twopence, and were intended for use in America.

Penny

ROSA AMERICANA

	V. Good	Fine	V. Fine	E. Fine
Twopence (no date)	$25.00	$80.00	$175.00	$300.00
1722 Halfpenny DEI GRATIS REX UTILE DULCI	22.00	60.00	90.00	200.00
1722 Penny	20.00	50.00	85.00	175.00
1722 Twopence	50.00	90.00	150.00	275.00

Halfpenny

1723 Halfpenny	20.00	70.00	100.00	200.00

Twopence

1723 Penny	20.00	70.00	100.00	200.00
1723 Twopence (illustrated)	40.00	80.00	150.00	300.00

WOOD'S HIBERNIA COINAGE

The type intended for Ireland had a seated figure with a harp on the reverse side and the word HIBERNIA. Denominations struck were halfpenny and farthing with dates 1722, 1723 and 1724. Hibernia coins were unpopular in Ireland, so many of them were sent to the American colonies.

1722 Hibernia Halfpenny — First Type — Second Type

	V. Good	V. Fine	E. Fine
1722 Farthing (2nd type)		$125.00	$250.00
1722 Halfpenny (1st or 2nd type)	$12.00	35.00	120.00

WOOD'S HIBERNIA COINAGE

1723 Hibernia Farthing

1724 Hibernia Halfpenny

	V. Good	*V. Fine*	*E. Fine*
1723 Farthing	$9.00	$22.00	$85.00
1723 Halfpenny....................................	9.00	20.00	80.00
1724 Farthing	18.00	35.00	110.00
1724 Halfpenny....................................	15.00	25.00	100.00

VIRGINIA HALFPENNY

In 1773 coinage of a copper halfpenny was authorized for Virginia by the English Crown. The style is similar to the regular English coinage. These pieces were never popular, but did circulate by necessity.

	V. Good	*V. Fine*	*Unc.*
1773 Halfpenny....................................	$15.00	$32.00	$325.00

III. EARLY AMERICAN TOKENS

Struck in America or England for use by American Merchants

LONDON ELEPHANT TOKENS

Struck c. 1672-1684 during the reign of Charles II, the London Token, an early historian states, was produced during the great plague raging in London. The legend on this piece relates directly to that crisis. It has also been stated that the London

LONDON ELEPHANT TOKENS

Token was to have been current in Tangier, Africa, but was never used in that locality. No date appears on this token.

It is unlikely that many ever circulated in America. They are associated with the 1694 pieces through use of a common obverse die.

	V. Good	Fine	V. Fine	E. Fine
(1680) Halfpenny GOD PRESERVE LONDON (Thick or thin planchet)	$38.00	$65.00	$150.00	$450.00

CAROLINA AND NEW ENGLAND ELEPHANT TOKENS

Although no law is known authorizing coinage for Carolina, very interesting pieces known as Elephant Tokens were made with the date 1694. These copper tokens were of halfpenny denomination. The reverse reads GOD PRESERVE CAROLINA AND THE LORDS PROPRIETERS. 1694.

The Carolina pieces were probably struck in England and perhaps intended only as tokens, or possibly as advertising to heighten interest in the Carolina Plantation.

Like the Carolina Tokens, the New England Elephant Tokens were believed to have been struck in England as a promotional piece to increase interest in the American Colonies.

	V. Good	Fine
1694 CAROLINA.	$550.00	$1,800

NEW ENGLAND ELEPHANT TOKEN

1694 NEW ENGLAND	9,500

THE NEW YORKE TOKEN

Little is known about the origin of this token. The design of displayed eagle on a regulated staff with oak leaf finials is identical to the crest found on the arms of William Lovelace, governor of New York 1663-1673. It seems likely that this piece is a token farthing struck by Lovelace for use in New York. Dies were possibibly cut in Bristol and tokens struck there.

UNDATED

	V. Good	Fine
Brass	$1,200	$3,000

GLOUCESTER TOKEN

This token appears to have been a private coinage by a merchant of Gloucester (county), Virginia. The only specimens known are struck in brass. The exact origin and use of these pieces is unknown.

1714 Shilling Brass . . . .

HIGLEY OR GRANBY COPPERS

The Higley coppers were never officially authorized. All the tokens were made of pure copper. There were seven obverse and four reverse dies. The first issue, in 1737, bore the legend THE VALUE OF THREEPENCE. After a time the quantity exceeded the local demand, and a protest arose against the value of the piece. The inscription was changed to VALUE ME AS YOU PLEASE.

	Good	V. Good
1737 THE • VALVE • OF • THREE • PENCE. — 3 Hammers — CONNECTICVT	$2,500	$4,000
1737 THE • VALVE • OF • THREE • PENCE. — 3 Hammers — I • AM • GOOD • COPPER	2,750	4,200
1737 VALUE • ME • AS • YOU • PLEASE — 3 Hammers — I • AM • GOOD • COPPER	2,350	3,750
(1737) VALUE • ME • AS • YOU • PLEASE — Broad Axe — J • CUT • MY • WAY • THROUGH	2,750	4,200
1739 VALUE • ME • AS • YOU • PLEASE — Broad Axe — J • CUT • MY • WAY • THROUGH	3,500	5,000

HIBERNIA-VOCE POPULI

These coins, struck in the year 1760, were made in Dublin. Like other Irish tokens, some of these pieces found their way to Colonial America.

Farthing 1760

Halfpenny 1760

	Good	*V. Fine*	*E. Fine*
1760 Farthing	$75.00	$200.00	$550.00
1760 Halfpenny..	22.00	100.00	160.00

PITT TOKENS

William Pitt is the subject of these pieces, probably intended as commemorative medalets. The halfpenny served as currency during a shortage of regular coinage.

E. Fine
1766 Farthing $2,200

1766 Halfpenny........ (illustrated)

V. Good	*Fine*	*E. Fine*
$80.00	$150.00	$500.00

RHODE ISLAND SHIP MEDAL

Although this medal has a Dutch inscription, the spelling and design indicate an English or Anglo-American origin. It is believed that this token was struck in England c. 1779-1780 as propaganda to pursuade the Dutch to sign the Treaty of Armed Neutrality. Specimens are known in brass, copper, tin and pewter. Modern copies exist.

1778-1779
Rhode Island
Ship Medal

V. Fine	*E. Fine*
$250.00	$475.00

J. CHALMERS — Annapolis, Maryland

John Chalmers, a silversmith, struck a series of silver tokens at Annapolis in 1783. The shortage of change and the refusal of the people to use underweight coins prompted the issuance of these pieces.

	V. Good	V. Fine
1783 Threepence	$275.00	$900.00
1783 Sixpence	350.00	1,300
1783 Shilling (Rev. illustrated)	300.00	1,200

IV. THE FRENCH COLONIES

None of the coins of the French regime is strictly American. They were all general issues for the French colonies of the New World. The copper of 1717 to 1722 was authorized by edicts of 1716 and 1721 for use in New France, Louisiana, and the French West Indies.

COPPER SOU OR NINE DENIERS

	V. Good	Fine
1721-B (Rouen)	$27.00	$50.00
1721-H (La Rochelle)	19.00	32.00
1722-H	13.00	25.00

FRENCH COLONIES IN GENERAL

Coined for use in the French colonies and only unofficially circulated in Louisiana along with other foreign coins and tokens. Most were counterstamped RF (République Française) for use in the West Indies.

	V. Good	V. Fine	E. Fine
1767 French Colonies, Sou	$15.00	$40.00	$150.00
1767 French Colonies, Sou. Counterstamped RF	12.00	35.00	125.00

V. SPECULATIVE ISSUES, TOKENS & PATTERNS

THE CONTINENTAL CURRENCY

The Continental Currency was probably a pattern issue only and never reached general circulation. It was the first silver dollar size coin ever proposed for the United States. The coins were probably struck in Philadelphia. Many modern copies and replicas exist.

	Good	Fine	E. Fine	Unc.
1776 CURENCY — Pewter	$550.00	$1,000	$3,000	$6,500
1776 CURENCY — Silver				25,000
1776 CURRENCY — Pewter	600.00	1,500	3,500	8,000
1776 CURRENCY — Pewter, EG FECIT above date	550.00	1,000	3,000	6,500

NOVA CONSTELLATIO COPPERS

The Nova Constellatio pieces were struck supposedly by order of Gouverneur Morris. Evidence indicates that they were all struck in Birmingham and imported for American circulation as a private business venture.

1783
"CONSTELLATIO"
Pointed Rays

V. Good	$15.00
Fine	30.00
V. Fine	60.00
Ex. Fine	200.00

1783
"CONSTELATIO"
Blunt Rays

V. Good	$17.00
Fine	35.00
V. Fine	75.00
Ex. Fine	225.00

NOVA CONSTELLATIO COPPERS

1785
"CONSTELATIO"
Blunt Rays

V. Good	$20.00
Fine.	45.00
V. Fine	95.00
Ex. Fine	250.00

1785
"CONSTELLATIO"
Pointed Rays

V. Good	$17.00
Fine.	35.00
V. Fine	75.00
Ex. Fine	230.00

IMMUNE COLUMBIA PIECES

These are considered experimental or pattern pieces. No laws describing them are known.

1785 Copper, Star reverse. $5,000

1785
George III Obverse

Good.	$650.00
Fine	1,200

1785
Vermon Auctori Obverse

Good.	$550.00
Fine	1,100

1787
IMMUNIS COLUMBIA
Eagle Reverse

V. Good.	$110.00
Fine	225.00
V. Fine	500.00
Ex. Fine	1,600

CONFEDERATIO COPPERS

The Confederatio Coppers are experimental or pattern pieces. This will explain why the die with the CONFEDERATIO legend was combined with other designs such as bust of George Washington, Libertas et Justitia of 1785, Immunis Columbia of 1786, the New York "Excelsiors," Inimica Tyrannis Americana and others. There were in all thirteen dies struck in fourteen combinations.

There are two types of the Confederatio reverse. In one instance the stars are contained in a small circle; in the other larger stars are in a larger circle.

Typical Obverse

Small Circle Reverse

Large Circle Reverse

	Fine
1785 Stars in small circle — various obverses	$5,000
1785 Stars in large circle — various obverses	5,000

SPECULATIVE PATTERNS

1786 IMMUNIS COLUMBIA

Eagle Reverse

Shield Reverse

1786 IMMUNIS COLUMBIA, eagle rev.	$9,000
1786 IMMUNIS COLUMBIA, shield rev.	6,000
1786 (No date) Washington obv.	18,000
1786 Eagle obverse	11,000
1786 Washington obverse, eagle reverse (Unique)	——

VI. COINAGE OF THE STATES

NEW HAMPSHIRE

New Hampshire was the first of the states to consider the subject of coinage following the Declaration of Independence.

NEW HAMPSHIRE

William Moulton was empowered to make a limited quantity of coins of pure copper authorized by the State House of Representatives in 1776.

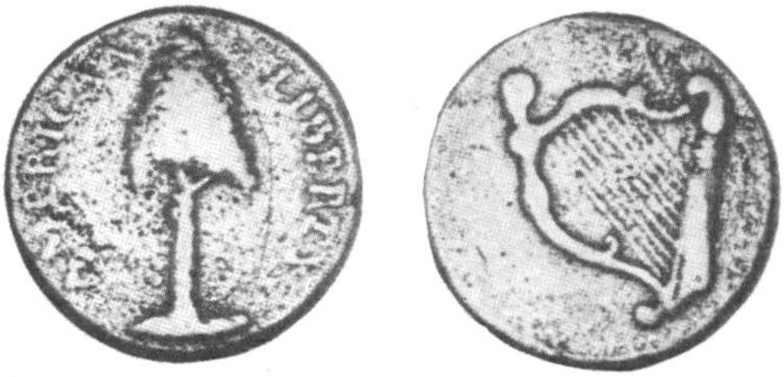

	V. Good
1776 New Hampshire copper	$6,000

MASSACHUSETTS

The coinage of Massachusetts copper cents and half cents in 1787 and 1788 was under the direction of Joshua Witherle. These were the first coins bearing the denomination Cent as established by Congress. Many varieties exist, the most valuable being that with arrows in the eagle's right talon.

1787 Half Cent	
Good	$15.00
Fine	35.00
V. Fine	100.00
Ex. Fine	265.00

	Good	*Fine*	*V. Fine*	*E. Fine*
1787 Cent, arrows in left talon (illustrated)	$15.00	$35.00	$100.00	$265.00
1787 Cent, arrows in right talon	—	2,500	—	—

1788 Half Cent	
Good	$15.00
Fine	35.00
Very Fine	115.00
Ex. Fine	295.00

MASSACHUSETTS

1788 Cent	
Good	$15.00
Fine	35.00
V. Fine	100.00
Ex. Fine	235.00

CONNECTICUT

Authority for establishing a mint near New Haven was granted by the State to Samuel Bishop, Joseph Hopkins, James Hillhouse and John Goodrich in 1785.

1785 Copper Bust Facing Right	
Good...........	$16.00
V. Good........	22.00
Fine	45.00
V. Fine.........	110.00

1785 Copper Bust Facing Left	
Good...........	$50.00
V. Good........	65.00
Fine	125.00
V. Fine.........	210.00

	Good	V. Good	Fine	V. Fine
1786 Bust facing right........................	$20.00	$30.00	$55.00	$125.00
1787 Mailed bust facing right.................	30.00	50.00	100.00	300.00

CONNECTICUT

	Good	V. Good	Fine	V. Fine
1786 Mailed bust facing left	$12.00	$18.00	$35.00	$85.00
1787 Mailed bust facing left	9.00	16.00	27.50	75.00

1787 Draped bust facing left....................	9.00	16.00	27.50	65.00

1788 Mailed bust facing right..................	12.00	20.00	45.00	110.00

1788 Mailed bust facing left	11.00	17.00	40.00	90.00

CONNECTICUT

	Good	*V. Good*	*Fine*	*V. Fine*
1788 Draped bust facing left....................	$11.00	$17.00	$50.00	$110.00

NEW YORK

THE BRASHER DOUBLOON

Perhaps the most famous pieces coined before the establishment of the U.S. Mint at Philadelphia were those produced by a well-known goldsmith and jeweler, Ephraim Brasher.

Brasher produced a gold piece weighing about 408 grains, approximately equal in value to a Spanish doubloon (about $15.00).

The punch-mark EB appears in either of two positions as illustrated. This mark is found on some foreign gold coins as well, and probably was so used by Brasher as evidence of his testing of their value.

1787 Doubloon, punch on breast. Gold (Unique)...........................	—
1787 Doubloon, punch on wing. Gold..	—

COPPER COINAGE

No coinage was authorized for New York following the Revolutionary War although several propositions were considered. The only coinage laws passed were those regulating coins already in use.

1786
NON VI VIRTUTE VICI

Good	$900
Fine...........	1,700
V. Fine	3,000

NEW YORK

	Good	Fine	V. Fine
1787 EXCELSIOR copper, eagle on globe facing right.	$325.00	$750.00	$1,650
1787 EXCELSIOR copper, eagle on globe facing left	275.00	650.00	1,400

1787 George Clinton

Good	$1,600
Fine.	3,750
V. Fine	7,000

1787
Indian and N.Y. Arms

Good	$1,250
Fine	3,000
V. Fine	4,500

1787
Indian and Eagle
on Globe

Good	$1,500
Fine.	3,500
V. Fine	6,000

NEW YORK
THE NOVA EBORACS

1787
NOVA EBORAC
Reverse Seated
Figure Facing Right

Fair	$12.00
Good	27.50
Fine	90.00
V. Fine	275.00

1787
NOVA EBORAC
Reverse Seated
Figure Facing Left

Fair	$10.00
Good	24.00
Fine	85.00
V. Fine	250.00

NEW JERSEY

On June 1, 1786, the New Jersey Colonial legislature granted to Thomas Goadsby, Albion Cox and Walter Mould authority to coin some three million coppers, not later than June 1788, on condition that they delivered to the Treasurer of the State, "one-tenth part of the full sum they shall strike and coin," in quarterly installments. These coppers were to pass current at 15 to the shilling.

Narrow Shield

Wide Shield

	Good	Fine	V. Fine
1786 Narrow shield	$12.00	$30.00	$100.00
1786 Wide shield	12.00	32.00	110.00

NEW JERSEY

Small Planchet

	Good	Fine	V. Fine
1787 Small planchet	$12.00	$30.00	$100.00
1787 Large planchet	12.00	30.00	100.00

	Good	Fine	V. Fine
1788 Horse's head facing right	13.00	32.00	110.00
1788 Horse's head facing left	45.00	160.00	350.00

VERMONT

Reuben Harmon, Jr., of Rupert, Vermont, was granted permission to coin copper pieces for a period of two years beginning July 1, 1785. The well-known Vermont plow coppers were first produced in that year. The franchise was extended for eight years in 1786.

	Good	Fine
1785 IMMUNE COLUMBIA	$550.00	$1,100

	Good	Fine
1785 Plow type	$65.00	$240.00
1786 Plow type	50.00	200.00

	Good	Fine
1786 Baby head	$80.00	$350.00

VERMONT

	Good	Fine
1786 Bust left . . .	$40.00	$220.00
1787 Bust left . . .	500.00	950.00

	Good	Fine
1787 BRITANNIA. .	$22.00	$75.00

1787 Bust right. .	$25.00	$80.00

1788 Bust right. .	$25.00	$85.00

1788 GEORGIVS III REX*	$75.00	$225.00

*This piece should not be confused with the common English halfpence with similar design and reverse legend BRITANNIA.

VII. PRIVATE TOKENS AFTER CONFEDERATION

NORTH AMERICAN TOKEN

This piece was struck in Dublin, Ireland. The obverse shows the seated figure of Hibernia facing left.

Copper or Brass

	V. Good	Fine	V. Fine
1781 . . .	$12.00	$24.00	$50.00

THE BAR "COPPER"

The Bar "Copper" is undated and of uncertain origin. It has thirteen parallel and unconnected bars on one side. On the other side is the large roman letter USA monogram. The design was supposedly copied from a Continental button.

	V. Good	*Fine*	*V. Fine*	*E. Fine*
Undated (about 1785) Bar "Copper"...........	$125.00	$250.00	$400.00	$750.00

AUCTORI PLEBIS TOKEN

This token is sometimes included with the coins of Connecticut as it greatly resembles issues of that state. It was struck in England by an unknown maker, possibly for use in America.

1787 AUCTORI PLEBIS	
Good.............	$17.00
V. Good..........	23.00
Fine..............	50.00
V. Fine...........	120.00

THE MOTT TOKEN

This was one of the first tradesman's tokens issued in America. Its exact date of manufacture and origin are unknown. They were distributed by Messrs. Mott of New York probably as a commemorative in 1839.

	V. Good	*Fine*	*V. Fine*	*E. Fine*
1789 Mott Token............................	$30.00	$50.00	$110.00	$260.00

STANDISH BARRY, BALTIMORE, MARYLAND

Standish Barry, a Baltimore silversmith, circulated a silver threepence in 1790. The tokens were believed to have been an advertising venture at a time when small change was scarce.

	Fine	*V. Fine*
1790 Threepence	$1,200	$4,000

KENTUCKY TOKEN

These tokens were struck in England about 1792-94. Each star in the triangle represents a state, identified by its initial letter. These pieces are usually called Kentucky Cents because the letter K (for Kentucky) happens to be at the top.

	V. Good	*V. Fine*	*E. Fine*	*Unc.*
Cent (1792-94)	$28.00	$65.00	$110.00	$375.00

FRANKLIN PRESS

This piece is an English tradesmans' token but, being associated with Benjamin Franklin, has accordingly been included in American collections.

	V. Good	*V. Fine*	*E. Fine*	*Unc.*
1794 Franklin Press Token	$24.00	$55.00	$100.00	$350.00

TALBOT, ALLUM & LEE CENTS

Talbot, Allum & Lee, engaged in the India trade and located in New York, placed a large quantity of English-made coppers in circulation during 1794 and 1795. ONE CENT appears on the 1794 issue.

1794 Cent with NEW YORK

V. Good	$15.00
V. Fine	35.00
Unc.	300.00

1794 Cent Without NEW YORK

V. Good	$40.00
V. Fine	175.00
Unc.	750.00

1795 Cent

V. Good	$15.00
V. Fine	35.00
E. Fine	85.00
Unc.	285.00

VIII. WASHINGTON PIECES

An interesting series of coins and tokens dated from 1783 to 1795 bear the portrait of George Washington. The likenesses in most instances were faithfully reproduced and were designed to honor Washington. Many of these pieces were of English origin and made later than the dates indicate.

	Fine	*V. Fine*	*E. Fine*
1783 Large military bust	$20.00	$35.00	$110.00

1783 Draped bust	20.00	35.00	110.00

WASHINGTON PIECES

UNITY STATES

V. Good	$20.00
V. Fine	50.00
Ex. Fine	110.00

Undated
Double Head
Cent

Fine	$25.00
V. Fine	60.00
Ex. Fine	125.00

Large Eagle

Small Eagle

	Fine	*E. Fine*	*Unc.*
1791 Cent, large eagle	$85.00	$200.00	$575.00
1791 Cent, small eagle	85.00	200.00	600.00

1791 Liverpool
Halfpenny
Lettered Edge

Fine	$185.00
Ex. Fine	375.00
Unc.	750.00

1792 Eagle with Stars

Copper	—
Silver	—
Gold	—

WASHINGTON PIECES

(1792) Undated Cent
"WASHINGTON BORN VIRGINIA"

	Fine
Copper	$700.00

1792 Cent
"WASHINGTON PRESIDENT"

	Fine
Plain edge	$1,200

	V. Good	Fine
1792 Small eagle. Copper	$1,200	$2,200

1793 Ship
Halfpenny

Fine	$55.00
V. Fine	85.00
Ex. Fine	200.00

1795 Halfpenny
Grate Token

	V. Fine	E. Fine	Unc.
1795 reeded edge	$40.00	$100.00	$275.00
1795 lettered edge	130.00	275.00	550.00

WASHINGTON PIECES

Liberty and Security Tokens

	Fine	V. Fine	E. Fine
1795 Halfpenny, plain edge	$40.00	$75.00	$185.00
1795 Halfpenny, lettered edge	30.00	60.00	160.00

Liberty and Security Penny

Fine	$60.00
V. Fine	100.00
Ex. Fine	200.00
Unc.	825.00

SUCCESS MEDALS

	Fine	V. Fine	E. Fine
Medal, large. Plain or reeded edge	$50.00	$100.00	$150.00
Medal, small. Plain or reeded edge	60.00	125.00	200.00

NORTH WALES HALFPENNY

	Good	Fine
1795 Halfpenny	$25.00	$75.00

IX. THE FUGIO CENTS

The first coins issued by authority of the United States were the "Fugio" cents.

The legends have been credited to Benjamin Franklin by many, and the coin, as a consequence, has been referred to as the Franklin Cent.

1787 WITH POINTED RAYS

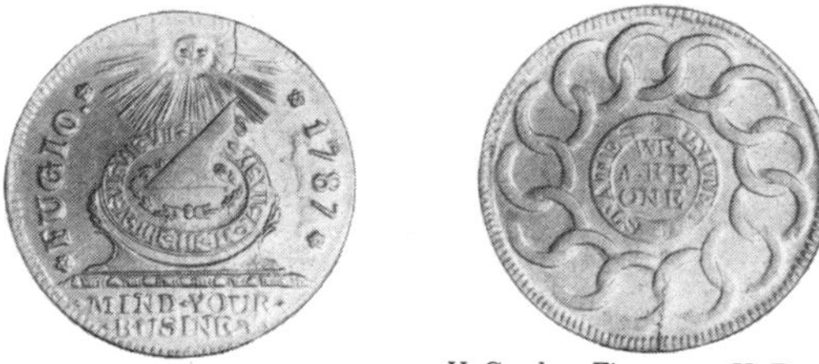

	V. Good	Fine	V. Fine	E. Fine	Unc.
STATES UNITED at sides of circle (illustrated)	$40.00	$75.00	$110.00	$200.00	$600.00
UNITED STATES at sides of circle	40.00	75.00	110.00	200.00	600.00

1787 WITH CLUB RAYS

	V. Good	Fine	V. Fine
Club Rays. Rounded ends	$60.00	$100.00	$300.00

MODERN PROOF COINS

Proof coins can usually be distinguished by their sharpness of detail, high wire edge, and extremely brilliant, mirrorlike surface. All proofs are originally sold by the mint at a premium.

Proof coins were not struck during 1943-1949 or 1965-67. Sets from 1936 through 1972 include the cent, nickel, dime, quarter and half; from 1973 through 1981 the dollar was also included. Proof sets may be ordered from the United States Mint, P.O. Box 13576, Philadelphia, PA 19162-0011. *Values shown are for original unblemished sets.*

Figures in parentheses represent the total number of full sets minted.

1936 (3,837)..................	$2,500
1937 (5,542)..................	1,400
1938 (8,045)..................	800.00
1939 (8,795)..................	750.00
1940 (11,246).................	600.00
1941 (15,287).................	525.00
1942 both nickels } (21,120)	550.00
1942 one nickel } (21,120)	510.00
1950 (51,386).................	300.00
1951 (57,500).................	230.00
1952 (81,980).................	100.00
1953 (128,800)................	75.00
1954 (233,300)................	45.00
1955 } .... Box	40.00
1955 } (378,200)..... Flat pack	45.00
1956 (669,384)................	$20.00
1957 (1,247,952)	12.00
1958 (875,652)................	17.00
1959 (1,149,291)	13.00
1960 (1,691,602 both kinds) with lg. date 1c	8.00
1960 with sm. date 1c	16.00
1961 (3,028,244)	6.00
1962 (3,218,019)	6.00
1963 (3,075,645)	6.00
1964 (3,950,762)	6.00
1968S (3,041,506).............	4.00
1969S (2,934,631).............	3.75
1970S (2,632,810).............	6.00
1970S small date 1¢	40.00

MODERN PROOF COINS

1971S (3,220,733)	$3.75
1972S (3,260,996)	4.00
1973S (2,760,339)	6.00
1974S (2,612,568)	6.25
1975S (2,845,450)	7.50
1976S (4,149,730)	6.00
1976S 3-pc. set (3,998,621)	8.50
1977S (3,251,152)	6.00
1978S (3,127,781)	6.00
1979S filled S } (3,677,175)	6.00
1979S clear S } (3,677,175)	52.00
1980S (3,554,806)	7.00
1981S (4,063,083)	6.75
1982S (3,857,479)	6.00
1983S (3,138,765)	5.50
1983S Prestige Set (140,361)	70.00
1984S (2,748,430)	9.00
1984S Prestige Set (316,680)	35.00
1985S (3,362,821)	$6.00
1986S (2,411,180)	16.00
1986S Prestige Set (599,317)	25.00
1987S (3,792,233)	6.00
1987S Prestige Set (435,495)	18.00
1988S (3,031,287)	10.00
1988S Prestige Set (231,661)	46.00
1989S (3,009,107)	8.00
1989S Prestige Set (211,087)	48.00
1990S 2,793,433	12.00
1990S Prestige Set 506,126	35.00
1991S	10.00
1991S Prestige Set	40.00
1992S	11.00
1992S Prestige Set	46.00

Original issue prices: 1936 thru 1942, $1.89; 1950 thru 1964, $2.10; 1968 thru 1972S, $5.00; 1973S thru 1976S, $7.00; 1977S thru 1979S, $9.00; 1980S, $10.00; 1981S to 1991, $11.00; 1992 to date $12.00.

UNCIRCULATED MINT SETS

Official Mint Sets are specially packaged by the government for sale to collectors. They contain uncirculated specimens of each year's coins for every denomination issued from each mint. Sets from 1947 through 1958 contain two examples of each regular issue coin. No official sets were produced in 1950, 1982 or 1983. Privately assembled sets are valued according to individual coin prices. Only official sets are included in the following list. Unlike the proof sets, these are normal coins intended for circulation and are not minted with any special consideration for quality. Current year sets may be ordered from The United States Mint, P.O. Box 13576, Philadelphia, PA 19162-0011.

1947 P-D-S		$600.00
1948 P-D-S		180.00
1949 P-D-S		500.00
1951 P-D-S	8,654	250.00
1952 P-D-S	11,499	175.00
1953 P-D-S	15,538	175.00
1954 P-D-S	25,599	80.00
1955 P-D-S	49,656	50.00
1956 P-D	45,475	40.00
1957 P-D	34,324	65.00
1958 P-D	50,314	60.00
1959 P-D	187,000	13.00
1960 P-D	260,485	10.00
1961 P-D	223,704	11.00
1962 P-D	385,285	14.00
1963 P-D	606,612	8.00
1964 P-D	1,008,108	6.00
1965	*2,360,000	3.00
1966	*2,261,583	3.50
1967	*1,863,344	4.50
1968 P-D-S	2,105,128	1.70
1969 P-D-S	1,817,392	1.80
1970 P-D-S	2,038,134	$8.50
1971 P-D-S	2,193,396	2.25
1972 P-D-S	2,750,000	1.90
1973 P-D-S	1,767,691	5.00
1974 P-D-S	1,975,981	3.75
1975 P-D-S	1,921,488	5.00
1976 3 pieces	4,908,319	7.00
1976 P-D	1,892,513	4.00
1977 P-D	2,006,869	4.00
1978 P-D	2,162,609	4.00
1979 P-D	2,526,000	4.00
1980 P-D-S	2,815,066	4.50
1981 P-D-S	2,908,145	5.00
1984 P-D	1,832,857	4.00
1985 P-D	1,710,571	6.00
1986 P-D	1,153,536	18.00
1987 P-D	2,890,758	4.00
1988 P-D	1,646,204	3.00
1989 P-D	1,987,915	3.00
1990 P-D	1,809,184	5.00
1991 P-D		6.50
1992 P-D		6.50

*Special Mint Sets

UNITED STATES REGULAR ISSUES

HALF CENTS — 1793-1857

The half cent was authorized to be coined April 2, 1792. Originally the weight was to have been 132 grains, but this was changed to 104 grains by the Act of January 14, 1793, before coinage commenced. The weight was again changed to 84 grains January 26, 1796 by presidential proclamation in conformity with the Act of March 3, 1795. Coinage was discontinued by the Act of February 21, 1857. All were coined at the Philadelphia Mint.

LIBERTY CAP TYPE — 1793-1797

AG-3 ABOUT GOOD—*Clear enough to identify.*
G-4 GOOD—*Outline of bust clear, no details. Date readable. Reverse lettering incomplete.*
VG-8 VERY GOOD—*Some hair details. Reverse lettering complete.*
F-12 FINE—*Most of hair detail shows. Leaves worn but all visible.*
VF-20 VERY FINE—*Hair near ear and forehead worn, other areas distinct. Some details in leaves show.*
EF-40 EXTREMELY FINE—*Light wear on highest parts of head and wreath.*

Head Facing Left 1793

	Quan. Minted	*AG-3*	*G-4*	*VG-8*	*F-12*	*VF-20*	*EF-40*
1793	35,334	$325.00	$900.00	$1,400	$1,800	$3,000	$5,000

Head Facing Right 1794-1797

1794	81,600	40.00	130.00	225.00	425.00	625.00	1,250

Pole to Cap

Punctuated Date

No Pole to Cap

	Quan. Minted	*AG-3*	*G-4*	*VG-8*	*F-12*	*VF-20*	*EF-40*
1795 All kinds	139,690						
1795 Lettered edge, with pole		$40.00	$110.00	$150.00	$275.00	$500.00	$1,200
1795 Lettered edge, punctuated date		40.00	110.00	150.00	265.00	475.00	1,000

HALF CENTS

	Quan. Minted	*AG-3*	*G-4*	*VG-8*	*F-12*	*VF-20*	*EF-40*
1795 Plain edge, punctuated date		$40.00	$100.00	$150.00	$275.00	$475.00	$1,100
1795 Pl. edge, no pole		40.00	100.00	150.00	275.00	475.00	1,100
1796 With pole .... }		1,200	2,500	4,000	6,000	9,000	——
1796 No pole .... }	1,390	2,000	5,000	8,000	10,000	22,000	

1797 Plain Edge

1797, 1 above 1, Plain Edge

	Quan. Minted	*AG-3*	*G-4*	*VG-8*	*F-12*	*VF-20*	*EF-40*
1797 All kinds	127,840						
1797 Lettered edge..................		90.00	200.00	325.00	650.00	1,300	——
1797 Plain edge....................		35.00	70.00	110.00	250.00	500.00	950.00
1797 Gripped edge		450.00	750.00	2,100	——	——	
1797, 1 above 1, plain edge		35.00	70.00	110.00	250.00	500.00	950.00

DRAPED BUST TYPE 1800-1808

AG-3 ABOUT GOOD—*Clear enough to identify.*
G-4 GOOD—*Bust outline clear, few details, date readable. Reverse lettering worn and incomplete.*
VG-8 VERY GOOD—*Some drapery shows. Date and legends complete.*
F-12 FINE—*Shoulder drapery and hair over brow worn smooth.*
VF-20 VERY FINE—*Only slight wear in above areas. Slight wear on reverse.*
EF-40 EXTREMELY FINE—*Light wear on highest parts of head and wreath.*

	Quan. Minted	*AG-3*	*G-4*	*VG-8*	*F-12*	*VF-20*	*EF-40*
1800	202,908	$7.00	$13.00	$21.00	$27.50	$45.00	$115.00
1802, 2 over 0	20,266	45.00	125.00	200.00	400.00	900.00	2,200
1803	92,000	7.50	14.00	22.00	30.00	47.50	130.00

Plain 4

Crosslet 4

Stemless Wreath

Stems to Wreath

	Quan. Minted	*AG-3*	*G-4*	*VG-8*	*F-12*	*VF-20*	*EF-40*
1804 All Kinds....	1,055,312						
1804 Plain 4, stems		6.00	12.00	19.00	25.00	40.00	120.00
1804 Pl. 4, stemless		6.00	11.00	18.00	20.00	38.00	90.00
1804 Cr. 4, stems		6.00	11.00	18.00	20.00	38.00	90.00
1804 Cr. 4, stemless		6.00	11.00	18.00	20.00	38.00	90.00

1804 "Spiked Chin"

Small 5

Large 5

	Quan. Minted	AG-3	G-4	VG-8	F-12	VF-20	EF-40
1804 "Spiked chin"	Inc. above	$7.50	$14.00	$19.00	$26.00	$50.00	$145.00
1805 All Kinds	814,464						
1805 Med. 5, stemless		6.50	13.00	20.00	22.00	42.00	90.00
1805 Small 5, stems		15.00	45.00	70.00	175.00	375.00	——
1805 Large 5, stems		6.00	12.00	20.00	22.00	42.00	90.00

Small 6

Large 6

1808, 8 over 7

Normal Date

	Quan. Minted	AG-3	G-4	VG-8	F-12	VF-20	EF-40
1806 All Kinds	356,000						
1806 Small 6, stems		10.00	25.00	40.00	80.00	125.00	250.00
1806 Sm. 6, stemless		6.50	13.00	20.00	22.00	42.00	90.00
1806 Large 6, stems		6.50	13.00	20.00	22.00	42.00	90.00
1807	476,000	6.50	13.00	20.00	22.00	42.00	90.00
1808, 8 over 7	} 400,000	18.00	30.00	50.00	95.00	250.00	400.00
1808 Normal date		6.50	13.00	20.00	24.00	45.00	110.00

CLASSIC HEAD TYPE 1809-1836

G-4 GOOD—*LIBERTY only partly visible on hair band. Lettering, date, stars, worn but visible.*
VG-8 VERY GOOD—*LIBERTY entirely visible on hair band. Lower curls worn.*
F-12 FINE—*Only part wear on LIBERTY and hair at top worn in spots.*
VF-20 VERY FINE—*Lettering clear-cut. Hair only slightly worn.*
EF-40 EXTREMELY FINE—*Light wear on highest points of hair and leaves.*
MS-60 UNCIRCULATED—*Typical brown to red surface. No trace of wear.*

Brilliant or red uncirculated coins are worth more than prices shown. Spotted, cleaned or discolored pieces are worth less.

	Quan. Minted	G-4	VG-8	F-12	VF-20	EF-40	MS-60
1809	1,154,572	$11.00	$13.00	$19.00	$32.50	$50.00	$180.00
1810	215,000	13.00	18.00	27.00	50.00	90.00	550.00
1811	63,140	40.00	60.00	125.00	375.00	600.00	1,350
1825	63,000	12.00	16.00	22.00	32.50	50.00	180.00
1826	234,000	10.00	12.00	18.00	28.00	40.00	180.00

HALF CENTS

13 Stars

12 Stars

	Quan. Minted	G-4	VG-8	F-12	VF-20	EF-40	MS-60	Proof-63
1828, 13 Stars	606,000	$10.00	$12.00	$16.00	$25.00	$35.00	$165.00	
1828, 12 Stars		11.00	14.00	20.00	35.00	50.00	250.00	
1829	487,000	10.00	12.00	16.00	25.00	35.00	165.00	
1831 (Beware of altered date)	2,200						—	$4,200
1832	51,000	10.00	13.00	17.00	26.00	40.00	150.00	1,700
1833	103,000	10.00	13.00	17.00	26.00	40.00	150.00	1,700
1834	141,000	10.00	13.00	17.00	26.00	40.00	150.00	1,700
1835	398,000	10.00	13.00	17.00	26.00	40.00	150.00	1,700
1836								3,100

CORONET TYPE 1840-1857

	Proof-63		Proof-63
1840 Original	$2,000	1845 Original	$2,850
1840 Restrike	1,900	1845 Restrike	2,600
1841 Original	2,100	1846 Original	2,600
1841 Restrike	2,000	1846 Restrike	2,100
1842 Original	2,300	1847 Original	2,100
1842 Restrike	2,000	1847 Restrike	2,100
1843 Original	2,100	1848 Original	2,100
1843 Restrike	2,100	1848 Restrike	2,100
1844 Original	2,850	1849 Original. Small date	2,400
1844 Restrike	2,100	1849 Restrike. Small date	2,400

Brilliant or red uncirculated coins are worth more than prices shown. Spotted, cleaned or discolored pieces are worth less.

G-4 GOOD—*Hair and bun show few details, parts of LIBERTY show.*
VG-8 VERY GOOD—*Beads uniformly distinct. Hairlines show in spots.*
F-12 FINE—*Hairlines above ear worn. Beads sharp.*
VF-20 VERY FINE—*Lowest curl shows wear, hair otherwise distinct.*
EF-40 EXTREMELY FINE—*Light wear on highest points of hair and leaves.*
MS-60 UNCIRCULATED—*No trace of wear, light blemishes.*

Small Date

Large Date

	Quan. Minted	G-4	VG-8	F-12	VF-20	EF-40	MS-60	Proof-63
1849 Large date	39,864	$15.00	$18.00	$21.00	$30.00	$45.00	$125.00	—
1850	39,812	15.00	18.00	21.00	30.00	45.00	125.00	—
1851	147,672	12.00	16.00	18.00	25.00	38.00	100.00	—
1852								$2,500
1853	129,694	12.00	16.00	18.00	25.00	38.00	100.00	
1854	55,358	12.00	16.00	18.00	25.00	38.00	100.00	2,500
1855	56,500	12.00	16.00	18.00	25.00	38.00	100.00	2,500
1856	40,430	14.00	17.00	20.00	30.00	45.00	125.00	2,500
1857	35,180	15.00	18.00	21.00	32.50	50.00	150.00	2,500

LARGE CENTS — 1793-1857

Cents and half cents were the first coins struck under the authority of the United States Government. Coinage began in 1793 with laws specifying that the cent should weigh exactly twice as much as the half cent. Large cents were coined every year from 1793 to 1857 with the exception of 1815, when a lack of copper prevented production. All were coined at the Philadelphia Mint. Varieties listed are those most significant to collectors. Numerous other die varieties may be found because each of the early dies was individually made.

FLOWING HAIR, CHAIN TYPE REVERSE 1793

AG-3 ABOUT GOOD—*Date and devices clear enough to identify.*
G-4 GOOD—*Lettering worn but readable. Bust has no detail.*
VG-8 VERY GOOD—*Date and lettering distinct, some details of head visible.*
F-12 FINE—*About half of hair, etc. details show.*
VF-20 VERY FINE—*Ear visible. Most of details can be seen.*
EF-40 EXTREMELY FINE—*Highest points of hair and back of temple show wear.*

Obverse

AMERI. Reverse

AMERICA Reverse

	Quan. Minted	*AG-3*	*G-4*	*VG-8*	*F-12*	*VF-20*	*EF-40*
1793 Chain	36,103						
1793 AMERI. in legend		$500.00	$1,300	$2,000	$3,500	$6,500	$12,000
1793 AMERICA		475.00	1,000	1,750	3,250	5,500	11,500

FLOWING HAIR, WREATH TYPE REVERSE 1793

Wreath Type

Strawberry Leaf Var.

	Quan. Minted	*AG-3*	*G-4*	*VG-8*	*F-12*	*VF-20*	*EF-40*
1793 Wreath	63,353						
1793 Vine/bars edge		$150.00	$425.00	$750.00	$1,100	$1,800	$4,000
1793 Lettered Edge		175.00	475.00	800.00	1,300	1,850	4,125
1793 Strawberry leaf				(4 known)			

LARGE CENTS
LIBERTY CAP TYPE 1793-1796

1793 Vine and Bar edge
Chain and Wreath Type Only

Lettered edge 1793-1795
ONE HUNDRED FOR A DOLLAR

Beaded Border, 1793 Only

1793-1794

"Head of 1793"
Head is in high
rounded relief

1794 Only

"Head of 1794"
Well defined hair,
hook on lowest curl

1794-1796

"Head of 1795"
Head in low relief,
no hook on lowest curl

	Quan. Minted	*AG-3*	*G-4*	*VG-8*	*F-12*	*VF-20*	*EF-40*
1793 Lib. Cap.	11,056	$300.00	$700.00	$1,200	$2,000	$4,100	$11,000
1794 All kinds	918,521						
1794 "Head of 1793"		75.00	160.00	275.00	650.00	1,600	4,000
1794 "Head of 1794"		20.00	60.00	95.00	175.00	425.00	1,100
1794 "Head of 1795"		20.00	60.00	95.00	175.00	425.00	1,100
1795 Ltd. ed.	37,000	20.00	60.00	110.00	200.00	450.00	1,300
1795 Plain ed.	501,500	19.00	50.00	75.00	150.00	400.00	825.00
1796 Lib. Cap.	109,825	20.00	50.00	90.00	175.00	400.00	1,000

DRAPED BUST TYPE 1796-1807

AG-3 ABOUT GOOD—*Clear enough to identify.*
G-4 GOOD—*Lettering worn, but clear; date clear. Bust lacks details.*
VG-8 VERY GOOD—*Drapery partly visible. Less wear in date and lettering.*
F-12 FINE—*Hair over brow is smooth, some details showing in other parts of hair.*
VF-20 VERY FINE—*Hairlines slightly worn. Hair over brow better defined.*
EF-40 EXTREMELY FINE—*Hair above forehead and left of eye outlined and detailed. Only slight wear on olive leaves.*

LARGE CENTS

LIBERTY error

Gripped Edge

Stems

Stemless

	Quan. Minted	AG-3	G-4	VG-8	F-12	VF-20	EF-40
1796 Draped Bust....	363,375	$20.00	$40.00	$70.00	$110.00	$325.00	$800.00
1796 LIHERTY error..........		25.00	50.00	100.00	195.00	500.00	1,500
1797 All kinds	897,510						
1797 Gr. edge, '96 rev		10.00	17.00	40.00	90.00	200.00	600.00
1797 Pl. edge, '96 rev		10.00	19.00	42.00	100.00	210.00	600.00
1797, '97 rev., Stems		8.00	16.00	30.00	60.00	170.00	400.00
1797, '97 rev., Stemless......		15.00	28.00	60.00	115.00	275.00	800.00

1798, 8 over 7

1799, 9 over 8

1800 over 1798

1800, 80 over 79

1798 All kinds	1,841,745						
1798, 8 over 7		10.00	21.00	55.00	125.00	300.00	850.00
1798		7.00	13.00	22.00	60.00	130.00	350.00
1799, 9 over 8	*	175.00	500.00	900.00	2,000	4,000	—
1799 Nor. date........	42,540	150.00	450.00	850.00	1,750	3,750	—
1800 All kds.	2,822,175						
1800 over 1798		6.00	11.00	19.00	40.00	120.00	400.00
1800, 80 over 79		4.50	10.00	18.00	35.00	120.00	275.00
1800 Normal date...........		4.50	10.00	18.00	35.00	120.00	275.00

*Mintage for 1799, 9 over 8 variety is included with the 1798 figure.

Fraction 1/000

Corrected Fraction

1801 Reverse, 3 Errors

1801 All kds.	1,362,837						
1801 Normal rev............		4.50	10.00	18.00	35.00	120.00	275.00
1801, 3 errors: 1/000, one stem & IINITED		10.00	20.00	40.00	120.00	250.00	800.00
1801 Fraction 1/000.........		6.00	12.00	25.00	60.00	125.00	390.00
1801, 1/100 over 1/000......		6.00	13.00	27.00	65.00	150.00	425.00
1802 All kds.	3,435,100						
1802 Normal rev............		4.25	9.00	16.00	30.00	90.00	210.00
1802 Fraction 1/000.........		6.00	12.00	21.00	40.00	110.00	275.00
1802 Stemless wreath		4.50	10.00	18.00	35.00	100.00	275.00

LARGE CENTS

1803 Sm. Date, Blunt 1

1803 Large Date, Pointed 1

Small Fraction

Large Fraction

	Quan. Minted	*AG-3*	*G-4*	*VG-8*	*F-12*	*VF-20*	*EF-40*
1803 All kds.	3,131,691						
1803 Sm. dt., sm. fract.		$4.00	$9.00	$16.00	$35.00	$100.00	$225.00
1803 Sm. dt., lg. fract.		4.00	9.00	16.00	35.00	100.00	225.00
1803 Lg. dt., sm. fract.		200.00	400.00	750.00	1,800	3,500	
1803 Lg. dt., lg. fract.		13.00	22.00	40.00	85.00	170.00	600.00
1803, 1/100 over 1/000		5.00	13.00	27.50	50.00	125.00	350.00
1803 Stemless wreath		5.00	10.00	22.00	40.00	115.00	300.00

1804 With Normal or Broken Dies (broken dies illustrated)

All genuine 1804 Cents have a crosslet 4 in the date and a large fraction. The 0 in the date is in line with the O in OF on the reverse of the coin.

1804	96,500	100.00	175.00	400.00	700.00	1,500	3,250
1805	941,116	4.00	9.00	16.00	35.00	125.00	250.00
1806	348,000	6.00	12.00	27.50	60.00	150.00	425.00

Sm. 1807, 7 over 6, blunt 1

Lg. 1807, 7 over 6, pointed 1

1807 All kinds	829,221						
1807 Small 7 over 6		100.00	250.00	500.00	1,200	2,500	—
1807 Large 7 over 6		4.00	9.00	16.00	35.00	125.00	275.00
1807 Small fraction		5.00	11.00	22.00	43.00	125.00	375.00
1807 Large fraction		4.00	9.00	16.00	32.00	125.00	300.00

CLASSIC HEAD TYPE 1808-1814

AG-3 ABOUT GOOD—*Details clear enough to identify.*

G-4 GOOD—*Legends, stars, date worn, but plain.*

VG-8 VERY GOOD—*LIBERTY all readable. Ear shows. Details worn but plain.*

F-12 FINE—*Hair on forehead and before ear nearly smooth. Ear and hair under ear sharp.*

VF-20 VERY FINE—*All hairlines show some detail. Leaves on rev. show slight wear.*

EF-40 EXTREMELY FINE—*All hairlines sharp. Very slight wear on high points.*

	Quan. Minted	AG-3	G-4	VG-8	F-12	VF-20	EF-40
1808	1,007,000	$6.25	$16.00	$27.00	$50.00	$140.00	$450.00
1809	222,867	17.00	35.00	60.00	125.00	325.00	700.00

1810, 10 over 09

1810 Normal Date

1811, last 1 over 0

1811 Normal Date

	Quan. Minted	AG-3	G-4	VG-8	F-12	VF-20	EF-40
1810 All kds.	1,458,500						
1810, 10 over 09		5.00	14.00	25.00	45.00	135.00	375.00
1810 Normal date		5.00	14.00	25.00	45.00	135.00	375.00
1811 All kds.	218,025						
1811 Last 1 over 0		12.00	23.00	45.00	110.00	250.00	625.00
1811 Normal date		10.00	20.00	40.00	100.00	235.00	600.00
1812	1,075,500	5.00	14.00	22.00	45.00	135.00	375.00
1813	418,000	7.50	17.00	30.00	65.00	175.00	400.00
1814	357,830	5.00	14.00	22.00	45.00	135.00	375.00

CORONET TYPE 1816-1857

G-4 GOOD—*Head details partly visible. Even wear in date and legends.*
VG-8 VERY GOOD—*LIBERTY, date, stars, legends clear. Part of hair cord visible.*
F-12 FINE—*All hairlines show. Hair cords show uniformly.*
VF-20 VERY FINE—*Hair cords only slightly worn. Hairlines only partly worn, all well defined.*
EF-40 EXTREMELY FINE—*Both hair cords stand out sharply. All hairlines sharp.*
MS-60 UNCIRCULATED—*Typical brown to red surface. No trace of wear.*

13 Stars

15 Stars

Brilliant or red uncirculated coins are worth more than prices shown. Spotted, cleaned or discolored pieces are worth less.

	Quan. Minted	G-4	VG-8	F-12	VF-20	EF-40	MS-60
1816	2,820,982	$4.00	$4.75	$7.50	$14.00	$35.00	$150.00
1817, 13 stars	3,948,400	4.00	4.75	6.50	13.00	35.00	125.00
1817, 15 stars		4.25	5.25	9.50	23.00	50.00	325.00
1818	3,167,000	4.00	4.75	6.50	13.00	35.00	125.00

LARGE CENTS

1819, 9 over 8

1820, 20 over 19

	Quan. Minted	G-4	VG-8	F-12	VF-20	EF-40	MS-60
1819, 9 over 8		$4.25	$5.25	$8.50	$14.00	$36.00	$190.00
1819	2,671,000	4.00	4.75	6.50	13.00	35.00	125.00
1820, 20 over 19		4.25	5.25	8.50	17.00	37.50	200.00
1820	4,407,550	4.00	4.75	6.50	13.00	35.00	125.00
1821	389,000	7.00	12.00	20.00	50.00	150.00	850.00
1822	2,072,339	4.00	4.75	6.50	14.00	40.00	200.00

1823, 3 over 2

1824, 4 over 2

1826, 6 over 5

	Quan. Minted	G-4	VG-8	F-12	VF-20	EF-40	MS-60
1823, 3 over 2	Included	12.00	16.00	35.00	85.00	225.00	—
1823 Normal date	with 1824	12.00	20.00	40.00	90.00	375.00	—
1824, 4 over 2		4.75	6.50	13.00	40.00	110.00	—
1824 Normal date	1,262,000	4.25	5.25	8.50	20.00	50.00	425.00
1825	1,461,100	4.00	4.75	7.50	15.00	37.50	200.00
1826, 6 over 5		5.00	9.00	14.00	32.00	80.00	275.00
1826 Normal date	1,517,425	4.00	4.75	6.50	13.00	32.00	150.00
1827	2,357,732	4.00	4.75	6.50	13.00	32.00	125.00

This date size appears on cents before 1828.

This date size appears on cents after 1828.

	Quan. Minted	G-4	VG-8	F-12	VF-20	EF-40	MS-60
1828 Lg. narrow date	2,260,624	4.00	4.75	6.50	13.00	32.00	190.00
1828 Sm. wide date		4.25	5.50	8.50	15.00	35.00	225.00
1829	1,414,500	4.00	4.75	6.50	13.00	32.00	135.00
1830	1,711,500	4.00	4.75	6.50	13.00	32.00	135.00
1831	3,359,260	3.75	4.50	6.00	12.00	30.00	125.00
1832	2,362,000	3.75	4.50	6.00	12.00	30.00	125.00
1833	2,739,000	3.75	4.50	6.00	12.00	30.00	125.00
1834	1,855,100	3.75	4.50	6.00	12.00	32.00	200.00
1835	3,878,400	3.75	4.50	6.00	12.00	32.00	175.00
1836	2,111,000	3.75	4.50	6.00	12.00	30.00	150.00

LARGE CENTS
Young Head 1835-1857

G-4 GOOD—*Considerably worn. LIBERTY readable.*
VG-8 VERY GOOD—*Hairlines smooth but visible, outline of ear clearly defined.*
F-12 FINE—*Hairlines at top of head and behind ear worn but visible. Braid over brow plain, ear clear.*
VF-20 VERY FINE—*All details more sharp. Hair over brow shows only slight wear.*
EF-40 EXTREMELY FINE—*Hair above ear detailed, but slightly worn.*
MS-60 UNCIRCULATED—*Typical brown to red surface. No trace of wear.*

1839 over 1836

Brilliant or red uncirculated coins are worth more than prices shown. Spotted, cleaned or discolored pieces are worth less.

	Quan. Minted	*G-4*	*VG-8*	*F-12*	*VF-20*	*EF-40*	*MS-60*
1837	5,558,300	$4.00	$4.75	$6.50	$11.00	$32.00	$150.00
1838	6,370,200	3.75	4.50	6.00	10.00	30.00	125.00
1839	} 3,128,661	3.75	5.25	6.50	13.00	36.00	150.00
1839, 9 over 6		40.00	80.00	175.00	300.00	900.00	——
1840	2,462,700	3.25	4.25	5.50	10.00	30.00	125.00
1841	1,597,367	3.25	4.25	5.50	9.00	27.00	125.00
1842	2,383,390	3.25	4.25	5.50	9.00	27.00	110.00

"Head of 1840"
Petite Head
1839-1843

"Head of 1844"
Mature Head
1843-1857

Small Letters

Large Letters

	Quan. Minted	*G-4*	*VG-8*	*F-12*	*VF-20*	*EF-40*	*MS-60*
1843 Petite, sm. let.	} 2,425,342	3.25	4.25	5.50	9.00	27.00	110.00
1843 Petite, lg. let.		5.25	8.50	13.00	25.00	45.00	250.00
1843 Mature, lg. let.		3.75	5.25	8.50	13.00	32.00	110.00
1844 Normal date	} 2,398,752	3.25	4.25	5.50	9.00	26.00	110.00
1844 over 81 (error-photo page 53)		4.25	5.25	9.50	17.00	60.00	325.00
1845	3,894,804	3.00	4.00	5.00	8.00	25.00	100.00
1846	4,120,800	3.25	4.25	5.25	9.00	27.00	110.00
1847	} 6,183,669	3.00	4.00	5.00	8.00	25.00	100.00
1847, 7 over "sm." 7		4.25	5.25	9.50	15.00	35.00	150.00

LARGE CENTS

	Quan. Minted	G-4	VG-8	F-12	VF-20	EF-40	MS-60
1848	6,415,799	$3.00	$4.00	$5.00	$8.00	$25.00	$100.00
1849	4,178,500	3.00	4.00	5.00	8.00	25.00	100.00
1850	4,426,844	3.00	3.00	5.00	8.00	25.00	100.00

1844, 44 over 81

1851, 51 over 81

1847, 7 over "Small" 7

Brilliant or red uncirculated coins are worth more than prices shown. Spotted, cleaned or discolored pieces are worth less.

	Quan. Minted	G-4	VG-8	F-12	VF-20	EF-40	MS-60
1851 Normal date	9,889,707	3.00	4.00	5.00	8.00	25.00	100.00
1851 over 81 (error)		4.25	5.25	8.50	17.00	30.00	160.00
1852	5,063,094	3.00	4.00	5.00	8.00	25.00	100.00
1853	6,641,131	3.00	4.00	5.00	8.00	25.00	100.00
1854	4,236,156	3.00	4.00	5.00	8.00	25.00	100.00

1855 Upright 5's

1855 Slanting 5's

1855 Knob on ear

	Quan. Minted	G-4	VG-8	F-12	VF-20	EF-40	MS-60
1855 All kinds	1,574,829						
1855 Upright 5's		3.00	4.00	5.00	8.00	25.00	100.00
1855 Slanting 5's		3.00	4.00	5.00	8.00	25.00	100.00
1855 Slanting 5's, knob on ear		3.25	4.25	6.00	12.00	27.00	110.00
1856 Upright 5	2,690,463	3.00	4.00	5.00	8.00	25.00	100.00
1856 Slanting 5		3.00	4.00	5.00	8.00	25.00	100.00

1857 Large Date

1857 Small Date

	Quan. Minted	G-4	VG-8	F-12	VF-20	EF-40	MS-60
1857 Large date	333,456	9.00	13.00	19.00	22.00	27.00	150.00
1857 Small date		10.00	15.00	22.00	26.00	30.00	175.00

SMALL CENTS — 1856 to Date

FLYING EAGLE TYPE 1856-1858

The Act of February 21, 1857 provided for the coinage of the small cent. The 1856 Eagle cent was not an authorized mint issue, as the law governing the new size coin was enacted after the date of issue. It is believed that about 1,000 of these pieces were struck. They are properly referred to as patterns.

G-4 GOOD—*All details worn, but readable.*
VG-8 VERY GOOD—*Feather details and eye of eagle are evident but worn.*
F-12 FINE—*Eagle head details and feather tips sharp.*
VF-20 VERY FINE—*Feathers in right wing and tail show considerable detail.*
EF-40 EXTREMELY FINE—*Slight wear, all details sharp.*
MS-60 UNCIRCULATED—*No trace of wear. Light blemishes.*

1858, 8 over 7

1856-1858 Large Letters

1858 Small Letters

Brilliant uncirculated and proof coins are worth more than prices shown. Spotted, cleaned or discolored pieces are worth less.

		Quan. Minted			*Quan. Minted*
1856		est. *1,000*	1858 Lg. letters	*(80)*	24,600,000
1857	*(485)*	17,450,000	1858 Sm. letters	*(200)*	

	G-4	*VG-8*	*F-12*	*VF-20*	*EF-40*	*MS-60*	*Proof-63*
1856	$1,000	$1,200	$1,500	$1,900	$2,300	$3,100	$3,500
1857	4.75	5.50	8.00	16.00	37.50	110.00	1,400
1858 Lg. let.	4.75	5.50	8.00	16.00	37.50	110.00	1,400
1858, 8 over 7		25.00	60.00	125.00	250.00	450.00	
1858 Sm let.	4.75	5.50	8.00	16.00	37.50	110.00	1,400

SMALL CENTS

INDIAN HEAD TYPE 1859-1909

The small cent was redesigned in 1859, and a representation of an Indian princess was adopted as the obverse device. The 1859 reverse was also changed to represent a laurel wreath. In 1860 the reverse was modified to display an oak wreath with a small shield at the top. From 1859 to 1863 cents were struck in copper-nickel. In 1864 the composition was changed to bronze, although copper-nickel cents were also struck during that year.

SMALL CENTS

G-4 GOOD—*No LIBERTY visible.*
VG-8 VERY GOOD—*At least three letters of LIBERTY readable on head band.*
F-12 FINE—*LIBERTY completely visible.*
VF-20 VERY FINE—*Slight but even wear on LIBERTY.*
EF-40 EXTREMELY FINE—*LIBERTY sharp. All other details sharp. Only slight wear on ribbon end.*
MS-60 UNCIRCULATED—*No trace of wear. Light blemishes.*

Without Shield at Top of Wreath
1859 Only

With Shield on Reverse
1860 to 1909

Brilliant uncirculated and proof coins are worth more than prices shown. Spotted, cleaned or discolored pieces are worth less.

Copper-nickel, Laurel Wreath Reverse 1859

	Quan. Minted	*G-4*	*VG-8*	*F-12*	*VF-20*	*EF-40*	*MS-60*	*Proof-63*
1859 . . . . *(800)*	36,400,000	$2.25	$2.50	$4.00	$11.00	$32.00	$95.00	$500.00

Copper-nickel, Oak Wreath with Shield Reverse 1860-1864

1860 . . . . *(1,000)*	20,566,000	2.00	2.50	4.00	7.00	15.00	65.00	425.00
1861 . . . . *(1,000)*	10,100,000	5.00	6.00	9.00	15.00	25.00	100.00	450.00
1862 . . . . *(550)*	28,075,000	1.25	1.50	2.25	5.00	10.00	60.00	400.00
1863 . . . . *(460)*	49,840,000	1.25	1.50	2.25	5.00	10.00	60.00	400.00
1864 . . . . *(370)*	13,740,000	4.00	5.00	7.00	10.00	15.00	65.00	425.00

Bronze 1864-1909

1864 Indian Head Cent with "L"

	Quan. Minted	*G-4*	*VG-8*	*F-12*	*VF-20*	*EF-40*	*MS-60*	*Proof-63*
1864 All kinds	39,233,714							
1864 No L.	*(150)*	$2.00	$2.75	$4.25	$9.00	$14.00	$35.00	$400.00
1864 L must show	*(20)*	17.00	23.00	30.00	55.00	80.00	200.00	——
1865 . . . . *(500)*	35,429,286	1.75	2.50	4.50	9.00	15.00	35.00	350.00
1866 . . . . *(725)*	9,826,500	11.00	13.00	20.00	35.00	50.00	85.00	300.00
1867 . . . . *(625)*	9,821,000	11.00	13.00	20.00	35.00	50.00	85.00	300.00
1868 . . . . *(600)*	10,266,500	11.00	13.00	20.00	35.00	50.00	85.00	275.00
1869 . . . . *(600)*	6,420,000	15.00	20.00	45.00	65.00	90.00	160.00	300.00

SMALL CENTS

Brilliant or red uncirculated coins are worth more than prices shown. Spotted, cleaned or discolored pieces are worth less.

	Quan. Minted	*G-4*	*VG-8*	*F-12*	*VF-20*	*EF-40*	*MS-60*	*Proof-63*
1870 *(1,000)*	5,275,000	$10.00	$15.00	$32.00	$50.00	$70.00	$135.00	$300.00
1871 *(960)*	3,929,500	15.00	20.00	45.00	55.00	85.00	150.00	325.00
1872 *(950)*	4,042,000	22.00	27.00	47.50	70.00	90.00	200.00	350.00
1873 *(1,100)*	11,676,500	5.00	6.00	9.00	16.00	27.00	60.00	165.00
1874 *(700)*	14,187,500	5.00	6.00	9.00	16.00	27.00	55.00	150.00
1875 *(700)*	13,528,000	5.00	6.00	9.00	16.00	27.00	55.00	150.00
1876 *(1,150)*	7,944,000	8.00	12.00	15.00	25.00	38.00	70.00	150.00
1877 *(510)*	852,500	125.00	150.00	225.00	350.00	500.00	900.00	1,200
1878 (2,350)	5,799,850	8.00	12.00	15.00	25.00	40.00	75.00	140.00
1879 (3,200)	16,231,200	1.50	2.00	3.00	5.00	12.00	30.00	125.00
1880 (3,955)	38,964,955	.50	.80	1.50	2.50	6.50	18.00	90.00
1881 (3,575)	39,211,575	.50	.80	1.50	2.50	6.50	18.00	90.00
1882 (3,100)	38,581,100	.50	.80	1.50	2.50	6.50	18.00	90.00
1883 (6,609)	45,598,109	.50	.80	1.50	2.50	6.50	18.00	90.00
1884 (3,942)	23,261,742	.75	1.25	2.25	4.00	8.00	22.00	100.00
1885 (3,790)	11,765,384	1.50	2.00	4.00	7.00	14.00	35.00	115.00
1886 (4,290)	17,654,290	.60	1.25	3.25	5.00	9.00	25.00	100.00
1887 (2,960)	45,226,483	.35	.50	.75	1.50	5.00	18.00	90.00
1888 (4,582)	37,494,414	.35	.50	.75	1.50	5.00	18.00	90.00
1889 (3,336)	48,869,361	.35	.50	.75	1.50	5.00	18.00	90.00
1890 (2,740)	57,182,854	.35	.50	.75	1.50	5.00	18.00	90.00
1891 (2,350)	47,072,350	.35	.50	.75	1.50	5.00	18.00	90.00
1892 (2,745)	37,649,832	.35	.50	.75	1.50	5.00	18.00	90.00
1893 (2,195)	46,642,195	.35	.50	.75	1.50	5.00	18.00	90.00
1894 (2,632)	16,752,132	.60	1.00	2.50	4.00	7.50	22.00	100.00
1895 (2,062)	38,343,636	.25	.35	.65	1.00	4.00	15.00	90.00
1896 (1,862)	39,057,293	.25	.35	.65	1.00	4.00	15.00	90.00
1897 (1,938)	50,466,330	.25	.35	.65	1.00	4.00	15.00	90.00
1898 (1,795)	49,823,079	.25	.35	.65	1.00	4.00	15.00	90.00
1899 (2,031)	53,600,031	.25	.35	.65	1.00	4.00	15.00	90.00
1900 (2,262)	66,833,764	.20	.25	.50	.75	3.00	13.00	75.00
1901 (1,985)	79,611,143	.20	.25	.50	.75	3.00	13.00	75.00
1902 (2,018)	87,376,722	.20	.25	.50	.75	3.00	13.00	75.00
1903 (1,790)	85,094,493	.20	.25	.50	.75	3.00	13.00	75.00
1904 (1,817)	61,328,015	.20	.25	.50	.75	3.00	13.00	75.00
1905 (2,152)	80,719,163	.20	.25	.50	.75	3.00	13.00	75.00
1906 (1,725)	96,022,255	.20	.25	.50	.75	3.00	13.00	75.00
1907 (1,475)	108,138,618	.20	.25	.50	.75	3.00	13.00	75.00

Location of mint mark S on reverse of Indian cent (1908 and 1909 only).

1908 (1,620)	32,327,987	.20	.25	.50	.75	3.00	16.00	80.00
1908S	1,115,000	10.00	12.00	15.00	20.00	30.00	75.00	
1909 (2,175)	14,370,645	.25	.30	.60	1.00	5.00	18.00	110.00
1909S	309,000	55.00	65.00	75.00	100.00	135.00	220.00	

SMALL CENTS

LINCOLN TYPE, WHEAT EARS REVERSE 1909-1958

Victor D. Brenner designed this cent which was issued to commemorate the hundredth anniversary of Lincoln's birth. The designer's initials VDB appear on the reverse of a limited quantity of cents of 1909. Later in the year they were removed from the dies but restored in 1918 as very small incuse letters beneath the shoulder. The Lincoln type was the first cent to have the motto IN GOD WE TRUST.

G-4 GOOD—*Date worn but apparent. Lines in wheat ears missing. Full rims.*
VG-8 VERY GOOD—*Half of lines show in upper wheat ears.*
F-12 FINE—*Wheat lines worn but visible.*
VF-20 VERY FINE—*Cheek and jaw bones worn but separated. No worn spots on wheat ears.*
EF-40 EXTREMELY FINE—*Slight wear. All details sharp.*
MS-60 UNCIRCULATED—*No trace of wear. Light blemishes or discoloration.*
MS-63 UNCIRCULATED—*No trace of wear. Slight blemishes.*

Location of mint mark S or D on obverse of Lincoln cent.

Location of designer's initials V.D.B. on 1909 only.

No V.D.B. on reverse 1909-1958.

Bronze 1909-1942

Brilliant uncirculated coins are worth more than prices shown. Spotted, cleaned, or discolored pieces are worth less.

	Quan. Minted	*G-4*	*VG-8*	*F-12*	*VF-20*	*EF-40*	*MS-60*
1909 V.D.B.	27,995,000	$.50	$.75	$1.00	$1.25	$1.50	$4.00
1909 V.D.B. Matte proof-63	(420)						900.00
1909S, V.D.B.	484,000	160.00	175.00	190.00	210.00	225.00	275.00
1909	72,702,618	.15	.20	.25	.40	.75	7.00
1909 Matte proof-63	(2,198)						125.00
1909S	1,825,000	21.00	23.00	27.50	35.00	45.00	85.00
1910	146,801,218	.05	.08	.10	.20	.50	7.00
1910 Matte proof-63	(2,405)						125.00
1910S	6,045,000	3.00	3.50	4.00	5.00	9.00	50.00
1911	101,177,787	.05	.08	.15	.40	.75	9.00
1911 Matte proof-63	(1,733)						125.00
1911D	12,672,000	2.00	2.25	3.00	5.00	15.00	55.00
1911S	4,026,000	6.00	7.00	8.00	10.00	16.00	65.00
1912	68,153,060	.05	.10	.40	1.00	1.75	13.00
1912 Matte proof-63	(2,145)						125.00
1912D	10,411,000	2.25	2.50	3.25	6.00	18.00	63.00
1912S	4,431,000	4.50	6.00	7.00	8.50	15.00	63.00
1913	76,532,352	.05	.10	.30	.75	1.25	11.00
1913 Matte proof-63	(2,848)						125.00
1913D	15,804,000	.50	1.00	1.50	2.75	10.00	48.00

SMALL CENTS

Brilliant uncirculated coins before 1934 are worth more than prices shown. Spotted, cleaned or discolored pieces are worth less

	Quan. Minted	*G-4*	*VG-8*	*F-12*	*VF-20*	*EF-40*	*MS-60*	*MS-63*
1913S	6,101,000	$3.00	$4.00	$4.50	$5.00	$11.00	$60.00	
1914	75,238,432	.05	.10	.30	.75	3.00	33.00	
1914 Matte proof-63	(1,365)	150.00						
1914D*	1,193,000	36.00	43.00	60.00	85.00	220.00	475.00	
1914S	4,137,000	4.75	5.50	6.00	7.00	16.00	100.00	
1915	29,092,120	.30	.50	1.25	2.00	14.00	60.00	
1915 Matte proof-63	(1,150)	225.00						
1915D	22,050,000	.20	.40	.60	1.25	3.75	20.00	
1915S	4,833,000	3.25	4.00	4.50	6.00	12.00	50.00	
1916	131,833,677	.03	.05	.10	.20	.80	5.50	
1916 Matte proof-63	(1,050)	300.00						
1916D	35,956,000	.08	.13	.40	1.00	2.50	20.00	
1916S	22,510,000	.30	.40	.75	1.25	3.50	27.50	
1917	196,429,785	.03	.05	.10	.20	.50	6.00	
1917D	55,120,000	.08	.13	.35	.80	2.50	25.00	
1917S	32,620,000	.08	.13	.35	.80	2.50	27.50	

Designer's initials restored starting 1918.

1918	288,104,634	.03	.05	.10	.20	.75	5.50	
1918D	47,830,000	.08	.13	.35	.80	2.50	25.00	
1918S	34,680,000	.08	.13	.35	.80	2.50	27.50	
1919	392,021,000	.02	.03	.05	.15	.50	4.00	
1919D	57,154,000	.04	.06	.10	.30	1.00	21.00	
1919S	139,760,000	.04	.06	.10	.25	.50	13.00	
1920	310,165,000	.02	.03	.05	.15	.50	3.50	
1920D	49,280,000	.04	.06	.10	.30	1.00	23.00	
1920S	46,220,000	.04	.06	.10	.30	1.25	25.00	
1921	39,157,000	.05	.08	.15	.35	1.50	17.00	
1921S	15,274,000	.35	.45	.70	1.25	6.00	65.00	
1922D	} 7,160,000	2.00	3.00	4.00	5.00	9.00	35.00	
1922 Plain†		85.00	100.00	125.00	225.00	500.00	2,200	
1923	74,723,000	.02	.03	.05	.15	.50	3.00	
1923S	8,700,000	.75	.85	1.25	2.00	6.00	65.00	
1924	75,178,000	.02	.03	.05	.15	.75	9.00	
1924D	2,520,000	4.50	5.00	6.00	10.00	25.00	125.00	
1924S	11,696,000	.35	.45	.70	1.00	2.00	50.00	
1925	139,949,000	.02	.03	.05	.15	.45	3.00	
1925D	22,580,000	.04	.06	.10	.30	1.50	22.00	
1925S	26,380,000	.04	.06	.10	.25	1.25	30.00	
1926	157,088,000	.02	.03	.05	.15	.45	3.00	
1926D	28,020,000	.04	.06	.10	.25	1.50	21.00	
1926S	4,550,000	.80	1.00	1.50	2.00	5.00	45.00	
1927	144,440,000	.02	.03	.05	.15	.45	3.00	
1927D	27,170,000	.04	.06	.10	.25	.85	12.50	
1927S	14,276,000	.25	.30	.50	.75	2.00	30.00	
1928	134,116,000	.02	.03	.05	.15	.45	3.00	
1928D	31,170,000	.04	.06	.10	.25	.75	10.00	
1928S	17,266,000	.06	.10	.25	.50	1.00	23.00	
1929	185,262,000	.02	.03	.05	.15	.25	2.00	
1929D	41,730,000	.04	.06	.10	.25	.60	6.00	
1929S	50,148,000	.03	.05	.10	.15	.40	3.00	
1930	157,415,000	.02	.03	.05	.15	.25	2.00	$4.00
1930D	40,100,000	.04	.06	.10	.25	.60	5.00	10.00

*Beware of altered date or mint mark. No VDB on shoulder of genuine 1914D cent.
†The 1922 without D caused by defective die. Beware removed mint mark.

SMALL CENTS

	Quan. Minted	G-4	VG-8	F-12	VF-20	EF-40	MS-60	MS-63
1930S	24,286,000	$.03	$.05	$.10	$.15	$.40	$2.50	$6.00
1931	19,396,000	.15	.20	.30	.40	.60	7.00	17.00
1931D	4,480,000	1.00	1.25	1.50	2.00	4.00	25.00	50.00
1931S	866,000	17.00	19.00	21.00	22.00	25.00	40.00	55.00
1932	9,062,000	.70	.80	1.00	1.15	1.75	9.00	20.00
1932D	10,500,000	.25	.35	.40	.50	.75	7.00	16.00
1933	14,360,000	.25	.35	.45	.60	1.00	8.00	17.00
1933D	6,200,000	.80	1.00	1.20	1.50	1.75	11.00	22.00
1934	219,080,000	.02	.02	.02	.03	.10	1.50	2.50
1934D	28,446,000	.04	.06	.08	.10	.25	9.00	17.00
1935	245,388,000	.02	.02	.02	.03	.06	.75	1.25
1935D	47,000,000	.02	.02	.02	.03	.10	1.25	3.25
1935S	38,702,000	.02	.03	.03	.04	.08	5.00	8.00
1936	309,637,569	.02	.02	.02	.03	.06	.50	.60
1936 Proof-63	(5,569)							45.00
1936D	40,620,000	.02	.02	.02	.03	.08	.75	1.50
1936S	29,130,000	.03	.03	.03	.04	.10	.90	1.60
1937	309,179,320	.02	.02	.02	.03	.05	.60	.70
1937 Proof-63	(9,320)							20.00
1937D	50,430,000	.02	.02	.02	.03	.06	.50	1.25
1937S	34,500,000	.03	.03	.03	.04	.06	.50	1.25
1938	156,696,734	.02	.02	.02	.03	.05	.60	.75
1938 Proof-63	(14,734)							15.00
1938D	20,010,000	.02	.03	.04	.06	.15	.80	1.25
1938S	15,180,000	.06	.08	.10	.12	.15	.90	1.50
1939	316,479,520	.02	.02	.02	.03	.05	.25	.40
1939 Proof-63	(13,520)							15.00
1939D	15,160,000	.06	.08	.10	.12	.15	.95	1.50
1939S	52,070,000	.03	.03	.03	.04	.10	.50	1.00
1940	586,825,872	.01	.01	.02	.02	.03	.20	.30
1940 Proof-63	(15,872)							12.00
1940D	81,390,000	.01	.01	.02	.02	.03	.25	.40
1940S	112,940,000	.01	.01	.02	.03	.04	.60	.80
1941	887,039,100	.01	.01	.02	.02	.03	.25	.40
1941 Proof-63	(21,100)							11.00
1941D	128,700,000	.01	.01	.02	.02	.03	.60	1.50
1941S	92,360,000	.01	.01	.02	.03	.04	.75	1.60
1942	657,828,600	.01	.01	.02	.02	.03	.10	.20
1942 Proof-63	(32,600)							11.00
1942D	206,698,000	.01	.01	.02	.02	.03	.10	.35
1942S	85,590,000	.01	.01	.02	.03	.05	1.00	2.75

Zinc-coated Steel 1943 Only

		F-12	VF-20	EF-40	MS-60	MS-63
1943	684,628,670	.02	.02	.08	.25	.40
1943D	217,660,000	.02	.04	.10	.30	.50
1943S	191,550,000	.03	.05	.15	.30	.75

Bronze Resumed 1944-1958

	Quan. Minted	VF-20	EF-40	MS-63
1944	1,435,400,000	$.02	$.02	$.25
1944D	430,578,000	.02	.02	.45
1944D, D over S (see illus. pg.60)		65.00	95.00	*225.00
1944S	282,760,000	.02	.03	.25
1945	1,040,515,000	.02	.02	.10
1945D	266,268,000	.02	.02	.35
1945S	181,770,000	.02	.03	.25
1946	991,655,000	.02	.02	.15
1946D	315,690,000	.02	.02	.15
1946S	198,100,000	.02	.03	.25
1947	190,555,000	.02	.02	.45

*Value for MS-60 uncirculated is $185.00.

SMALL CENTS

1944D, D over S

1955 Doubled Die Error

		Quan. Minted	VF-20	EF-40	MS-63	Proof-63
1947D		194,750,000	$.02	$.02	$.25	
1947S		99,000,000	.02	.03	.45	
1948		317,570,000	.02	.02	.30	
1948D		172,637,500	.02	.02	.50	
1948S		81,735,000	.02	.03	.50	
1949		217,775,000	.02	.02	.75	
1949D		153,132,500	.02	.02	.55	
1949S		64,290,000	.03	.05	1.50	
1950	(51,386)	272,686,386	.02	.02	.80	$15.00
1950D		334,950,000	.02	.02	.15	
1950S		118,505,000	.02	.03	.45	
1951	(57,500)	284,633,500	.02	.02	.55	10.00
1951D		625,355,000	.02	.02	.20	
1951S		136,010,000	.02	.03	.85	
1952	(81,980)	186,856,980	.02	.02	.30	6.00
1952D		746,130,000	.02	.02	.35	
1952S		137,800,004	.02	.03	.50	
1953	(128,800)	256,883,800	.02	.03	.15	4.00
1953D		700,515,000	.02	.02	.20	
1953S		181,835,000	.02	.03	.25	
1954	(233,300)	71,873,350	.03	.05	.25	1.75
1954D		251,552,500	.02	.02	.10	
1954S		96,190,000	.02	.03	.10	
1955 Doubled die obv	}	330,958,200	220.00	250.00	*550.00	
1955	(378,200) }		.02	.02	.08	1.50
1955D		563,257,500	.02	.02	.08	
1955S		44,610,000	.10	.15	.25	
1956	(669,384)	421,414,384	.02	.02	.08	.70
1956D		1,098,201,100	.02	.02	.05	
1957	(1,247,952)	283,787,952	.02	.02	.05	.50
1957D		1,051,342,000	.02	.02	.03	
1958	(875,652)	253,400,652	.02	.02	.03	.65
1958D		800,953,300	.02	.02	.03	

*Value for MS-60 Uncirculated is $450.00.

LINCOLN TYPE, MEMORIAL REVERSE 1959 TO DATE

Small Date

Large Date

		Quan. Minted	MS-63	Proof-63
1959	(1,149,291)	610,864,291	$.01	$.40
1959D		1,279,760,000	.01	
1960 Large date	} (1,691,602)	588,096,602	.01	.25
1960 Sm. date			.75	3.00

	Quan. Minted	MS-63	Proof-63
1960D Large date	}	$.01	
1960D Small date	} 1,580,884,000	.02	
1961 (3,028,244)	756,373,244	.01	$.20
1961D	1,753,266,700	.01	
1962 (3,218,019)	609,263,019	.01	.20
1962D	1,793,148,400	.01	
1963 (3,075,645)	757,185,645	.01	.20
1963D	1,774,020,400	.01	

Small Date
Numbers aligned at top

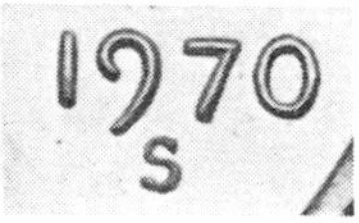

Large Date
Low 7 to date

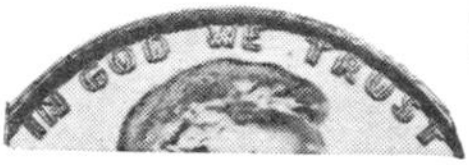

Enlarged Detail of 1972
Doubled Die Error

1969S Doubled Die
Error

	Quan. Minted	MS-63	Proof-63
1964 (3,950,762)	2,652,525,762	$.01	$.20
1964D	3,799,071,500	.01	
1965	1,497,224,900	.02	
1966	2,188,147,783	.04	
1967	3,048,667,100	.03	
1968	1,707,880,970	.02	
1968D	2,886,269,600	.01	
1968S (3,041,506)	261,311,507	.02	.20
1969	1,136,910,000	.06	
1969D	4,002,832,200	.04	
1969S (2,934,631)	547,309,631	.03	.20
1969S Doubled die obv		——	
1970	1,898,315,000	.04	
1970D	2,891,438,900	.02	
1970S (2,632,810)	693,192,814		
1970S Sm. date		6.00	35.00
1970S Lg. date (low 7)		.04	.20
1971	1,919,490,000	.05	
1971D	2,911,045,600	.03	
1971S (3,220,733)	528,354,192	.03	.20
1972 Doubled die obv		100.00	
1972	2,933,255,000	.01	
1972D	2,665,071,400	.02	
1972S (3,260,996)	380,200,104	.02	.20
1973	3,728,245,000	.01	
1973D	3,549,576,588	.01	

	Quan. Minted	MS-63	Proof-63
1973S (2,760,339)	319,937,634	$.02	$.20
1974	4,232,140,523	.01	
1974D	4,235,098,000	.01	
1974S (2,612,568)	412,039,228	.03	.20
1975	5,451,476,142	.01	
1975D	4,505,275,300	.01	
1975S Proof	(2,845,450)		2.00
1976	4,674,292,426	.01	
1976D	4,221,592,455	.02	
1976S Proof	(4,149,730)		1.00
1977	4,469,930,000	.01	
1977D	4,194,062,300	.01	
1977S Proof	(3,251,152)		1.00
1978	5,558,605,000	.01	
1978D	4,280,233,400	.01	
1978S Proof	(3,127,781)		1.10
1979	6,018,515,000	.01	
1979D	4,139,357,254	.01	
1979S Proof	(3,677,175)		
Filled S			1.10
Clear S			1.50
1980	7,414,705,000	.01	
1980D	5,140,098,660	.01	
1980S Proof	(3,554,806)		.60
1981	7,491,750,000	.01	
1981D	5,373,235,677	.01	
1981S Proof	(4,063,083)		.60
1982	10,712,525,000		
Lg. Date		.01	
Sm. Date		.02	

Large Date

Small Date

	Quan. Minted	MS-63	Proof-63
1982D	6,012,979,368		
Lg. Date		$.01	
1982S Proof	(3,857,479)		$.75

Copper Plated Zinc

	Quan. Minted	MS-63	Proof-63
1982 Lg. Date	inc. above	.01	
1982 Sm. Date	inc. above	.01	
1982D Lg. Date	inc. above	.05	
1982D Sm. Date	inc. above	.01	
1983	7,752,355,000	.01	
1983D	6,467,199,428	.01	
1983S Proof	(3,279,126)	.01	1.00
1984	8,151,079,000	.01	
1984D	5,569,238,906	.01	
1984S Proof	(3,065,110)		2.00
1985	5,648,489,887	.01	
1985D	5,287,399,926	.01	
1985S Proof	(3,362,821)		1.00
1986	4,491,395,493	.01	

	Quan. Minted	MS-63	Proof-63
1986D	4,442,866,698	$.01	
1986S Proof	(3,010,497)		$2.25
1987	4,682,466,931	.01	
1987D	4,879,389,511	.01	
1987S Proof	(4,227,728)		2.00
1988	6,092,810,000	.01	
1988D	5,253,740,443	.01	
1988S Proof	(3,262,948)		1.75
1989	7,261,535,000	.01	
1989D	5,345,467,111	.01	
1989S Proof	(3,220,194)		2.00
1990	6,851,765,000	.01	
1990D	4,922,894,553	.01	
1990S Proof	(3,299,559)		2.00
1991	5,165,940,000	.01	
1991D	4,158,442,076	.01	
1991S Proof			1.50
1992		.01	
1992D		.01	
1992S Proof			1.50

TWO-CENT PIECES — 1864-1873

The Act of April 22, 1864, which changed the weight and composition of the cent, included a provision for the bronze two-cent piece. The weight was specified as 96 grains, the alloy being the same as for the cent.

There are two varieties for the first year of issue, 1864: the small motto and the large motto. The differences are explained in the illustrations below.

1864 Small Motto

1864 Large Motto

On the obverse the D in GOD is narrow on the large motto. The stem to the leaf shows plainly on the small motto variety.

G-4 GOOD—*At least IN GOD visible.*
VG-8 VERY GOOD—*WE weakly visible.*
F-12 FINE—*Complete motto visible. WE weak.*
EF-40 EXTREMELY FINE—*WE is bold.*
MS-60 UNCIRCULATED—*No trace of wear. Light blemishes.*

Brilliant red choice uncirculated and proof coins are worth more than prices shown. Cleaned or discolored pieces are worth less.

		Quan. Minted	G-4	VG-8	F-12	EF-40	MS-60	Proof-63
1864 Sm. motto	(100+)	19,847,500	$20.00	$25.00	$55.00	$135.00	$275.00	——
1864 Lg. motto			2.00	3.00	4.00	15.00	40.00	$325.00
1865	(500+)	13,640,000	2.00	3.00	4.00	15.00	40.00	275.00
1866	(725+)	3,177,000	2.00	3.00	4.00	15.00	40.00	275.00
1867	(625+)	2,938,750	2.00	3.00	4.00	15.00	40.00	275.00
1868	(600+)	2,803,750	2.00	3.00	4.00	15.00	40.00	275.00
1869	(600+)	1,546,500	2.50	3.50	6.00	20.00	100.00	325.00
1870	(1,000+)	861,250	3.00	4.50	8.50	25.00	125.00	350.00
1871	(960+)	721,250	3.25	4.75	10.00	30.00	150.00	500.00
1872	(950+)	65,000	30.00	40.00	80.00	200.00	475.00	700.00
1873 Proofs only	(1,000+)							1,000

SILVER THREE-CENT PIECES 1851-1873

This smallest of United States silver coins was authorized by Congress March 3, 1851. The first three-cent silver pieces had no lines bordering the six-pointed star. From 1854 through 1858 there were three lines, while issues of the last fifteen years show only two lines. Issues from 1854 through 1873 have an olive sprig over the III and a bundle of three arrows beneath.

No outline around star.

Mint Mark
O

G-4 GOOD—*Star worn smooth. Legend and date readable.*
VG-8 VERY GOOD—*Outline of shield defined. Legend and date clear.*
F-12 FINE—*Only star points worn smooth.*
VF-20 VERY FINE—*Only partial wear on star ridges.*
EF-40 EXTREMELY FINE—*Ridges on star points show.*
MS-60 UNCIRCULATED—*No trace of wear. Light blemishes.*

Well struck specimens command higher prices.

	Quan. Minted	*G-4*	*VG-8*	*F-12*	*VF-20*	*EF-40*	*MS-60*	*Proof-63*
1851	5,447,400	$4.75	$6.50	$9.00	$14.00	$27.00	$90.00	——
1851O	720,000	7.50	11.00	16.50	27.00	50.00	210.00	
1852	18,663,500	4.50	6.00	8.00	13.00	25.00	90.00	——
1853	11,400,000	4.50	6.00	8.00	13.00	25.00	90.00	

Three outlines to star, large date.

	Quan. Minted	*G-4*	*VG-8*	*F-12*	*VF-20*	*EF-40*	*MS-60*	*Proof-63*
1854	671,000	6.00	8.00	10.00	20.00	42.00	175.00	——
1855	139,000	9.00	13.00	20.00	35.00	85.00	300.00	$1,300
1856	1,458,000	4.75	6.50	10.00	18.00	40.00	160.00	1,200
1857	1,042,000	4.75	6.50	10.00	18.00	40.00	160.00	1,200
1858	1,604,000	4.75	6.50	10.00	18.00	40.00	160.00	1,000

Two outlines to star, small date.

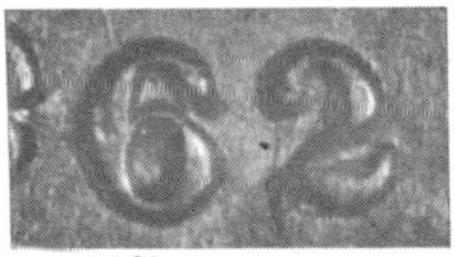

1862 2 over 1

	Quan. Minted	*G-4*	*VG-8*	*F-12*	*VF-20*	*EF-40*	*MS-60*	*Proof-63*
1859 (800)	365,000	4.75	6.50	10.00	17.00	30.00	90.00	350.00
1860 (1,000)	287,000	4.75	6.50	10.00	17.00	30.00	90.00	350.00
1861 (1,000)	498,000	4.75	6.50	10.00	17.00	30.00	90.00	350.00
1862, 2 over 1	343,550	6.00	8.00	12.00	20.00	40.00	125.00	
1862 (550)		4.75	6.50	10.00	17.00	30.00	90.00	350.00
1863 (460)	21,460						300.00	400.00
1864 (470)	12,470						300.00	400.00
1865 (500)	8,500						325.00	400.00
1866 (725)	22,725						325.00	400.00
1867 (625)	4,625						325.00	400.00
1868 (600)	4,100						325.00	400.00
1869 (600)	5,100						325.00	400.00
1870 (1,000)	4,000						325.00	400.00
1871 (960)	4,360						325.00	400.00
1872 (950)	1,950						325.00	400.00
1873 (600)	600 (Proof only)							900.00

THREE-CENT PIECES (NICKEL)

ISSUED 1865-1889

The three-cent pieces struck in nickel composition were designed to replace the silver three cent coins. Composition is 75% copper and 25% nickel. All were coined at Philadelphia and have plain edges.

G-4 GOOD—*Date and legends complete though worn. III smooth.*

VG-8 VERY GOOD—*III is half worn. Rims complete.*

F-12 FINE—*Hair curls well defined.*

EF-40 EXTREMELY FINE—*Slight, even wear.*

MS-60 UNCIRCULATED—*No trace of wear. Light blemishes.*

Brilliant choice uncirculated and proof coins are worth more than prices shown. Spotted, cleaned or discolored pieces are worth less.

	Quan. Minted	*G-4*	*VG-8*	*F-12*	*VF-20*	*EF-40*	*MS-60*	*Proof-63*
1865 .... *(500+)*	11,382,000	$2.50	$3.00	$3.25	$4.00	$8.50	$40.00	$550.00
1866 .... *(725+)*	4,801,000	2.50	3.00	3.25	4.00	8.50	40.00	150.00
1867 .... *(625+)*	3,915,000	2.50	3.00	3.25	4.00	8.50	40.00	150.00
1868 .... *(600+)*	3,252,000	2.50	3.00	3.25	4.00	8.50	40.00	150.00
1869 .... *(600+)*	1,604,000	2.50	3.00	3.25	4.00	8.50	40.00	150.00
1870 .... *(1,000+)*	1,335,000	2.25	3.25	4.00	5.00	9.50	40.00	150.00
1871 .... *(960+)*	604,000	2.25	3.25	4.00	5.00	9.50	45.00	150.00
1872 .... *(950+)*	862,000	2.25	3.25	4.00	5.00	9.50	45.00	150.00
1873 .... *(1,100+)*	1,173,000	2.25	3.25	4.00	5.00	9.50	40.00	150.00
1874 .... *(700+)*	790,000	3.00	3.75	4.50	5.50	11.00	45.00	150.00
1875 .... *(700+)*	228,000	3.00	4.00	5.00	6.00	14.00	90.00	150.00
1876 .... *(1,150+)*	162,000	3.00	5.00	6.00	7.00	14.00	100.00	175.00
1877 .... *(510+)*	510 (Proofs only)					500.00		800.00
1878 .... (2,350)	2,350					300.00		500.00
1879 .... (3,200)	41,200	20.00	30.00	35.00	40.00	50.00	125.00	175.00
1880 .... (3,955)	24,955	25.00	40.00	50.00	55.00	75.00	140.00	175.00
1881 .... (3,575)	1,080,575	2.50	3.00	3.25	4.00	8.50	40.00	175.00
1882 .... (3,100)	25,300	21.00	35.00	40.00	50.00	60.00	150.00	225.00
1883 .... (6,609)	10,609	48.00	75.00	95.00	115.00	135.00	225.00	375.00
1884 .... (3,942)	5,642	125.00	160.00	175.00	200.00	250.00	350.00	425.00
1885 .... (3,790)	4,790	160.00	200.00	220.00	250.00	300.00	425.00	500.00
1886 .... (4,290)	4,290					200.00		300.00
1887, 7 over 6 } (2,960)						200.00		300.00
1887 All kinds }	7,961	85.00	125.00	150.00	175.00	225.00	275.00	325.00
1888 .... (4,582)	41,083	15.00	20.00	25.00	30.00	40.00	125.00	165.00
1889 .... (3,436)	21,561	25.00	35.00	45.00	50.00	60.00	140.00	175.00

NICKEL FIVE-CENT PIECES — 1866 to Date

SHIELD TYPE 1866-1883

The shield type nickel was made possible by the Act of May 16, 1866. Its weight was set at 77-16/100 grains with the same composition as the nickel three-cent piece which was authorized in 1865.

Rays Between Stars 1866-1867

G-4 GOOD—*All letters in motto readable.*

VG-8 VERY GOOD—*Motto stands out clearly. Rims worn slightly but even. Part of shield lines visible.*

F-12 FINE—*Half of each olive leaf is smooth.*

EF-40 EXTREMELY FINE—*Leaf tips show slight wear. Cross over shield slightly worn.*

MS-6C UNCIRCULATED—*No trace of wear. Light blemishes.*

NICKEL FIVE-CENT PIECES

Brilliant choice uncirculated and proof coins are worth more than prices shown. Spotted, cleaned or discolored pieces are worth less.

	Quan. Minted	*G-4*	*VG-8*	*F-12*	*EF-40*	*MS-60*	*Proof-63*
1866 Rays .... *(125+)*	14,742,500	$6.00	$7.25	$11.00	$45.00	$115.00	$1,250
1867 Rays .... *(25+)*	2,019,000	7.00	8.00	13.00	50.00	175.00	4,250

Without Rays 1867-1883

Typical example of 1883, 3 over 2. Other varieties exist.

	Quan. Minted	*G-4*	*VG-8*	*F-12*	*EF-40*	*MS-60*	*Proof-63*
1867 No rays .... *(600+)*	28,890,500	4.00	4.50	6.00	15.00	50.00	150.00
1868 .... *(600+)*	28,817,000	4.00	4.50	6.00	15.00	50.00	150.00
1869 .... *(600+)*	16,395,000	4.00	4.50	6.00	15.00	50.00	150.00
1870 .... *(1,000+)*	4,806,000	4.00	4.50	6.00	16.00	65.00	150.00
1871 .... *(960+)*	561,000	15.00	18.00	25.00	50.00	150.00	200.00
1872 .... *(950+)*	6,036,000	4.00	4.50	6.00	16.00	50.00	150.00
1873 Closed 3 ...... *(1,100+)*	436,050	4.00	4.50	6.00	16.00	65.00	150.00
1873 Open 3	4,113,950	4.00	4.50	6.00	16.00	65.00	
1874 .... *(700+)*	3,538,000	5.00	6.00	7.00	16.00	65.00	150.00
1875 .... *(700+)*	2,097,000	6.00	7.00	10.00	20.00	75.00	150.00
1876 .... *(1,150+)*	2,530,000	6.00	7.00	10.00	20.00	65.00	150.00
1877 Est. Issued .... *(510+)*	510				600.00		850.00
1878 .... (2,350)	2,350				350.00		450.00
1879 .... (3,200)	29,100	125.00	150.00	180.00	275.00	300.00	325.00
1880 .... (3,955)	19,955	140.00	170.00	200.00	300.00	375.00	375.00
1881 .... (3,575)	72,375	85.00	110.00	135.00	190.00	225.00	400.00
1882 .... (3,100)	11,476,000	3.00	4.00	5.00	15.00	50.00	150.00
1883 .... (5,419)	1,456,919	3.00	4.00	5.00	15.00	50.00	150.00
1883, 3 over 2			15.00	25.00	65.00	175.00	

LIBERTY HEAD TYPE 1883-1913

In 1883 the design was changed to the familiar "Liberty head." This type first appeared without the word CENTS on the coin, merely a large letter "V." These "centless" coins were goldplated and passed for five dollars. Later in that year the word CENTS was added.

Without CENTS 1883 Only

G-4 GOOD—*No details in head. LIBERTY obliterated.*
VG-8 VERY GOOD—*At least 3 letters in LIBERTY readable.*
F-12 FINE—*All letters in LIBERTY show.*
VF-20 VERY FINE—*LIBERTY bold, including letter I.*
EF-40 EXTREMELY FINE—*LIBERTY sharp. Corn grains at bottom of wreath show, on reverse.*
MS-60 UNCIRCULATED—*No trace of wear. Light blemishes.*

	Quan. Minted	*G-4*	*VG-8*	*F-12*	*VF-20*	*EF-40*	*MS-60*	*Proof-63*
1883 without CENTS .... (5,219)	5,479,519	$1.00	$1.50	$2.00	$2.50	$3.75	$16.00	$175.00

NICKEL FIVE-CENT PIECES

With CENTS 1883-1913

Location of mint mark

Brilliant choice uncirculated and proof coins are worth more than prices shown. Spotted, cleaned or discolored pieces are worth less.

	Quan. Minted	*G-4*	*VG-8*	*F-12*	*VF-20*	*EF-40*	*MS-60*	*Proof-63*
1883 with CENTS .... (6,783)	16,032,983	$2.00	$3.00	$5.00	$10.00	$15.00	$55.00	$130.00
1884 .... (3,942)	11,273,942	2.50	3.50	5.50	11.00	16.00	70.00	140.00
1885 .... (3,790)	1,476,490	90.00	110.00	175.00	225.00	400.00	500.00	500.00
1886 .... (4,290)	3,330,290	25.00	32.00	55.00	90.00	125.00	225.00	250.00
1887 .... (2,960)	15,263,652	2.00	3.00	6.00	8.00	15.00	50.00	125.00
1888 .... (4,582)	10,720,483	3.50	4.50	7.00	12.00	18.00	70.00	125.00
1889 .... (3,336)	15,881,361	2.00	3.00	5.00	8.00	15.00	50.00	125.00
1890 .... (2,740)	16,259,272	2.00	3.00	5.00	8.00	15.00	50.00	125.00
1891 .... (2,350)	16,834,350	2.00	3.00	5.00	8.00	15.00	50.00	125.00
1892 .... (2,745)	11,699,642	2.00	3.00	5.00	8.00	15.00	50.00	125.00
1893 .... (2,195)	13,370,195	2.00	3.00	5.00	8.00	15.00	50.00	125.00
1894 .... (2,632)	5,413,132	2.00	3.00	6.00	12.00	19.00	80.00	125.00
1895 .... (2,062)	9,979,884	1.50	3.00	5.00	7.00	13.00	45.00	125.00
1896 .... (1,862)	8,842,920	2.00	3.25	6.00	8.00	15.00	45.00	125.00
1897 .... (1,938)	20,428,735	.50	.75	2.00	3.50	9.00	45.00	125.00
1898 .... (1,795)	12,532,087	.50	.75	2.00	3.50	9.00	45.00	125.00
1899 .... (2,031)	26,029,031	.50	.75	2.00	3.50	9.00	45.00	125.00
1900 .... (2,262)	27,255,995	.25	.35	1.00	2.00	8.00	40.00	100.00
1901 .... (1,985)	26,480,213	.25	.35	1.00	2.00	8.00	40.00	100.00
1902 .... (2,018)	31,489,579	.25	.35	1.00	2.00	8.00	40.00	100.00
1903 .... (1,790)	28,006,725	.25	.35	1.00	2.00	8.00	40.00	100.00
1904 .... (1,817)	21,404,984	.25	.35	1.00	2.00	8.00	40.00	100.00
1905 .... (2,152)	29,827,276	.25	.35	1.00	2.00	8.00	40.00	100.00
1906 .... (1,725)	38,613,725	.25	.35	1.00	2.00	8.00	40.00	100.00
1907 .... (1,475)	39,214,800	.25	.35	1.00	2.00	8.00	40.00	100.00
1908 .... (1,620)	22,686,177	.25	.35	1.00	2.00	8.00	40.00	100.00
1909 .... (4,763)	11,590,526	.25	.35	1.00	3.00	10.00	45.00	100.00
1910 .... (2,405)	30,169,353	.25	.35	1.00	2.00	8.00	40.00	100.00
1911 .... (1,733)	39,559,372	.25	.35	1.00	2.00	8.00	40.00	100.00
1912 .... (2,145)	26,236,714	.25	.35	1.00	2.00	8.00	40.00	100.00
1912D	8,474,000	.40	.50	2.00	4.00	21.00	100.00	
1912S	238,000	20.00	24.00	35.00	95.00	200.00	350.00	
1913 Liberty Head (5 known)								400,000

INDIAN HEAD or BUFFALO TYPE 1913-1938

The Buffalo nickel was designed by James E. Fraser, whose initial F is below the date. He modeled the bison after Black Diamond in the New York Zoological Gardens. The three Indians used in the portrait were Irontail, Two Moons, and John Big Tree.

NICKEL FIVE-CENT PIECES

Variety 1 — FIVE CENTS on Raised Ground

G-4 GOOD—*Legends and date readable. Horn worn off.*
VG-8 VERY GOOD—*Half horn shows.*
F-12 FINE—*Three-quarters of horn shows. Obv. rim intact.*
VF-20 VERY FINE—*Full horn shows. Indian's cheekbone worn.*
EF-40 EXTREMELY FINE—*Full horn. Slight wear on Indian's hair ribbon.*
MS-60 UNCIRCULATED—*No trace of wear. Light blemishes. Attractive mint luster.*

Brilliant choice uncirculated coins are worth more than prices shown. Spotted, cleaned, weakly struck or discolored pieces are worth less.

	Quan. Minted	*G-4*	*VG-8*	*F-12*	*VF-20*	*EF-40*	*MS-60*	*Matte Proof-63*
1913 Var. 1. (1,520)	30,993,520	$1.25	$2.00	$2.50	$3.00	$6.50	$16.00	$600.00
1913D Var. 1	5,337,000	2.50	3.00	3.50	6.00	12.00	27.00	
1913S Var. 1	2,105,000	5.50	6.50	8.00	11.00	22.00	43.00	

Variety 2 — FIVE CENTS in Recess

Mint mark below FIVE CENTS

1916 Doubled Die Obverse

1918D, 8 over 7

1913 Var. 2. (1,514)	29,858,700	1.50	2.25	3.00	3.75	6.50	15.00	500.00
1913D Var. 2	4,156,000	18.00	20.00	25.00	30.00	40.00	85.00	
1913S Var. 2	1,209,000	30.00	42.00	55.00	70.00	100.00	185.00	
1914 .... (1,275)	20,665,738	2.00	2.50	3.00	4.00	9.00	25.00	500.00
1914D..............	3,912,000	15.00	18.00	22.50	30.00	55.00	135.00	
1914S..............	3,470,000	2.00	3.00	5.00	8.00	18.00	55.00	
1915 .... (1,050)	20,987,270	1.00	1.25	2.00	3.00	7.00	25.00	500.00
1915D..............	7,569,000	3.00	4.00	6.50	15.00	25.00	75.00	
1915S..............	1,505,000	5.00	6.50	10.00	30.00	60.00	135.00	
1916 .... (600)	63,498,066	.35	.50	.90	1.40	2.80	19.00	1,000
1916 Doubled die obv..........		400.00	700.00	850.00	1,200	2,500	7,000	
1916D..............	13,333,000	2.00	3.00	4.50	12.00	25.00	75.00	
1916S..............	11,860,000	1.50	2.00	3.00	12.00	25.00	75.00	
1917	51,424,019	.30	.40	.75	1.00	5.00	25.00	
1917D..............	9,910,000	2.50	3.00	6.00	20.00	40.00	110.00	
1917S..............	4,193,000	2.00	2.50	5.00	23.00	55.00	125.00	
1918	32,086,314	.25	.50	1.00	3.00	8.00	37.50	
1918D, 8 over 7....... }	8,362,000	175.00	275.00	450.00	900.00	2,200	6,000	
1918D.............. }		2.50	3.50	6.50	35.00	60.00	165.00	
1918S..............	4,882,000	2.00	3.00	6.00	22.00	45.00	140.00	
1919	60,868,000	.25	.35	.55	1.00	4.00	22.00	
1919D†..............	8,006,000	2.00	3.00	7.50	45.00	65.00	200.00	
1919S†..............	7,521,000	1.50	2.00	4.00	30.00	50.00	170.00	
1920	63,093,000	.25	.35	.55	1.50	4.00	22.00	
1920D†..............	9,418,000	1.75	2.50	5.00	35.00	75.00	175.00	
1920S..............	9,689,000	.75	1.25	2.50	20.00	60.00	100.00	
1921	10,663,000	.25	.50	1.00	3.00	10.00	45.00	
1921S†..............	1,557,000	7.50	10.00	20.00	125.00	250.00	450.00	

†Uncirculated pieces with full sharp details are worth considerably more.

NICKEL FIVE-CENT PIECES

Brilliant choice uncirculated coins are worth more than prices shown. Spotted, cleaned, weakly struck or discolored pieces are worth less.

	Quan. Minted	G-4	VG-8	F-12	VF-20	EF-40	MS-60
1923	35,715,000	$.20	$.20	$.30	$.90	$3.00	$22.00
1923S†	6,142,000	1.00	1.50	2.50	20.00	50.00	80.00
1924	21,620,000	.20	.20	.30	1.00	4.50	30.00
1924D	5,258,000	1.25	1.75	3.00	25.00	50.00	125.00
1924S	1,437,000	2.00	3.00	7.50	150.00	350.00	500.00
1925	35,565,100	.20	.25	.30	1.00	3.00	18.00
1925D†	4,450,000	2.00	3.00	5.00	32.00	70.00	150.00
1925S	6,256,000	1.00	1.50	3.00	20.00	40.00	100.00
1926	44,693,000	.20	.25	.30	.50	1.50	18.00
1926D†	5,638,000	1.00	1.50	4.00	30.00	50.00	75.00
1926S	970,000	2.00	3.00	7.00	100.00	300.00	500.00
1927	37,981,000	.20	.25	.30	.50	1.50	18.00
1927D	5,730,000	.40	.85	1.00	6.00	25.00	60.00
1927S	3,430,000	.25	.35	.75	8.00	35.00	80.00
1928	23,411,000	.20	.25	.20	.50	1.50	18.00
1928D	6,436,000	.25	.35	.65	2.00	6.00	21.00
1928S	6,936,000	.20	.30	.50	1.00	4.50	35.00
1929	36,446,000	.20	.25	.30	.40	1.50	15.00
1929D	8,370,000	.25	.40	.60	1.75	6.00	27.50
1929S	7,754,000	.20	.25	.30	.75	3.50	20.00
1930	22,849,000	.20	.25	.30	.50	1.75	15.00
1930S	5,435,000	.20	.25	.30	.50	3.50	20.00
1931S	1,200,000	1.50	1.75	2.00	2.50	5.00	25.00
1934	20,213,003	.15	.20	.25	.35	1.10	13.00
1934D	7,480,000	.15	.20	.25	.35	2.00	20.00
1935	58,264,000	.15	.20	.25	.25	.60	9.00
1935D	12,092,000	.15	.20	.25	.35	1.10	14.00
1935S	10,300,000	.15	.20	.25	.30	.90	12.00
1936	119,001,420	.15	.20	.25	.30	.50	7.00
1936 Proof-63	(4,420)						475.00
1936D	24,814,000	.15	.20	.25	.30	.60	7.00
1936S	14,930,000	.15	.20	.25	.30	.60	6.00
1937	79,485,769	.15	.20	.25	.30	.50	6.00
1937 Proof-63	(5,769)						450.00
1937D	17,826,000	.15	.20	.25	.30	.60	7.00
1937D 3-Legged*		45.00	70.00	85.00	100.00	150.00	400.00
1937S	5,635,000	.15	.20	.25	.30	.60	7.00
1938D	7,020,000	.15	.20	.25	.30	.60	6.00
1938D, D over S				2.00	3.00	4.00	10.00

†Uncirculated pieces with full sharp details are worth considerably more.
*Beware of removed leg.

1937D "3-Legged" Variety

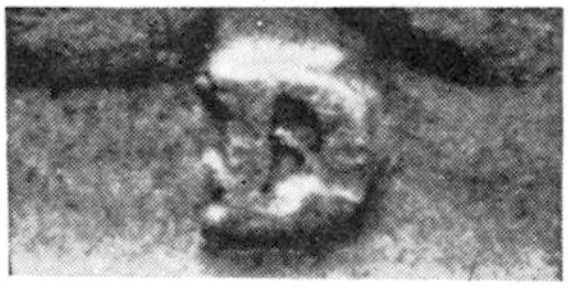

1938D, D over S

JEFFERSON TYPE 1938 to Date

This nickel was designed by Felix Schlag. He won an award of $1,000 in a competition with some 390 artists. It established the definite public approval of portrait and pictorial rather than symbolic devices on our coinage. On October 8, 1942, the wartime five-cent piece composed of copper (56%), silver (35%) and manganese (9%) was introduced to eliminate nickel, a critical war material. A larger mint mark was placed above the dome. Letter P (Philadelphia) was used for the first time, indicating the change of alloy. The designer's initials FS were added below the bust starting in 1966. Mint mark position was moved to the obverse starting in 1968.

VG-8 VERY GOOD—*Second porch pillar from right nearly gone, other three still visible but weak.*
F-12 FINE—*Cheekbone worn flat. Hairlines and eyebrow faint. Second pillar weak, especially at bottom.*
VF-20 VERY FINE—*Second pillar plain and complete on both sides.*
EF-40 EXTREMELY FINE—*Cheekbone, hairlines, eyebrow slightly worn but well defined. Base of triangle above pillars visible but weak.*
MS-63 UNCIRCULATED—*No trace of wear. Slight blemishes.*

Mint mark located at right of building

Wartime Silver

Mint mark location starting 1968

Uncirculated pieces with fully struck steps are valued higher.

	Quan. Minted	VG-8	F-12	VF-20	EF-40	MS-63	Proof-63
1938	(19,365) 19,515,365	$.06	$.08	$.10	$.20	$.75	$15.00
1938D	5,376,000	.30	.40	.50	.75	3.00	
1938S	4,105,000	.50	.75	1.00	1.25	3.75	
1939	(12,535) 120,627,535	.06	.08	.10	.20	.65	15.00
1939D	3,514,000	1.00	1.50	2.00	4.00	20.00	
1939S	6,630,000	.20	.25	.30	1.00	10.00	
1940	(14,158) 176,499,158			.05	.08	.50	12.50
1940D	43,540,000			.05	.08	.60	
1940S	39,690,000			.05	.10	.60	
1941	(18,720) 203,283,720			.05	.08	.35	12.00
1941D	53,432,000			.05	.08	1.00	
1941S	43,445,000			.05	.09	1.25	
1942	(29,600) 49,818,600			.05	.08	.90	12.00
1942D	13,938,000	.06	.08	.20	.40	9.00	

Wartime Silver Five-Cent Pieces 1942-1945

	Quan. Minted	VG-8	F-12	VF-20	EF-40	MS-63	Proof-63
1942P	(27,600) 579,900,600	*.15*	*.15*	*.20*	.35	4.50	40.00
1942S	32,900,000	*.15*	*.25*	*.20*	.35	3.00	
1943P, 3 over 2	271,165,000		20.00	30.00	60.00	200.00	
1943P		*.15*	*.15*	*.20*	.35	1.00	
1943D	15,294,000	*.15*	.30	.35	.50	1.25	
1943S	104,060,000	*.15*	*.15*	*.20*	.35	1.00	
1944P	119,150,000	*.15*	*.15*	*.20*	.35	1.00	
1944D	32,309,000	*.15*	*.15*	*.20*	.35	2.00	
1944S	21,640,000	*.15*	*.15*	*.20*	.35	2.00	
1945P	119,408,100	*.15*	*.15*	*.20*	.35	1.50	
1945D	37,158,000	*.15*	*.15*	*.20*	.35	1.50	
1945S	58,939,000	*.15*	*.15*	*.20*	.35	1.00	

Prewar composition and mint mark style resumed 1946-1964

	Quan. Minted	VG-8	F-12	VF-20	EF-40	MS-63	Proof-63
1946	161,116,000			.05	.05	.25	
1946D	45,292,200			.05	.05	.30	
1946S	13,560,000			.05	.06	.30	
1947	95,000,000			.05	.05	.20	
1947D	37,822,000			.05	.05	.30	
1947S	24,720,000			.05	.06	.30	
1948	89,348,000			.05	.05	.25	

Italic prices indicate unsettled values due to fluctuating bullion market. See Bullion Chart.

NICKEL FIVE-CENT PIECES

		Quan. Minted	*VF-20*	*EF-40*	*MS-63*	*Proof-63*
1948D		44,734,000	$.05	$.06	$.50	
1948S		11,300,000	.05	.06	.40	
1949		60,652,000	.05	.05	.60	
1949D		36,498,000	.05	.05	.45	
1949D, D over S			15.00	25.00	100.00	
1949S		9,716,000	.05	.10	.85	
1950	(51,386)	9,847,386	.05	.10	.75	$14.00
1950D		2,630,030	3.00	3.50	4.00	
1951	(57,500)	28,609,500	.05	.05	.50	12.00
1951D		20,460,000	.05	.05	.50	
1951S		7,776,000	.05	.10	1.00	
1952	(81,980)	64,069,980	.05	.05	.30	8.00
1952D		30,638,000	.05	.05	.50	
1952S		20,572,000	.05	.05	.50	
1953	(128,800)	46,772,800	.05	.05	.10	4.00
1953D		59,878,600	.05	.05	.10	
1953S		19,210,900	.05	.05	.20	
1954	(233,300)	47,917,350	.05	.05	.10	2.75
1954D		117,183,060	.05	.05	.10	
1954S		29,384,000	.05	.05	.12	
1954S, S over D			2.50	5.00	15.00	
1955	(378,200)	8,266,200	.06	.08	.25	1.50
1955D		74,464,100	.05	.05	.07	
1955D, D over S*			3.00	5.00	27.50	

1943, 3 over 2

1954S, S over D

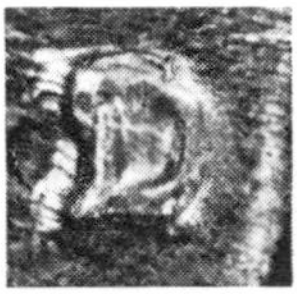

1955D, D over S*

		Quan. Minted	*VF-20*	*EF-40*	*MS-63*	*Proof-63*
1956	(669,384)	35,885,384		.05	.06	.40
1956D		67,222,940		.05	.06	
1957	(1,247,952)	39,655,952		.05	.07	.30
1957D		136,828,900		.05	.07	
1958	(875,652)	17,963,652		.05	.08	.50
1958D		168,249,120		.05	.06	
1959	(1,149,291)	28,397,291		.05	.06	.30
1959D		160,738,240		.05	.05	
1960	(1,691,602)	57,107,602		.05	.05	.25
1960D		192,582,180		.05	.05	
1961	(3,028,144)	76,668,244		.05	.05	.20
1961D		229,342,760		.05	.05	
1962	(3,218,019)	100,602,019		.05	.05	.20
1962D		280,195,720		.05	.07	
1963	(3,075,645)	178,851,645		.05	.05	.20
1963D		276,829,460			.05	
1964	(3,950,762)	1,028,622,762			.05	.20
1964D		1,787,297,160			.05	
1965		136,131,380			.05	
1966		156,208,283			.05	
1967		107,325,800			.05	
1968D		91,227,880			.05	
1968S		103,437,510			.05	
1968S Proof		(3,041,506)				.20
1969D		202,807,500			.05	
1969S		123,009,631			.05	
1969S Proof		(2,934,631)				.20
1970D		515,485,380			.05	

*Varieties exist. Value is for that illustrated.

NICKEL FIVE-CENT PIECES

	Quan. Minted	MS-63	Proof-63
1970S	241,464,814	$.05	
1970S Proof	(2,632,810)		$.25
1971	106,884,000	.20	
1971D	316,144,800	.05	
1971S Proof	(3,220,733)		.50
1972	202,036,000	.05	
1972D	351,694,600	.05	
1972S Proof	(3,260,996)		.50
1973	384,396,000	.05	
1973D	261,405,000	.05	
1973S Proof	(2,760,339)		.50
1974	601,752,000	.05	
1974D	277,373,000	.06	
1974S Proof	(2,612,568)		.50
1975	181,772,000	.06	
1975D	401,875,300	.06	
1975S Proof	(2,845,450)		.50
1976	367,124,000	.05	
1976D	563,964,147	.05	
1976S Proof	(4,149,730)		.20
1977	585,376,000	.05	
1977D	297,313,422	.06	
1977S Proof	(3,251,152)		.20
1978	391,308,000	.05	
1978D	313,092,780	.05	
1978S Proof	(3,127,781)		.30
1979	463,188,000	.05	
1979D	325,867,672	.05	
1979S Proof	(3,677,175)		
Filled S			.25
Clear S			.60
1980P	593,004,000	.05	
1980D	502,323,448	.05	
1980S Proof	(3,554,806)		.25
1981P	657,504,000	.05	
1981D	364,801,843	$.05	
1981S Proof	(4,063,083)		$.25
1982P	292,355,000	.05	
1982D	373,726,544	.05	
1982S Proof	(3,857,479)		.35
1983P	561,615,000	.05	
1983D	536,726,276	.05	
1983S Proof	(3,279,126)		.50
1984P	746,769,000	.05	
1984D	517,675,146	.05	
1984S Proof	(3,065,110)		1.50
1985P	647,114,962	.05	
1985D	459,747,446	.05	
1985S Proof	(3,362,821)		1.25
1986P	536,883,483	.05	
1986D	361,819,140	.05	
1986S Proof	(3,010,497)		1.50
1987P	371,499,481	.05	
1987D	410,590,604	.05	
1987S Proof	(4,227,728)		1.00
1988P	771,360,000	.05	
1988D	663,771,652	.05	
1988S Proof	(3,262,948)		1.00
1989P	898,812,000	.05	
1989D	570,842,474	.05	
1989S Proof	(3,220,194)		1.00
1990P	661,636,000	.05	
1990D	663,938,503	.05	
1990S Proof			1.00
1991P	614,104,000	.05	
1991D	436,496,678	.05	
1991S Proof	(3,299,559)		1.00
1992P		.05	
1992D		.05	
1992S Proof			.75

HALF DIMES 1794-1873

The half dime types present the same general characteristics as larger United States silver coins. Authorized by the Act of April 2, 1792, they were not coined until February, 1795, although dated 1794. At first the weight was 20.8 grains, and fineness 892.4. By the Act of January 18, 1837, the weight was slightly reduced to 20 5/8 grains and the fineness changed to .900. Finally the weight was reduced to 19.2 grains by the Act of February 21, 1853.

FLOWING HAIR TYPE 1794-1795

AG-3 ABOUT GOOD—*Details clear enough to identify.*

G-5 GOOD—*Eagle, wreath, bust outlined but lack details.*

VG-8 VERY GOOD—*Some details remain on face. All lettering readable.*

F-12 FINE—*Hair ends show. Hair at top smooth.*

VF-20 VERY FINE—*Hairlines at top show. Hair about ear defined.*

EF-40 EXTREMELY FINE—*Hair above forehead and at neck well defined but shows some wear.*

MS-60 UNCIRCULATED—*No trace of wear. Light blemishes.*

Weakly struck uncirculated coins are worth less than values shown.

	Quan. Minted	AG-3	G-4	VG-8	F-12	VF-20	EF-40	MS-60
1794	86,416 (1794 and 1795)	$160.00	$350.00	$400.00	$700.00	$1,100	$1,850	$5,000
1795		150.00	350.00	375.00	500.00	850.00	1,250	3,000

HALF DIMES

DRAPED BUST TYPE, SMALL EAGLE REVERSE 1796-1797

AG-3 ABOUT GOOD—*Details clear enough to identify.*
G-4 GOOD—*Date, stars, LIBERTY readable. Bust outlined but no details.*
VG-8 VERY GOOD—*Some details show.*
F-12 FINE—*Hair and drapery lines worn, but visible.*
VF-20 VERY FINE—*Only left of drapery indistinct.*
EF-40 EXTREMELY FINE—*All hairlines show details.*
MS-60 UNCIRCULATED—*No trace of wear. Light blemishes.*

	Quan. Minted	*AG-3*	*G-4*	*VG-8*	*F-12*	*VF-20*	*EF-40*	*MS-60*
1796, 6 over 5		$200.00	$450.00	$550.00	$800.00	$1,300	$2,500	$5,500
1796 Nor. dt.	10,230	160.00	400.00	475.00	650.00	1,100	1,850	4,500
1796 LIBERTY		200.00	450.00	550.00	750.00	1,300	2,250	4,500
1797, 15 Stars		150.00	400.00	475.00	650.00	1,100	1,850	5,000
1797, 16 stars	44,527	150.00	400.00	475.00	650.00	1,100	1,850	4,500
1797, 13 stars		150.00	400.00	475.00	650.00	1,100	1,850	4,500

DRAPED BUST TYPE, HERALDIC EAGLE REVERSE 1800-1805

1800 LIBEKTY

1800	24,000	85.00	250.00	300.00	450.00	650.00	1,300	3,500
1800 LIBEKTY	16,000	85.00	250.00	300.00	450.00	650.00	1,300	4,000
1801	27,760	85.00	250.00	300.00	450.00	650.00	1,400	4,500
1802	3,060	1,500	4,000	6,000	11,000	18,000	30,000	——
1803	37,850	85.00	250.00	300.00	450.00	650.00	1,400	3,500
1805	15,600	85.00	300.00	400.00	525.00	750.00	3,000	——

CAPPED BUST TYPE 1829-1837

G-4 GOOD—*Bust outlined, no detail. Date and legend readable.*
VG-8 VERY GOOD—*Complete legend and date plain. At least 3 letters of LIBERTY show clearly.*
F-12 FINE—*All letters in LIBERTY show.*
VF-20 VERY FINE—*Full rims. Ear and shoulder clasp show plainly.*
EF-40 EXTREMELY FINE—*Ear very distinct, eyebrow and hair well defined.*
MS-60 UNCIRCULATED—*No trace of wear. Light blemishes.*

	Quan. Minted	*G-4*	*VG-8*	*F-12*	*VF-20*	*EF-40*	*MS-60*
1829	1,230,000	$6.00	$9.00	$13.00	$25.00	$55.00	$175.00
1830	1,240,000	6.00	9.00	13.00	25.00	55.00	175.00
1831	1,242,700	6.00	9.00	13.00	25.00	55.00	175.00
1832	965,000	6.00	9.00	13.00	25.00	55.00	175.00
1833	1,370,000	6.00	9.00	13.00	25.00	55.00	175.00
1834	1,480,000	6.00	9.00	13.00	25.00	55.00	175.00
1835	2,760,000	6.00	9.00	13.00	25.00	55.00	175.00
1836	1,900,000	6.00	9.00	13.00	25.00	55.00	175.00
1837 Small 5c.	871,000	7.00	14.00	23.00	40.00	100.00	500.00
1837 Large 5c		6.00	9.00	13.00	25.00	55.00	175.00

HALF DIMES

LIBERTY SEATED TYPE 1837-1873

No Stars on Obverse 1837-1838

G-4 GOOD—*LIBERTY On shield smooth. Date and letters readable.*
VG-8 VERY GOOD—*At least 3 letters in LIBERTY are visible.*
F-12 FINE—*Entire LIBERTY visible, weak spots.*
VF-20 VERY FINE—*Entire LIBERTY strong and even.*
EF-40 EXTREMELY FINE—*LIBERTY and scroll edges distinct.*
MS-60 UNCIRCULATED—*No trace of wear. Light blemishes.*

	Quan. Minted	*G-4*	*VG-8*	*F-12*	*VF-20*	*EF-40*	*MS-60*
1837	1,405,000	$15.00	$20.00	$27.50	$47.50	$125.00	$300.00
1838O No stars	70,000	30.00	45.00	75.00	150.00	350.00	1,250

Stars on Obverse 1838-1853

From 1838 through 1859 mint mark is located above bow on reverse. Large, medium or small mint mark varieties occur for several dates.

1838	2,255,000	3.00	4.00	6.00	13.00	28.00	200.00
1839	1,069,150	3.00	4.00	6.00	13.00	28.00	150.00
1839O	1,034,039	4.00	6.00	9.00	15.00	35.00	250.00
1840	1,344,085	2.00	3.50	5.50	11.00	28.00	200.00
1840O	935,000	3.00	5.00	9.00	17.00	45.00	300.00
1841	1,150,000	2.00	3.50	5.50	11.00	28.00	125.00
1841O	815,000	5.00	8.00	12.00	20.00	35.00	325.00
1842	815,000	2.00	3.50	5.00	11.00	22.00	110.00
1842O	350,000	6.00	10.00	17.00	40.00	125.00	—
1843	1,165,000	2.00	3.50	5.00	11.00	22.00	100.00
1844	430,000	2.00	3.50	5.00	11.00	22.00	100.00
1844O	220,000	15.00	21.00	45.00	125.00	315.00	—
1845	1,564,000	2.00	3.50	5.00	11.00	22.00	100.00
1846	27,000	60.00	75.00	125.00	250.00	500.00	—
1847	1,274,000	2.00	3.50	5.00	11.00	22.00	100.00
1848	668,000	2.00	3.50	5.00	11.00	22.00	100.00
1848O	600,000	5.00	10.00	13.00	25.00	35.00	250.00
1849, 9 over 6		3.50	6.00	9.00	12.00	25.00	200.00
1849, 9 over 8	1,309,000	4.00	7.00	10.00	15.00	35.00	225.00
1849 Nor. date		2.00	3.50	5.00	11.00	22.00	100.00
1849O	140,000	12.00	20.00	35.00	100.00	225.00	—
1850	955,000	3.00	3.50	5.00	11.00	22.00	100.00
1850O	690,000	5.00	10.00	13.00	20.00	35.00	300.00
1851	781,000	2.00	3.50	5.00	11.00	22.00	100.00
1851O	860,000	5.00	8.00	12.00	20.00	35.00	250.00
1852	1,000,500	2.00	3.50	5.00	11.00	22.00	100.00
1852O	260,000	11.00	16.00	25.00	60.00	110.00	—
1853 No arrows	135,000	6.00	12.00	18.00	25.00	50.00	275.00
1853O No arrows	160,000	60.00	90.00	125.00	200.00	400.00	—

Arrows at Date 1853-1855

As on the dimes, quarters and halves, arrows were placed at the sides of the date for a short period starting in 1853 to denote reduction of weight.

HALF DIMES

	Quan. Minted	G-4	VG-8	F-12	VF-20	EF-40	MS-60	Proof-63
1853	13,210,020	$2.00	$3.50	$5.00	$10.00	$21.00	$110.00	
1853O	2,200,000	4.00	5.00	7.00	12.00	30.00	130.00	
1854	5,740,000	2.00	3.50	5.00	9.00	19.00	110.00	
1854O	1,560,000	2.00	3.50	6.00	11.00	23.00	250.00	
1855	1,750,000	2.00	3.50	5.00	10.00	21.00	110.00	$2,500
1855O	600,000	4.00	7.00	10.00	17.00	40.00	275.00	

No Arrows at Date 1856-1859

1856	4,880,000	2.00	3.00	5.00	10.00	18.00	100.00	900.00
1856O	1,100,000	2.00	3.00	6.00	11.00	20.00	200.00	
1857	7,280,000	2.00	3.00	5.00	10.00	18.00	100.00	900.00
1857O	1,380,000	2.00	3.00	6.00	11.00	20.00	200.00	

1858 over Inverted Date

1858	3,500,000	2.00	3.00	5.00	10.00	17.00	100.00	800.00
1858 over inv. date		9.00	15.00	30.00	60.00	115.00	225.00	
1858O	1,660,000	2.00	3.00	6.00	11.00	20.00	175.00	
1859	340,000	5.00	8.00	12.00	20.00	30.00	150.00	800.00
1859O	560,000	5.00	8.00	12.00	20.00	30.00	200.00	

Legend on Obverse 1860-1873

1860 .... (1,000)	799,000	2.00	3.00	4.00	7.00	15.00	100.00	350.00
1860O	1,060,000	2.00	3.00	5.00	8.00	18.00	150.00	
1861 .... (1,000)	3,361,000	2.00	3.00	4.00	7.00	14.00	100.00	325.00
1862 ..... (550)	1,492,550	2.00	3.00	4.00	7.00	14.00	100.00	325.00
1863 ..... (460)	18,460	30.00	40.00	60.00	90.00	125.00	300.00	350.00
1863S	100,000	7.00	9.00	12.00	21.00	45.00	400.00	
1864 ..... (470)	48,470	75.00	100.00	125.00	175.00	250.00	650.00	750.00
1864S	90,000	10.00	15.00	25.00	40.00	100.00	425.00	
1865 ..... (500)	13,500	30.00	40.00	60.00	90.00	125.00	275.00	325.00
1865S	120,000	6.00	9.00	13.00	22.00	40.00	325.00	
1866 ..... (725)	10,725	50.00	75.00	100.00	125.00	200.00	350.00	325.00
1866S	120,000	6.00	9.00	12.00	21.00	40.00	325.00	
1867 ..... (625)	8,625	65.00	100.00	135.00	170.00	275.00	450.00	350.00
1867S	120,000	6.00	9.00	12.00	21.00	30.00	325.00	
1868 ..... (600)	89,200	9.00	15.00	25.00	50.00	100.00	275.00	300.00
1868S	280,000	4.00	6.00	7.00	10.00	19.00	150.00	
1869 ..... (600)	208,600	4.00	5.00	6.00	9.00	15.00	100.00	300.00
1869S	230,000	4.00	6.00	7.00	10.00	19.00	175.00	
1870 .... (1,000)	536,000	2.00	3.00	4.00	7.00	15.00	100.00	300.00
1870S	Unique							
1871 ..... (960)	1,873,960	2.00	3.00	4.00	7.00	15.00	100.00	300.00
1871S	161,000	5.00	8.00	15.00	30.00	45.00	250.00	
1872 ..... (950)	2,947,950	2.00	3.00	4.00	7.00	15.00	100.00	300.00
1872S	837,000	2.00	3.00	4.00	7.00	15.00	100.00	
1873 ..... (600)	712,600	2.00	3.00	4.00	7.00	15.00	100.00	300.00
1873S	324,000	2.00	3.00	4.00	7.00	15.00	100.00	

DIMES — 1796 to Date

The designs of the dimes, first coined in 1796, follow closely those of the half dimes up through the Liberty seated type. The dimes in each instance weigh twice as much as the half dimes.

DRAPED BUST TYPE, SMALL EAGLE REVERSE 1796-1797

AG-3 ABOUT GOOD—*Details clear enough to identify.*

G-4 GOOD—*Date readable. Bust outlined, but no detail.*

VG-8 VERY GOOD—*All but deepest drapery folds worn smooth. Hairlines nearly gone and curls lack detail.*

F-12 FINE—*All drapery lines visible. Hair partly worn.*

VF-20 VERY FINE—*Only left side of drapery is indistinct.*

EF-40 EXTREMELY FINE—*Hair well outlined and shows details.*

MS-60 UNCIRCULATED—*No trace of wear. Light blemishes.*

1797, 16 Stars

1797, 13 Stars

	Quan. Minted	*AG-3*	*G-4*	*VG-8*	*F-12*	*VF-20*	*EF-40*	*MS-60*
1796	22,135	$225.00	$525.00	$800.00	$1,000	$1,400	$2,500	$6,000
1797 16 stars	25,261 (both varieties)	225.00	500.00	750.00	900.00	1,200	2,000	5,000
1797 13 stars		225.00	500.00	750.00	900.00	1,200	2,000	5,000

DRAPED BUST TYPE, HERALDIC EAGLE REVERSE 1798-1807

	Quan. Minted	*AG-3*	*G-4*	*VG-8*	*F-12*	*VF-20*	*EF-40*	*MS-60*
1798 All kinds	27,550							
1798 over 97, 16 stars on rev.		80.00	225.00	250.00	450.00	600.00	1,000	3,000
1798 over 97, 13 stars				500.00	900.00	1,700	—	
1798		80.00	225.00	250.00	450.00	700.00	1,000	3,000
1800	21,760	80.00	225.00	250.00	450.00	575.00	700.00	2,300
1801	34,640	80.00	225.00	250.00	450.00	575.00	700.00	2,300
1802	10,975	80.00	225.00	250.00	450.00	575.00	700.00	2,300
1803	33,040	80.00	225.00	250.00	450.00	575.00	700.00	2,300
1804	8,265	225.00	450.00	750.00	1,000	1,700	3,500	5,000
1805	120,780	80.00	225.00	250.00	425.00	550.00	675.00	2,200
1807	165,000	80.00	225.00	250.00	425.00	550.00	675.00	2,200

CAPPED BUST TYPE 1809-1837

G-4 GOOD—*Date, letters and stars discernible. Bust outlined, no details.*

VG-8 VERY GOOD—*Legends and date plain. Minimum of 3 letters in LIBERTY.*

F-12 FINE—*Full LIBERTY. Ear and shoulder clasp visible. Part of rim shows both sides.*

VF-20 VERY FINE—*LIBERTY distinct. Full rim. Ear and clasp plain and distinct.*

EF-40 EXTREMELY FINE—*LIBERTY sharp. Ear distinct. Hair above eye well defined.*

MS-60 UNCIRCULATED—*No trace of wear. Light blemishes.*

DIMES

Wide Border 1809-1828

	Quan. Minted	G-4	VG-8	F-12	VF-20	EF-40	MS-60
1809	51,065	$40.00	$60.00	$100.00	$200.00	$350.00	$2,000
1811 over 9	65,180	20.00	37.00	50.00	100.00	225.00	1,700
1814	421,500	12.00	14.00	20.00	60.00	175.00	650.00
1820	942,587	7.50	10.00	15.00	50.00	150.00	500.00
1821	1,186,512	7.50	10.00	15.00	50.00	150.00	500.00
1822	100,000	50.00	75.00	150.00	300.00	600.00	2,500
1823, 3 over 2, all kinds	440,000						
1823, 3 over 2, sm. E's		7.50	10.00	15.00	45.00	125.00	600.00
1823, 3 over 2, lg. E's		7.50	10.00	15.00	45.00	125.00	600.00

1823, 3 over 2

1824, 4 over 2

1828 Large Date

1828 Small Date

	Quan. Minted	G-4	VG-8	F-12	VF-20	EF-40	MS-60
1824, 4 over 2	} 510,000	13.00	16.00	22.50	60.00	175.00	800.00
1825	}	7.50	10.00	15.00	45.00	125.00	550.00
1827	1,215,000	7.50	10.00	15.00	45.00	125.00	550.00
1828 Both vars	125,000						
1828 Lg. date, curl base 2		15.00	20.00	40.00	80.00	200.00	900.00

Modified Design 1828-1837

1829 Small 10c

Large 10c

1830, 30 over 29

	Quan. Minted	G-4	F-12	VF-20	EF-40	MS-60
1828 Small date, sq. base 2		$14.00	$23.00	$45.00	$125.00	$600.00
1829 Small 10c	}	5.00	11.00	25.00	90.00	400.00
1829 Medium 10c	} 770,000	5.00	11.00	22.00	90.00	350.00
1829 Large 10c	}	10.00	18.00	30.00	100.00	400.00
1830, 30 over 29	}	25.00	50.00	100.00	175.00	500.00
1830 Large 10c	} 510,000	5.00	11.00	22.00	90.00	350.00
1830 Small 10c	}	5.00	11.00	22.00	90.00	350.00

DIMES

	Quan. Minted	G-4	F-12	VF-20	EF-40	MS-60
1831	771,350	$5.00	$11.00	$22.00	$90.00	$350.00
1832	522,500	5.00	11.00	22.00	90.00	350.00
1833	485,000	5.00	11.00	22.00	90.00	350.00
1834	635,000	5.00	11.00	22.00	90.00	400.00
1835	1,410,000	5.00	11.00	22.00	90.00	350.00
1836	1,190,000	5.00	11.00	22.00	90.00	350.00
1837	359,500	5.00	11.00	22.00	90.00	350.00

LIBERTY SEATED TYPE 1837-1891

No Stars on Obverse 1837-1838

G-4 GOOD—*LIBERTY on shield smooth. Date and letters readable.*
F-12 FINE—*Entire LIBERTY visible, weak spots.*
VF-20 VERY FINE—*Entire LIBERTY strong and even.*
EF-40 EXTREMELY FINE—*LIBERTY and scroll edges distinct.*
MS-60 UNCIRCULATED—*No trace of wear. Light blemishes.*

No Drapery from Elbow
No Stars on Obverse

Mint marks on Liberty seated dimes are placed on the reverse, within or below the wreath.

1837	682,500	12.00	30.00	100.00	175.00	650.00
1838O	406,034	15.00	50.00	125.00	250.00	1,600

Stars on Obverse 1838-1853

1838 Small Stars

No Drapery from Elbow
Tilted Shield

1838 Large Stars

1838 Small stars	1,992,500	6.50	16.00	35.00	70.00	550.00
1838 Large stars		3.50	6.00	10.00	30.00	155.00
1838 Partial drapery		6.50	15.00	25.00	50.00	500.00
1839	1,053,115	2.50	5.00	9.00	25.00	135.00
1839O	1,323,000	3.00	7.00	14.00	27.00	175.00
1840	981,500	2.50	5.00	9.00	20.00	135.00
1840O	1,175,000	3.00	7.00	15.00	27.00	475.00

DIMES

Drapery from Elbow
Upright Shield

	Quan. Minted	G-4	F-12	VF-20	EF-40	MS-60	Proof-63
1840	377,500	$10.00	$25.00	$50.00	$200.00	—	
1841	1,622,500	2.00	3.50	7.00	18.00	$135.00	
1841O	2,007,500	3.00	7.00	12.00	25.00	500.00	
1842	1,887,500	2.00	3.50	7.00	18.00	135.00	
1842O	2,020,000	2.00	3.50	10.00	30.00	—	
1843	1,370,000	2.00	3.50	7.00	18.00	135.00	
1843O	150,000	13.00	45.00	120.00	310.00	—	
1844	72,500	13.00	45.00	90.00	165.00	1,000	
1845	1,755,000	2.00	3.50	7.00	18.00	135.00	
1845O	230,000	6.50	20.00	60.00	300.00	—	
1846	31,300	25.00	50.00	135.00	350.00	—	
1847	245,000	4.50	14.00	25.00	75.00	375.00	
1848	451,500	2.50	5.00	12.00	30.00	200.00	
1849	839,000	2.00	3.50	7.00	18.00	175.00	
1849O	300,000	4.50	10.00	40.00	120.00	—	
1850	1,931,500	2.00	3.50	7.00	18.00	135.00	
1850O	510,000	3.50	7.00	30.00	65.00	425.00	
1851	1,026,500	2.00	3.50	7.00	18.00	160.00	
1851O	400,000	4.50	10.00	25.00	75.00	650.00	
1852	1,535,500	2.00	3.50	7.00	18.00	150.00	
1852O	430,000	4.50	12.00	35.00	90.00	800.00	
1853 No arrows	95,000	17.50	32.50	65.00	135.00	425.00	

Arrows at Date 1853-1855

1853-1855
Arrows at Date

1856-1860
Small Date, Arrows Removed

	Quan. Minted	G-4	F-12	VF-20	EF-40	MS-60	Proof-63
1853 With arrows	12,078,010	1.50	3.50	8.00	25.00	150.00	
1853O	1,100,000	1.75	4.00	11.00	45.00	300.00	
1854	4,470,000	1.50	3.50	8.00	25.00	150.00	$6,000
1854O	1,770,000	2.50	4.00	10.00	40.00	275.00	
1855	2,075,000	1.50	3.50	8.00	25.00	175.00	3,000

No Arrows at Date 1856-1860

	Quan. Minted	G-4	F-12	VF-20	EF-40	MS-60	Proof-63
1856 Lg. date	5,780,000 (1856 Lg. date and Sm. date)	1.50	3.25	7.00	16.00	140.00	
1856 Sm. date		1.50	3.25	7.00	16.00	140.00	1,100
1856O	1,180,000	1.50	3.25	9.00	20.00	135.00	
1856S	70,000	18.00	40.00	80.00	200.00	—	
1857	5,580,000	1.50	3.25	7.00	15.00	135.00	1,000
1857O	1,540,000	1.50	3.25	7.00	15.00	150.00	

DIMES

	Quan. Minted	G-4	F-12	VF-20	EF-40	MS-60	Proof-63
1858	1,540,000	$1.50	$3.25	$7.00	$15.00	$135.00	$1,100
1858O	290,000	4.50	12.00	30.00	75.00	300.00	
1858S	60,000	20.00	45.00	100.00	225.00	—	
1859 (800)	430,000	1.75	4.00	10.00	25.00	135.00	1,000
1859O	480,000	1.75	5.00	17.00	35.00	150.00	
1859S	60,000	25.00	50.00	110.00	225.00	950.00	
1860S	140,000	4.50	15.00	40.00	100.00	—	

Legend on Obverse 1860-1873

	Quan. Minted	G-4	F-12	VF-20	EF-40	MS-60	Proof-63
1860 (1,000)	607,000	1.25	3.50	6.50	13.00	120.00	325.00
1860O	40,000	150.00	350.00	550.00	1,100	—	
1861 (1,000)	1,884,000	1.25	3.50	6.50	13.00	120.00	325.00
1861S	172,500	6.50	18.00	40.00	100.00	500.00	
1862 (550)	847,550	1.25	3.50	6.50	13.00	110.00	325.00
1862S	180,750	6.50	15.00	35.00	100.00	500.00	
1863 (460)	14,460	30.00	60.00	100.00	200.00	550.00	350.00
1863S	157,500	8.50	20.00	40.00	65.00	450.00	
1864 (470)	11,470	50.00	110.00	160.00	275.00	450.00	350.00
1864S	230,000	5.50	15.00	30.00	60.00	500.00	
1865 (500)	10,500	60.00	90.00	150.00	225.00	500.00	350.00
1865S	175,000	5.50	15.00	30.00	100.00	500.00	
1866 (725)	8,725	100.00	175.00	250.00	400.00	600.00	350.00
1866S	135,000	6.50	15.00	30.00	100.00	550.00	
1867 (625)	6,625	80.00	160.00	250.00	350.00	750.00	350.00
1867S	140,000	5.50	14.00	30.00	65.00	600.00	
1868 (600)	464,600	2.25	5.00	14.00	30.00	175.00	325.00
1868S	260,000	4.50	10.00	30.00	70.00	175.00	
1869 (600)	256,600	2.25	5.00	14.00	30.00	175.00	325.00
1869S	450,000	3.50	7.00	15.00	35.00	200.00	
1870 (1,000)	471,500	1.50	3.50	8.00	17.00	110.00	325.00
1870S	50,000	20.00	50.00	100.00	200.00	1,200	
1871 (960)	907,710	1.50	3.50	6.50	13.00	100.00	325.00
1871CC	20,100	160.00	425.00	600.00	1,200	—	
1871S	320,000	4.50	14.00	25.00	60.00	300.00	
1872 (950)	2,396,450	1.50	3.50	6.50	13.00	75.00	325.00
1872CC	35,480	100.00	250.00	600.00	1,000	—	
1872S	190,000	7.50	20.00	35.00	90.00	400.00	
1873 Closed 3 (1,100)	1,508,000	1.50	3.50	6.50	13.00	120.00	325.00
1873 Open 3	60,000	10.00	20.00	30.00	70.00	160.00	
1873CC (Unique)	12,400						

Arrows at Date 1873-1874

In 1873 the dime was increased in weight to 2.50 grams. Arrows at date in 1873 and 1874 indicate this change.

DIMES

	Quan. Minted	G-4	F-12	VF-20	EF-40	MS-60	Proof-63
1873	(800) 2,378,500	$3.50	$9.00	$20.00	$50.00	$325.00	$700.00
1873CC	18,791	200.00	425.00	650.00	1,300	——	
1873S	455,000	7.50	16.00	30.00	55.00	400.00	
1874	(700) 2,940,000	3.50	9.00	20.00	50.00	325.00	700.00
1874CC	10,817	400.00	900.00	1,500	2,400	——	
1874S	240,000	8.50	20.00	45.00	75.00	325.00	

No Arrows at Date 1875-1891

	Quan. Minted	G-4	F-12	VF-20	EF-40	MS-60	Proof-63
1875	(700) 10,350,700	1.25	3.00	5.00	11.00	80.00	300.00
1875CC	4,645,000	1.25	3.00	5.00	11.00	90.00	
1875S	9,070,000	1.25	3.00	5.00	11.00	80.00	
1876	(1,150) 11,461,150	1.25	3.00	5.00	11.00	80.00	300.00
1876CC	8,270,000	1.25	3.00	5.00	11.00	90.00	
1876S	10,420,000	1.25	3.00	5.00	11.00	80.00	
1877	(510) 7,310,510	1.25	3.00	5.00	11.00	80.00	325.00
1877CC	7,700,000	1.25	3.00	5.00	11.00	90.00	
1877S	2,340,000	1.25	3.00	5.00	11.00	90.00	
1878	(800) 1,678,000	1.25	3.00	5.00	11.00	80.00	300.00
1878CC	200,000	12.00	37.50	50.00	125.00	350.00	
1879	(1,100) 15,100	50.00	100.00	150.00	200.00	350.00	325.00
1880	(1,355) 37,355	24.00	60.00	85.00	140.00	275.00	325.00
1881	(975) 24,975	35.00	80.00	110.00	175.00	300.00	325.00
1882	(1,100) 3,911,100	1.25	3.00	5.00	11.00	80.00	300.00
1883	(1,039) 7,675,712	1.25	3.00	5.00	11.00	80.00	300.00
1884	(875) 3,366,380	1.25	3.00	5.00	11.00	80.00	300.00
1884S	564,969	4.50	10.00	20.00	30.00	300.00	
1885	(930) 2,533,427	1.25	3.00	5.00	11.00	80.00	300.00
1885S	43,690	60.00	125.00	225.00	350.00	1,500	
1886	(886) 6,377,570	1.25	3.00	5.00	11.00	80.00	300.00
1886S	206,524	4.50	10.00	18.00	25.00	225.00	
1887	(710) 11,283,939	1.25	3.00	5.00	11.00	80.00	300.00
1887S	4,454,450	1.25	3.00	5.00	11.00	80.00	
1888	(832) 5,496,487	1.25	3.00	5.00	11.00	80.00	300.00
1888S	1,720,000	1.25	3.00	5.00	11.00	90.00	
1889	(711) 7,380,711	1.25	3.00	5.00	11.00	80.00	300.00
1889S	972,678	4.50	10.00	20.00	35.00	200.00	
1890	(590) 9,911,541	1.25	3.00	5.00	11.00	80.00	300.00
1890S	1,423,076	1.25	3.50	6.00	12.00	90.00	
1891	(600) 15,310,600	1.25	3.00	5.00	11.00	80.00	300.00
1891O	4,540,000	1.25	3.00	5.00	18.00	100.00	
1891S	3,196,116	1.25	3.00	5.00	13.00	80.00	

BARBER or LIBERTY HEAD TYPE 1892-1916

This type was designed by Charles E. Barber, Chief Engraver of the Mint. His initial B is at the truncation of the neck. He also designed quarters and half dollars of the same period.

G-4 GOOD—*Date and letters plain. LIBERTY Is obliterated.*

VG-8 VERY GOOD—*At least 3 letters visible in LIBERTY.*

F-12 FINE—*All letters in LIBERTY visible, though some are weak.*

VF-20 VERY FINE—*All letters of LBERTY evenly plain.*

EF-40 EXTREMELY FINE—*All letters in LIBERTY are sharp, distinct. Headband edges are distinct.*

MS-60 UNCIRCULATED—*No trace ot wear. Light blemishes.*

Mint mark location is on the reverse below the wreath.

DIMES

	Quan. Minted	G-4	VG-8	F-12	VF-20	EF-40	MS-60	Proof-63
1892 (1,245)	12,121,245	$ *.60*	$1.25	$3.00	$4.00	$9.00	$70.00	$400.00
1892O	3,841,700	2.25	3.00	4.00	6.00	14.00	90.00	
1892S (792)	990,710	14.00	20.00	25.00	30.00	50.00	175.00	
1893, 3 over 2	3,340,792				—	50.00	185.00	450.00
1893		2.00	2.75	3.75	5.00	13.00	90.00	400.00
1893O	1,760,000	7.00	8.00	20.00	35.00	40.00	150.00	
1893S	2,491,401	3.00	6.00	8.00	12.00	20.00	135.00	
1894 (972)	1,330,972	3.00	6.00	20.00	30.00	45.00	125.00	400.00
1894O	720,000	18.00	25.00	40.00	75.00	150.00	550.00	
1894S	24						50,000	
1895 (880)	690,880	30.00	35.00	75.00	100.00	150.00	350.00	400.00
1895O	440,000	80.00	100.00	175.00	200.00	400.00	1,000	
1895S	1,120,000	8.00	12.00	25.00	30.00	45.00	175.00	
1896 (762)	2,000,762	2.00	4.00	8.00	12.00	20.00	90.00	400.00
1896O	610,000	24.00	30.00	60.00	85.00	150.00	400.00	
1896S	575,056	20.00	24.00	35.00	50.00	100.00	300.00	
1897 (731)	10,869,264	*.50*	*.60*	1.35	3.50	9.00	80.00	400.00
1897O	666,000	20.00	25.00	50.00	75.00	140.00	350.00	
1897S	1,342,844	3.00	5.00	12.00	20.00	40.00	160.00	
1898 (735)	16,320,735	*.30*	*.50*	1.35	3.50	9.00	75.00	400.00
1898O	2,130,000	*.70*	3.00	10.00	20.00	35.00	175.00	
1898S	1,702,507	*.70*	2.00	5.00	10.00	18.00	110.00	
1899 (846)	19,580,846	*.30*	*.50*	1.35	3.50	9.00	75.00	400.00
1899O	2,650,000	*.70*	3.00	8.00	15.00	35.00	175.00	
1899S	1,867,493	*.70*	2.00	5.00	9.00	15.00	100.00	
1900 (912)	17,600,912	*.50*	*.60*	1.35	3.50	9.00	75.00	400.00
1900O	2,010,000	2.00	3.00	10.00	15.00	50.00	225.00	
1900S	5,168,270	*.70*	1.25	2.50	4.00	12.00	90.00	
1901 (813)	18,860,478	*.50*	*.60*	1.35	3.50	9.00	70.00	400.00
1901O	5,620,000	*.70*	1.25	2.50	6.00	20.00	175.00	
1901S	593,022	20.00	24.00	50.00	80.00	150.00	425.00	
1902 (777)	21,380,777	*.30*	*.50*	1.35	3.50	9.00	75.00	400.00
1902O	4,500,000	*.70*	1.25	2.50	4.00	14.00	135.00	
1902S	2,070,000	2.00	3.00	6.00	15.00	35.00	160.00	
1903 (755)	19,500,755	*.30*	*.50*	1.35	3.50	9.00	75.00	400.00
1903O	8,180,000	*.70*	1.25	2.00	4.00	13.00	135.00	
1903S	613,300	15.00	20.00	50.00	90.00	200.00	375.00	
1904 (670)	14,601,027	*.30*	*.50*	1.35	3.50	9.00	75.00	400.00
1904S	800,000	10.00	14.00	20.00	36.00	65.00	300.00	
1905 (727)	14,552,350	*.30*	*.50*	1.35	3.50	9.00	75.00	400.00
1905O	3,400,000	*.30*	1.25	3.00	6.00	12.00	110.00	
1905S	6,855,199	*.30*	1.25	2.50	4.50	12.00	110.00	
1906 (675)	19,958,406	*.30*	*.50*	1.35	3.50	9.00	75.00	400.00
1906D	4,060,000	*.30*	1.25	2.50	4.50	11.00	80.00	
1906O	2,610,000	*.70*	2.00	4.00	7.00	15.00	110.00	
1906S	3,136,640	*.60*	1.25	2.50	5.00	13.00	110.00	
1907 (575)	22,220,575	*.30*	*.50*	1.35	3.50	9.00	75.00	400.00
1907D	4,080,000	*.30*	1.00	2.25	4.25	12.00	110.00	
1907O	5,058,000	*.30*	1.00	2.25	4.25	12.00	80.00	
1907S	3,178,470	*.70*	1.25	2.50	5.00	14.00	120.00	
1908 (545)	10,600,545	*.30*	*.60*	1.35	3.50	9.00	75.00	400.00
1908D	7,490,000	*.30*	1.00	2.25	2.75	10.00	80.00	
1908O	1,789,000	*.70*	1.75	4.00	9.00	18.00	135.00	
1908S	3,220,000	*.30*	1.00	2.25	4.00	12.00	110.00	

Italic prices indicate unsettled values due to fluctuating bullion market. See Bullion Chart.

DIMES

	Quan. Minted	G-4	VG-8	F-12	VF-20	EF-40	MS-60	Proof-63
1909 .... (650)	10,240,650	*$.50*	*$.60*	$1.35	$2.75	$9.00	$75.00	$400.00
1909D.................	954,000	1.25	2.75	7.00	14.00	30.00	140.00	
1909O...............	2,287,000	1.00	1.50	3.00	7.00	15.00	90.00	
1909S...............	1,000,000	1.25	2.75	6.00	10.00	40.00	150.00	
1910 .... (551)	11,520,551	*.30*	*.50*	1.35	2.75	9.00	75.00	400.00
1910D...............	3,490,000	*.30*	1.25	2.25	4.00	14.00	100.00	
1910S...............	1,240,000	*.30*	1.25	3.25	7.00	15.00	150.00	
1911 .... (543)	18,870,543	*.30*	*.50*	1.35	2.75	9.00	75.00	400.00
1911D..............	11,209,000	*.30*	*.50*	1.35	2.75	9.00	75.00	
1911S...............	3,520,000	*.30*	1.25	2.25	4.00	10.00	90.00	
1912 .... (700)	19,350,000	*.30*	*.50*	1.35	2.75	9.00	75.00	400.00
1912D..............	11,760,000	*.30*	*.50*	1.35	2.75	9.00	75.00	
1912S...............	3,420,000	*.30*	1.25	2.25	4.00	10.00	100.00	
1913 .... (622)	19,760,622	*.30*	*.50*	1.35	2.75	9.00	75.00	400.00
1913S.................	510,000	3.00	5.00	12.00	27.00	55.00	225.00	
1914 .... (425)	17,360,655	*.30*	*.50*	1.35	2.75	9.00	75.00	400.00
1914D..............	11,908,000	*.30*	*.50*	1.35	2.75	9.00	75.00	
1914S...............	2,100,000	*.30*	1.25	2.25	4.00	10.00	90.00	
1915 .... (450)	5,620,450	*.30*	*.50*	1.35	2.75	9.00	75.00	400.00
1915S.................	960,000	*.60*	1.50	2.75	4.25	15.00	95.00	
1916	18,490,000	*.30*	*.50*	1.35	2.75	9.00	75.00	
1916S...............	5,820,000	*.30*	*.50*	1.35	2.75	9.00	75.00	

WINGED LIBERTY HEAD or "MERCURY" TYPE 1916-1945

Although this coin is commonly called the "Mercury Dime," the main device is in fact a representation of Liberty. The wings crowning her cap are intended to symbolize liberty of thought. The designer's monogram AW is right of neck.

Mint mark location is on reverse left of fasces.

G-4 GOOD—*Letters and date clear. Lines and bands in fasces are obliterated.*
VG-8 VERY GOOD—*One-half of sticks discernible in fasces.*
F-12 FINE—*All sticks in fasces are defined. Diagonal bands worn nearly flat.*
VF-20 VERY FINE—*The two crossing diagonal bands must show.*
EF-40 EXTREMELY FINE—*Diagonal bands show only slight wear. Braids and hair before ear show clearly.*
MS-60 UNCIRCULATED—*No trace of wear. Light blemishes.*
MS-63 UNCIRCULATED—*No trace of wear. Slight blemishes.*

Uncirculated values shown are for average pieces with minimum blemishes, those with sharp strikes and split bands on reverse are worth much more.

	Quan. Minted	G-4	VG-8	F-12	VF-20	EF-40	MS-60	MS-63
1916	22,180,080	*$.30*	*$.40*	*$.50*	$1.50	$2.50	$10.00	$20.00
1916D.................	264,000	175.00	300.00	475.00	800.00	1,100	1,800	3,200
1916S..............	10,450,000	*.30*	*.40*	*.70*	3.00	7.00	18.00	25.00
1917	55,230,000	*.30*	*.30*	*.50*	1.25	2.50	9.00	15.00
1917D...............	9,402,000	*.30*	*.40*	*.80*	5.00	12.50	50.00	150.00
1917S..............	27,330,000	*.30*	*.40*	*.50*	1.50	3.50	20.00	60.00
1918	26,680,000	*.30*	*.30*	*.50*	3.00	9.00	25.00	60.00
1918D..............	22,674,800	*.30*	*.30*	*.50*	3.00	9.00	40.00	100.00
1918S..............	19,300,000	*.30*	*.30*	*.40*	2.00	5.00	25.00	65.00
1919	35,740,000	*.30*	*.30*	*.40*	1.50	2.50	15.00	40.00
1919D..............	9,939,000	*.30*	*.30*	1.00	5.00	15.00	65.00	185.00

Italic prices indicate unsettled values due to fluctuating bullion market. See Bullion Chart.

DIMES

	Quan. Minted	G-4	VG-8	F-12	VF-20	EF-40	MS-60	MS-63
1919S	8,850,000	*$.30*	*$.30*	*$.40*	$4.50	$10.00	$70.00	$175.00
1920	59,030,000	*.30*	*.30*	*.40*	2.00	3.00	10.00	30.00
1920D	19,171,000	*.30*	*.30*	*.40*	3.00	8.00	40.00	150.00
1920S	13,820,000	*.30*	*.30*	*.40*	2.50	7.00	30.00	100.00
1921	1,230,000	10.00	15.00	35.00	70.00	225.00	500.00	800.00
1921D	1,080,000	15.00	20.00	45.00	85.00	225.00	500.00	900.00
1923	50,130,000	*.30*	*.30*	*.40*	1.00	1.75	8.00	20.00
1923S	6,440,000	*.30*	*.30*	*.50*	2.50	10.00	45.00	175.00
1924	24,010,000	*.30*	*.30*	*.40*	1.25	3.00	20.00	45.00
1924D	6,810,000	*.30*	*.30*	1.00	2.50	10.00	75.00	150.00
1924S	7,120,000	*.30*	*.30*	1.00	2.25	10.00	65.00	250.00
1925	25,610,000	*.30*	*.30*	*.40*	1.25	2.25	15.00	30.00
1925D	5,117,000	1.50	2.00	4.00	12.00	35.00	130.00	225.00
1925S	5,850,000	*.30*	*.30*	1.00	2.25	10.00	60.00	200.00
1926	32,160,000	*.30*	*.30*	*.40*	1.25	2.00	10.00	15.00
1926D	6,828,000	*.30*	*.30*	*.40*	2.00	6.00	30.00	90.00
1926S	1,520,000	2.50	3.50	7.00	15.00	75.00	300.00	800.00
1927	28,080,000	*.30*	*.30*	*.40*	1.00	1.75	8.00	15.00
1927D	4,812,000	*.30*	*.30*	1.00	5.00	12.00	90.00	225.00
1927S	4,770,000	*.30*	*.30*	*.40*	1.30	5.00	50.00	125.00
1928	19,480,000	*.30*	*.30*	*.40*	1.00	1.75	8.00	20.00
1928D	4,161,000	*.30*	*.30*	1.75	5.00	11.00	65.00	150.00
1928S	7,400,000	*.30*	*.30*	*.40*	1.25	4.00	28.00	80.00
1929	25,970,000	*.30*	*.30*	*.40*	1.00	1.50	6.00	10.00
1929D	5,034,000	*.30*	*.30*	*.40*	1.75	3.00	15.00	20.00
1929S	4,730,000	*.30*	*.30*	*.40*	1.25	2.00	15.00	20.00
1930	6,770,000	*.30*	*.30*	*.40*	1.00	2.00	10.00	20.00
1930S	1,843,000	*.30*	1.00	1.25	1.50	3.00	30.00	45.00
1931	3,150,000	*.30*	*.30*	*.40*	1.50	3.50	15.00	30.00
1931D	1,260,000	2.50	3.00	4.75	8.00	18.00	40.00	50.00
1931S	1,800,000	*.30*	1.00	1.50	2.00	4.00	35.00	45.00

	Quan. Minted	VG-8	F-12	VF-20	EF-40	MS-60	MS-63	Proof-63
1934	24,080,000	*$.30*	*$.30*	*$.35*	*$.40*	$6.00	$10.00	
1934D	6,772,000	*.30*	*.30*	*.35*	*.40*	15.00	20.00	
1935	58,830,000	*.30*	*.30*	*.35*	*.40*	5.00	8.00	
1935D	10,477,000	*.30*	*.30*	*.35*	*.40*	15.00	20.00	
1935S	15,840,000	*.30*	*.30*	*.35*	*.40*	10.00	16.00	
1936 (4,130)	87,504,130	*.30*	*.30*	*.35*	*.40*	6.00	9.00	$275.00
1936D	16,132,000	*.30*	*.30*	*.35*	*.40*	11.00	15.00	
1936S	9,210,000	*.30*	*.30*	*.35*	*.40*	8.00	10.00	
1937 (5,756)	56,865,756	*.30*	*.30*	*.35*	*.40*	6.00	10.00	150.00
1937D	14,146,000	*.30*	*.30*	*.35*	*.40*	10.00	14.00	
1937S	9,740,000	*.30*	*.30*	*.35*	*.40*	7.00	10.00	
1938 (8,728)	22,198,728	*.30*	*.30*	*.35*	*.40*	5.00	10.00	125.00
1938D	5,537,000	*.30*	*.30*	*.35*	*.40*	9.00	12.00	
1938S	8,090,000	*.30*	*.30*	*.35*	*.40*	7.00	12.00	
1939 (9,321)	67,749,321	*.30*	*.30*	*.35*	*.40*	4.00	7.00	110.00
1939D	24,394,000	*.30*	*.30*	*.35*	*.40*	4.00	7.00	
1939S	10,540,000	*.30*	*.30*	*.35*	*.40*	10.00	15.00	
1940 (11,827)	65,361,827	*.30*	*.30*	*.35*	*.40*	4.00	8.00	100.00
1940D	21,198,000	*.30*	*.30*	*.35*	*.40*	4.00	8.00	
1940S	21,560,000	*.30*	*.30*	*.35*	*.40*	4.00	8.00	
1941 (16,557)	175,106,557	*.30*	*.30*	*.35*	*.40*	4.00	7.00	95.00
1941D	45,634,000	*.30*	*.30*	*.35*	*.40*	4.00	8.00	
1941S	43,090,000	*.30*	*.30*	*.35*	*.40*	4.00	7.00	

Italic prices indicate unsettled values due to fluctuating bullion market. See Bullion Chart.

1942, 2 over 1

1942D, 2 over 1

	Quan. Minted	VG-8	F-12	VF-20	EF-40	MS-60	MS-63	Proof-63
1942, 2 over 1 ...	205,432,329	$100.00	$125.00	$135.00	$160.00	$600.00	$1,200	
1942 ..... (22,329)		.30	.30	.35	.40	4.00	6.00	$95.00
1942D, 2 over 1..	60,740,000	100.00	125.00	155.00	200.00	650.00	1,300	
1942D..........		.30	.30	.35	.40	5.00	8.00	
1942S..............	49,300,000	.30	.30	.35	.40	6.50	10.00	
1943..............	191,710,000	.30	.30	.35	.40	4.00	6.00	
1943D..............	71,949,000	.30	.30	.35	.40	5.00	8.00	
1943S..............	60,400,000	.30	.30	.35	.40	5.00	8.00	
1944..............	231,410,000	.30	.30	.35	.40	4.00	7.00	
1944D..............	62,224,000	.30	.30	.35	.40	4.00	7.00	
1944S..............	49,490,000	.30	.30	.35	.40	4.00	7.00	
1945..............	159,130,000	.30	.30	.35	.40	3.00	5.00	
1945D..............	40,245,000	.30	.30	.35	.40	4.00	6.00	
1945S Normal S .	41,920,000	.30	.30	.35	.40	5.00	7.00	
1945S Micro S.....		.30	.30	.35	.40	8.00	11.00	

ROOSEVELT TYPE 1946 to Date

John R. Sinnock (whose initials JS are at the truncation of the neck) designed this dime showing a portrait of Franklin D. Roosevelt. The design has heavier lettering and a more modernistic character than preceding types.

VF-20 VERY FINE—*Hair above ear slightly worn. All vertical lines on torch plain.*
EF-40 EXTREMELY FINE—*All lines of torch, flame and hair very plain.*
MS-63 UNCIRCULATED—*No trace of wear. Slight blemishes.*

SILVER COINAGE — 1946-1964

Mint mark on reverse 1946-1964.

	Quan. Minted	VF-20	EF-40	MS-63	Proof-63
1946..............................	255,250,000	$.20	$.30	$.75	
1946D..............................	61,043,500	.20	.30	.90	
1946S..............................	27,900,000	.20	.30	1.85	
1947..............................	121,520,000	.20	.30	1.25	
1947D..............................	46,835,000	.20	.30	1.50	
1947S..............................	34,840,000	.20	.30	1.50	
1948..............................	74,950,000	.20	.30	3.50	
1948D..............................	52,841,000	.20	.30	2.50	
1948S..............................	35,520,000	.20	.30	3.00	
1949..............................	30,940,000	.20	.30	8.00	
1949D..............................	26,034,000	.20	.30	4.00	
1949S..............................	13,510,000	.20	.30	15.00	
1950........................ (51,386)	50,181,500	.20	.30	1.40	$13.00

Italic prices indicate unsettled values due to fluctuating bullion market. See Bullion Chart.

DIMES

		Quan. Minted	VF-20	EF-40	MS-63	Proof-63
1950D		46,803,000	*$.20*	*$.30*	$1.45	
1950S		20,440,000	*.20*	*.30*	7.00	
1951	(57,500)	103,937,602	*.20*	*.30*	.75	$9.00
1951D		56,529,000	*.20*	*.30*	.85	
1951S		31,630,000	*.20*	*.30*	5.00	
1952	(81,980)	99,122,073	*.20*	*.30*	1.00	8.00
1952D		122,100,000	*.20*	*.30*	.75	
1952S		44,419,500	*.20*	*.30*	2.00	
1953	(128,800)	53,618,920	*.20*	*.30*	1.00	4.50
1953D		136,433,000	*.20*	*.30*	.75	
1953S		39,180,000	*.20*	*.30*	.75	
1954	(233,300)	114,243,503	*.20*	*.30*	.75	2.00
1954D		106,397,000	*.20*	*.30*	.75	
1954S		22,860,000	*.20*	*.30*	.75	
1955	(378,200)	12,828,381	*.20*	*.30*	.90	2.00
1955D		13,959,000	*.20*	*.30*	.75	
1955S		18,510,000	*.20*	*.30*	.75	
1956	(669,384)	109,309,384	*.20*	*.30*	.75	.90
1956D		108,015,100	*.20*	*.30*	.75	
1957	(1,247,952)	161,407,952	*.20*	*.30*	*.50*	.80
1957D		113,354,330	*.20*	*.30*	*.50*	
1958	(875,652)	32,785,652	*.20*	*.30*	*.60*	.90
1958D		136,564,600	*.20*	*.30*	*.40*	
1959	(1,149,291)	86,929,291	*.20*	*.30*	*.40*	.75
1959D		164,919,790	*.20*	*.30*	*.40*	
1960	(1,691,602)	72,081,602	*.20*	*.30*	*.40*	.75
1960D		200,160,400	*.20*	*.30*	*.40*	
1961	(3,028,244)	96,758,244	*.20*	*.30*	*.40*	.65
1961D		209,146,550	*.20*	*.30*	*.40*	
1962	(3,218,019)	75,668,019	*.20*	*.30*	*.40*	.65
1962D		334,948,380	*.20*	*.30*	*.40*	
1963	(3,075,645)	126,725,645	*.20*	*.30*	*.40*	.65
1963D		421,476,530	*.20*	*.30*	*.40*	
1964	(3,950,762)	933,310,762	*.20*	*.30*	*.40*	.65
1964D		1,357,517,180	*.20*	*.30*	*.40*	

Clad Coinage

Mint mark on obverse starting 1968

	Quan. Minted	MS-63	Proof-63
1965	1,652,140,570	$.12	
1966	1,382,734,540	.12	
1967	2,244,007,320	.12	
1968	424,470,400	.11	
1968D	480,748,280	.11	
1968S Proof	(3,041,506)		$.20
1969	145,790,000	.15	
1969D	563,323,870	.12	
1969S Proof	(2,934,631)		.20
1970	345,570,000	.12	
1970D	754,942,100	.12	

	Quan. Minted	MS-63	Proof-63
1970S Proof	(2,632,810)		$.30
1971	162,690,000	$.15	
1971D	377,914,240	.14	
1971S Proof	(3,220,733)		.30
1972	431,540,000	.13	
1972D	330,290,000	.12	
1972S Proof	(3,260,996)		.30
1973	315,670,000	.12	
1973D	455,032,426	.12	
1973S Proof	(2,760,339)		.20
1974	470,248,000	.12	

Italic prices indicate unsettled values due to fluctuating bullion market. See Bullion Chart.

	Quan. Minted	MS-63	Proof-63
1974D	571,083,000	$.12	
1974S Proof	(2,612,568)		$.30
1975	585,673,900	.13	
1975D	313,705,300	.12	
1975S Proof	(2,845,450)		.30
1976	568,760,000	.13	
1976D	695,222,774	.13	
1976S Proof	(4,149,730)		.20
1977	796,930,000	.12	
1977D	376,607,228	.12	
1977S Proof	(3,251,152)		.20
1978	663,980,000	.12	
1978D	282,847,540	.12	
1978S Proof	(3,127,781)		.30
1979	315,440,000	.12	
1979D	390,921,184	.12	
1979S Proof	(3,677,175)		
Filled S			.40
Clear S			1.00
1980P	735,170,000	.20	
1980D	719,354,321	.12	
1980S Proof	(3,554,806)		.30
1981P	676,650,000	.12	
1981D	712,284,143	.12	
1981S Proof	(4,063,083)		.30
1982 (no mint mark)		50.00	
1982P	519,475,000	.12	
1982D	542,713,584	.11	
1982S Proof	(3,857,479)		.50
1983P	647,025,000	.12	
1983D	730,129,224	$.12	
1983S Proof	(3,279,126)		$.75
1984P	856,669,000	.12	
1984D	704,803,976	.12	
1984S Proof	(3,065,110)		.75
1985P	705,200,962	.10	
1985D	587,979,970	.10	
1985S Proof	(3,362,821)		.50
1986P	682,649,693	.12	
1986D	473,326,970	.10	
1986S Proof	(3,010,497)		1.00
1987P	762,709,481	.10	
1987D	653,203,402	.10	
1987S Proof	(4,227,728)		.50
1988P	1,030,550,000	.12	
1988D	962,385,488	.12	
1988S Proof	(3,262,948)		.50
1989P	1,298,400,000	.10	
1989D	896,535,597	.10	
1989S Proof	(3,220,194)		.50
1990P	1,034,340,000	.10	
1990D	839,995,824	.10	
1990S Proof	(3,299,559)		.50
1991P	927,228,000	.10	
1991D	601,241,114	.10	
1991S Proof			.50
1992P		.10	
1992D		.10	
1992S Proof			.50

TWENTY-CENT PIECES — 1875-1878

This short-lived coin was authorized by the Act of March 3, 1875. The edge of the coin is plain. Most of the 1876CC coins were melted at the mint and never released. Mint mark is on the reverse below the eagle.

G-4 GOOD—*LIBERTY on shield obliterated. Letters and date legible.*
VG-8 VERY GOOD—*One or two letters in LIBERTY may show. Other details will be bold.*
F-12 FINE—*At least 3 letters of LIBERTY show.*
VF-20 VERY FINE—*LIBERTY completely readable, but partly weak.*
EF-40 EXTREMELY FINE—*LIBERTY sharp. Only slight wear on high points of coin.*
MS-60 UNCIRCULATED—*No trace of wear. Light blemishes.*

	Quan. Minted	G-4	VG-8	F-12	VF-20	EF-40	MS-60	Proof-63
1875 (2,790)	39,700	$25.00	$30.00	$40.00	$65.00	$110.00	$400.00	$1,000
1875CC	133,290	25.00	30.00	40.00	65.00	120.00	425.00	
1875S	1,155,000	23.00	28.00	38.00	55.00	70.00	350.00	—
1876 (1,260)	15,900	34.00	42.00	60.00	80.00	155.00	525.00	1,200
1876CC	10,000						—	
1877 (350)	350							1,525
1878 (600)	600							1,600

QUARTER DOLLARS — 1796 to Date

Authorized in 1792, this denomination was not issued until four years later. The first type weighed 104 grains which remained standard until modified to 103⅛ grains by the Act of January 18, 1837. As with the dime and half dime, the weight was reduced and arrows placed at the date in 1853. Rays were placed in the field of the reverse during that year only.

DRAPED BUST TYPE, SMALL EAGLE REVERSE 1796

AG-3 ABOUT GOOD—*Details clear enough to identify.*

G-4 GOOD—*Date readable. Bust outlined, but no detail.*

VG-8 VERY GOOD—*All but deepest drapery folds worn smooth. Hairlines nearly gone and curls lack detail.*

F-12 FINE—*All drapery lines visible. Hair partly worn.*

VF-20 VERY FINE—*Only left side of drapery is indistinct.*

EF-40 EXTREMELY FINE—*Hair well outlined and detailed.*

MS-60 UNCIRCULATED—*No trace of wear. Light blemishes.*

	Quan. Minted	*AG-3*	*G-4*	*VG-8*	*F-12*	*VF-20*	*EF-40*	*MS-60*
1796	6,146	$1,000	$2,500	$3,300	$4,300	$7,000	$11,000	$18,000

DRAPED BUST TYPE, HERALDIC EAGLE REVERSE 1804-1807

1804	6,738	175.00	400.00	550.00	1,500	2,400	4,500	—
1805	121,394	50.00	110.00	150.00	230.00	500.00	900.00	3,200
1806 6 over 5	206,124	50.00	110.00	150.00	230.00	500.00	900.00	3,200
1806	(incl. above)	50.00	110.00	150.00	230.00	500.00	900.00	3,200
1807	220,643	50.00	110.00	150.00	230.00	500.00	900.00	3,200

CAPPED BUST TYPE 1815-1838

Large Size 1815-1828

AG-3 ABOUT GOOD—*Details clear enough to identify.*

G-4 GOOD—*Date, letters and stars readable. Hair under headband smooth. Cap lines worn smooth.*

VG-8 VERY GOOD—*Rim well defined. Main details visible. Full LIBERTY on cap. Hair above eye nearly smooth.*

F-12 FINE—*All hairlines show but drapery has only part details. Shoulder clasp distinct.*

VF-20 VERY FINE—*All details show, but some wear. Clasp and ear sharp.*

EF-40 EXTREMELY FINE—*All details show distinctly. Hair well outlined.*

MS-60 UNCIRCULATED—*No trace of wear. Light blemishes.*

QUARTER DOLLARS

Quan. Minted	AG-3	G-4	VG-8	F-12	VF-20	EF-40	MS-60
1815 89,235	$12.00	$24.00	$35.00	$55.00	$150.00	$450.00	$1,100
1818 8 over 5 } 361,174	12.00	24.00	35.00	55.00	150.00	425.00	1,300
1818 Normal }	12.00	24.00	30.00	50.00	135.00	400.00	1,000
1819 144,000	12.00	24.00	30.00	50.00	135.00	400.00	1,000
1820 127,444	12.00	24.00	30.00	50.00	135.00	400.00	1,000
1821 216,851	12.00	24.00	30.00	50.00	135.00	400.00	1,000
1822 All kinds . . 64,080	12.00	24.00	30.00	50.00	135.00	400.00	1,100
1822, 25 over 50c	100.00	200.00	300.00	500.00	900.00	1,750	3,500
1823, 3 over 2 . . 17,800	800.00	2,000	3,750	6,750	10,000	15,000	——
1824 . . . . } 168,000	14.00	30.00	37.00	75.00	200.00	500.00	1,800
1825 . . . . }	10.00	20.00	27.50	45.00	125.00	400.00	1,100
1827 Original (Curled base 2 in 25c) 4,000 Minted							——
1827 Restrike (Square base 2 in 25c)							——
1828 All kds . . . 102,000	9.00	20.00	27.50	45.00	125.00	400.00	1,200
1828, 25 over 50c	20.00	40.00	75.00	140.00	300.00	550.00	2,300

Reduced Size, No Motto on Reverse 1831-1838

G-4 GOOD—*Bust well defined. Hair under headband smooth. Date, letters, stars readable. Scant rims.*
VG-8 VERY GOOD—*Details apparent but worn on high spots. Rims strong. Full LIBERTY.*
F-12 FINE—*All hairlines visible. Drapery partly worn. Shoulder clasp distinct.*
VF-20 VERY FINE—*Only top spots worn. Clasp sharp. Ear distinct.*
EF-40 EXTREMELY FINE—*Hair details and clasp are bold and clear.*
MS-60 UNCIRCULATED—*No trace of wear. Light blemishes.*

Quan. Minted	G-4	VG-8	F-12	VF-20	EF-40	MS-60
1831 398,000	$16.00	$20.00	$27.00	$55.00	$110.00	$550.00
1832 320,000	16.00	20.00	27.00	55.00	110.00	550.00
1833 156,000	17.00	22.00	30.00	60.00	150.00	700.00
1834 286,000	16.00	20.00	27.00	55.00	110.00	550.00
1835 1,952,000	16.00	20.00	27.00	55.00	110.00	550.00
1836 472,000	16.00	20.00	27.00	55.00	110.00	550.00
1837 252,400	16.00	20.00	27.00	55.00	110.00	550.00
1838 366,000	16.00	20.00	27.00	55.00	110.00	550.00

QUARTER DOLLARS

LIBERTY SEATED TYPE 1838-1891

No Motto Above Eagle 1838-1853

G-4 GOOD—*Scant rim. LIBERTY on shield worn off. Date and letters readable.*
VG-8 VERY GOOD—*Rim fairly defined, at least 3 letters in LIBERTY evident.*
F-12 FINE—*LIBERTY complete, but partly weak.*
VF-20 VERY FINE—*LIBERTY strong.*
EF-40 EXTREMELY FINE—*Complete LIBERTY and edges of scroll. Clasp shows plainly.*
MS-60 UNCIRCULATED—*No trace of wear. Light blemishes.*

Mint mark location is on the reverse below the eagle.

	Quan. Minted	*G-4*	*VG-8*	*F-12*	*VF-20*	*EF-40*	*MS-60*
1838	466,000	$4.50	$6.00	$11.00	$21.00	$90.00	$700.00
1839	491,146	4.50	6.00	11.00	21.00	90.00	700.00
1840	188,127	7.00	9.00	20.00	40.00	70.00	550.00
1840O	425,200	4.50	6.00	15.00	30.00	70.00	800.00
1841	120,000	15.00	25.00	40.00	60.00	125.00	400.00
1841O	452,000	4.50	6.00	11.00	24.00	80.00	450.00

Small Date

Large Date

1842 Small date. Proof only							12,000
1842	88,000	30.00	40.00	70.00	130.00	175.00	600.00
1842O Small date	769,000	100.00	175.00	300.00	500.00	1,000	—
1842O Large date		5.00	7.00	11.00	15.00	40.00	550.00
1843	645,600	4.50	6.00	9.00	14.00	25.00	275.00
1843O	968,000	7.00	12.00	20.00	35.00	100.00	600.00
1844	421,200	4.50	6.00	11.00	15.00	35.00	225.00
1844O	740,000	4.50	6.00	11.00	21.00	50.00	600.00
1845	922,000	4.50	6.00	9.00	14.00	30.00	200.00
1846	510,000	4.50	6.00	11.00	15.00	30.00	200.00
1847	734,000	4.50	6.00	11.00	14.00	30.00	200.00
1847O	368,000	9.00	14.00	24.00	40.00	90.00	500.00
1848	146,000	8.00	12.00	24.00	40.00	80.00	450.00
1849	340,000	7.00	9.00	15.00	21.00	65.00	300.00
1849O	†incl. below	140.00	230.00	410.00	825.00	1,400	—
1850	190,800	4.50	9.00	14.00	25.00	50.00	400.00
1850O	412,000	12.00	16.00	22.00	35.00	65.00	550.00
1851	160,000	4.50	9.00	14.00	21.00	60.00	400.00
1851O	88,000	65.00	100.00	200.00	300.00	650.00	1,400
1852	177,060	9.00	14.00	21.00	30.00	60.00	325.00
1852O	96,000	80.00	120.00	175.00	350.00	550.00	1,400
1853 No arrows or rays	44,200	70.00	90.00	125.00	225.00	325.00	1,600

†Coinage for 1849O included with 1850O.

Arrows at Date, Rays Around Eagle 1853 Only

1853, 3 over 4

QUARTER DOLLARS

	Quan. Minted	*G-4*	*VG-8*	*F-12*	*VF-20*	*EF-40*	*MS-60*
1853	15,210,020	$4.00	$6.00	$9.00	$16.00	$60.00	$500.00
1853, 3 over 4		25.00	50.00	100.00	150.00	300.00	——
1853O	1,332,000	5.00	7.00	11.00	22.00	80.00	700.00

Arrows at Date, No Rays 1854-1855

1854	12,380,000	4.00	5.00	8.00	15.00	35.00	250.00
1854O	1,484,000	4.00	5.00	8.00	15.00	35.00	300.00
1855	2,857,000	4.00	5.00	8.00	15.00	35.00	275.00
1855O	176,000	22.00	35.00	50.00	100.00	170.00	875.00
1855S	396,400	22.00	35.00	50.00	90.00	150.00	850.00

No Motto Above Eagle 1856-1865

	Quan. Minted	*G-4*	*VG-8*	*F-12*	*VF-20*	*EF-40*	*MS-60*	*Proof-63*
1856	7,264,000	$4.00	$5.00	$7.00	$10.00	$21.00	$165.00	$1,300
1856O	968,000	5.00	7.00	11.00	16.00	30.00	350.00	
1856S	286,000	10.00	14.00	21.00	50.00	100.00	1,100	
1857	9,644,000	4.00	5.00	7.00	10.00	21.00	165.00	1,200
1857O	1,180,000	4.00	6.00	8.00	11.00	21.00	300.00	
1857S	82,000	20.00	32.00	45.00	120.00	225.00	900.00	
1858	7,368,000	4.00	5.00	7.00	10.00	20.00	165.00	1,000
1858O	520,000	4.00	6.00	8.00	12.00	25.00	400.00	
1858S	121,000	16.00	18.00	30.00	90.00	150.00	700.00	
1859 .... (800)	1,344,000	4.00	5.00	7.00	10.00	21.00	165.00	600.00
1859O	260,000	6.00	10.00	16.00	25.00	40.00	400.00	
1859S	80,000	25.00	40.00	75.00	125.00	250.00	1,000	
1860 .. (1,000)	805,400	4.00	5.00	7.00	10.00	21.00	165.00	600.00
1860O	388,000	5.00	7.00	10.00	14.00	30.00	400.00	
1860S	56,000	40.00	65.00	120.00	210.00	450.00	1,350	
1861 .. (1,000)	4,854,600	4.00	5.00	7.00	10.00	21.00	165.00	600.00
1861S	96,000	10.00	14.00	21.00	45.00	150.00	1,200	
1862 .... (550)	932,550	4.00	5.00	7.00	10.00	21.00	165.00	600.00
1862S	67,000	11.00	15.00	22.00	50.00	150.00	1,200	
1863 .... (460)	192,060	7.00	9.00	14.00	20.00	40.00	350.00	625.00
1864 .... (470)	94,070	11.00	15.00	22.00	40.00	80.00	475.00	625.00
1864S	20,000	50.00	85.00	150.00	225.00	500.00	——	
1865 .... (500)	59,300	16.00	21.00	35.00	50.00	90.00	400.00	625.00
1865S	41,000	15.00	20.00	30.00	60.00	135.00	1,300	

Motto Above Eagle 1866-1873

1866 .... (725)	17,525	60.00	100.00	150.00	250.00	350.00	700.00	600.00
1866S	28,000	20.00	30.00	60.00	100.00	200.00	1,200	
1867 .... (625)	20,625	20.00	30.00	70.00	110.00	200.00	450.00	600.00
1867S	48,000	18.00	25.00	40.00	65.00	100.00	1,200	
1868 .... (600)	30,000	19.00	27.00	45.00	70.00	125.00	400.00	600.00

QUARTER DOLLARS

	Quan. Minted	G-4	VG-8	F-12	VF-20	EF-40	MS-60	Proof-63
1868S	96,000	$11.00	$17.00	$30.00	$40.00	$90.00	$600.00	
1869 .... (600)	16,600	20.00	30.00	75.00	110.00	185.00	500.00	$500.00
1869S	76,000	11.00	17.00	28.00	35.00	90.00	500.00	
1870 .. (1,000)	87,400	11.00	15.00	22.00	37.00	60.00	275.00	500.00
1870CC	8,340	450.00	750.00	1,200	1,500	2,750	—	
1871 .... (960)	119,160	4.00	6.00	10.00	18.00	30.00	225.00	
1871CC	10,890	250.00	400.00	650.00	1,100	1,800	—	
1871S	30,900	35.00	65.00	125.00	175.00	270.00	1,300	
1872 .... (950)	182,950	4.00	6.00	9.00	14.00	30.00	200.00	500.00
1872CC	22,850	125.00	175.00	275.00	450.00	1,100	3,000	
1872S	83,000	50.00	75.00	125.00	200.00	300.00	1,800	
1873 .... (600)	212,600	4.00	9.00	14.00	21.00	150.00	200.00	500.00
1873CC	4,000						—	

Arrows at Date 1873-1874

	Quan. Minted	G-4	VG-8	F-12	VF-20	EF-40	MS-60	Proof-63
1873 .... (540)	1,271,700	6.00	8.00	14.00	35.00	90.00	475.00	1,000
1873CC	12,462	275.00	350.00	500.00	800.00	1,200	3,750	
1873S	156,000	9.00	10.00	18.00	40.00	100.00	650.00	
1874 .... (700)	471,900	6.00	8.00	14.00	35.00	90.00	500.00	1,000
1874S	392,000	9.00	10.00	18.00	40.00	100.00	650.00	

No Arrows at Date 1875-1891

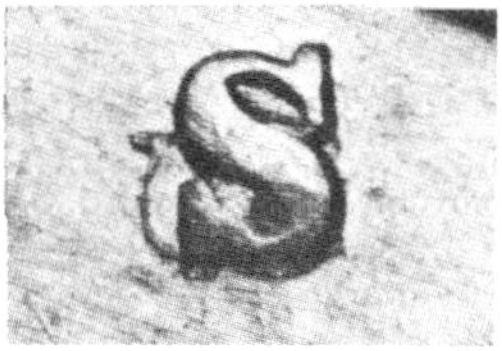

1877S, S over horizontal S

	Quan. Minted	G-4	VG-8	F-12	VF-20	EF-40	MS-60	Proof-63
1875 .... (700)	4,293,500	3.00	4.00	5.00	10.00	20.00	225.00	450.00
1875CC	140,000	16.00	22.00	55.00	80.00	175.00	650.00	
1875S	680,000	4.00	6.00	10.00	18.00	30.00	250.00	
1876 .. (1,150)	17,817,150	3.00	4.00	5.00	10.00	20.00	225.00	450.00
1876CC	4,944,000	4.00	5.00	7.00	14.00	30.00	250.00	
1876S	8,596,000	3.00	4.00	5.00	10.00	20.00	225.00	
1877 .... (510)	10,911,710	3.00	4.00	5.00	10.00	20.00	200.00	450.00
1877CC	4,192,000	4.00	5.00	7.00	14.00	30.00	250.00	
1877S	} 8,996,000	3.00	4.00	5.00	10.00	20.00	200.00	
1877S over horizontal S	}	4.00	6.00	40.00	50.00	90.00	300.00	
1878 .... (800)	2,260,800	3.00	4.00	5.00	10.00	20.00	200.00	450.00
1878CC	996,000	4.00	5.00	7.00	11.00	25.00	300.00	
1878S	140,000	27.00	37.00	65.00	90.00	125.00	1,200	
1879 .. *(1,100)*	14,700	35.00	40.00	55.00	75.00	100.00	325.00	500.00

QUARTER DOLLARS

	Quan. Minted	G-4	VG-8	F-12	VF-20	EF-40	MS-60	Proof-63
1880 .. (1,355)	14,955	$35.00	$40.00	$55.00	$75.00	$100.00	$325.00	$450.00
1881 .... (975)	12,975	35.00	40.00	55.00	75.00	100.00	300.00	500.00
1882 .. (1,100)	16,300	35.00	40.00	55.00	75.00	100.00	300.00	500.00
1883 .. (1,039)	15,439	35.00	40.00	55.00	75.00	100.00	300.00	500.00
1884 .... (875)	8,875	40.00	50.00	65.00	90.00	125.00	350.00	500.00
1885 .... (930)	14,530	35.00	40.00	55.00	75.00	110.00	325.00	500.00
1886 .... (886)	5,886	45.00	60.00	70.00	100.00	150.00	350.00	500.00
1887 .... (710)	10,710	35.00	40.00	55.00	75.00	110.00	325.00	500.00
1888 .... (832)	10,833	35.00	40.00	55.00	75.00	110.00	325.00	500.00
1888S	1,216,000	4.00	5.00	6.00	11.00	20.00	180.00	
1889 .... (711)	12,711	33.00	37.00	50.00	65.00	90.00	325.00	500.00
1890 .... (590)	80,590	20.00	25.00	33.00	45.00	70.00	275.00	450.00
1891 .... (600)	3,920,600	3.00	4.00	5.00	10.00	20.00	180.00	450.00
1891O...............	68,000	50.00	65.00	100.00	150.00	275.00	1,500	
1891S	2,216,000	3.00	5.00	7.00	12.00	23.00	180.00	

BARBER or LIBERTY HEAD TYPE 1892-1916

Like other silver coins of this type the quarter dollars minted from 1892 to 1916 were designed by Charles E. Barber. His initial B is found at the truncation of the neck of Liberty.

G-4 GOOD—*Date and legends readable. LIBERTY worn off headband.*

VG-8 VERY GOOD—*Minimum of 3 letters in LIBERTY readable.*

F-12 FINE—*LIBERTY completely readable but not sharp.*

VF-20 VERY FINE—*All letters in LIBERTY evenly plain.*

EF-40 EXTREMELY FINE—*LIBERTY bold, and its ribbon distinct.*

MS-60 UNCIRCULATED—*No trace of wear. Light blemishes.*

Mint mark location is on the reverse below the eagle.

	Quan. Minted	G-4	VG-8	F-12	VF-20	EF-40	MS-60	Proof-63
1892 .. (1,245)	8,237,245	*$1.00*	*$1.50*	$5.00	$10.00	$26.00	$125.00	$500.00
1892O............	2,640,000	*1.00*	3.00	6.00	11.00	30.00	150.00	
1892S..............	964,079	7.00	8.00	13.00	22.00	50.00	200.00	
1893 .... (792)	5,444,815	*.75*	*1.00*	5.00	11.00	27.00	150.00	500.00
1893O............	3,396,000	*.75*	*1.00*	7.00	12.00	28.00	175.00	
1893S	1,454,535	*1.00*	3.50	9.00	14.00	35.00	175.00	
1894 .... (972)	3,432,972	*.75*	*1.00*	5.00	11.00	27.00	140.00	500.00
1894O............	2,852,000	*.75*	*1.00*	7.00	11.00	30.00	175.00	
1894S	2,648,821	*.75*	*1.00*	7.00	11.00	30.00	175.00	
1895 .... (880)	4,440,880	*.75*	*1.00*	5.00	10.00	25.00	140.00	500.00
1895O............	2,816,000	*.75*	*1.00*	7.00	11.00	28.00	200.00	
1895S	1,764,681	*.75*	*1.00*	8.00	12.00	25.00	175.00	
1896 .... (762)	3,874,762	*.75*	*1.00*	5.00	11.00	28.00	140.00	500.00
1896O............	1,484,000	*1.00*	3.00	12.00	40.00	110.00	425.00	
1896S..............	188,039	120.00	150.00	325.00	475.00	700.00	1,800	
1897 .... (731)	8,140,731	*1.00*	*1.25*	5.00	10.00	24.00	100.00	500.00
1897O............	1,414,800	*1.75*	3.50	9.00	24.00	75.00	425.00	
1897S..............	542,229	5.00	7.00	14.00	28.00	60.00	200.00	
1898 .... (735)	11,100,735	*1.00*	*1.25*	5.00	10.00	24.00	100.00	500.00

Italic prices indicate unsettled values due to fluctuating bullion market. See Bullion Chart.

QUARTER DOLLARS

	Quan. Minted	G-4	VG-8	F-12	VF-20	EF-40	MS-60	Proof-63
1898O	1,868,000	*$1.00*	*$1.75*	$7.00	$16.00	$60.00	$325.00	
1898S	1,020,592	*1.00*	*1.75*	6.00	12.00	30.00	200.00	
1899 .... (846)	12,624,846	*.75*	*1.25*	5.00	10.00	24.00	100.00	$500.00
1899O	2,644,000	*.75*	*1.25*	6.00	12.00	25.00	225.00	
1899S	708,000	4.50	6.00	9.00	18.00	35.00	175.00	
1900 .... (912)	10,016,912	*.75*	*1.25*	5.00	10.00	24.00	100.00	500.00
1900O	3,416,000	*1.00*	3.50	8.00	18.00	35.00	250.00	
1900S	1,858,585	*.75*	*1.25*	6.00	11.00	25.00	150.00	
1901 .... (813)	8,892,813	*.75*	*1.25*	5.00	10.00	24.00	100.00	500.00
1901O	1,612,000	5.00	8.00	18.00	50.00	100.00	450.00	
1901S	72,664	550.00	800.00	1,250	1,800	2,500	6,000	
1902 .... (777)	12,197,744	*.75*	*1.00*	5.00	10.00	24.00	100.00	500.00
1902O	4,748,000	*.75*	*1.00*	6.00	10.00	25.00	200.00	
1902S	1,524,612	*1.00*	4.00	7.00	16.00	38.00	185.00	
1903 .... (755)	9,670,064	*.75*	*1.00*	5.00	10.00	24.00	100.00	500.00
1903O	3,500,000	*.75*	*1.00*	8.00	12.00	27.00	175.00	
1903S	1,036,000	*1.00*	*2.00*	9.00	14.00	30.00	200.00	
1904 .... (670)	9,588,813	*.75*	*1.00*	5.00	10.00	24.00	100.00	500.00
1904O	2,456,000	*1.00*	*2.00*	9.00	13.00	55.00	350.00	
1905 .... (727)	4,968,250	*.75*	*1.00*	5.00	10.00	24.00	100.00	500.00
1905O	1,230,000	*1.00*	*2.00*	9.00	12.00	30.00	185.00	
1905S	1,884,000	*.75*	*1.00*	6.00	11.00	25.00	175.00	
1906 .... (675)	3,656,435	*.75*	*1.00*	5.00	10.00	24.00	100.00	500.00
1906D	3,280,000	*.75*	*1.00*	5.00	10.00	24.00	150.00	
1906O	2,056,000	*.75*	*1.00*	5.00	10.00	24.00	150.00	
1907 .... (575)	7,192,575	*.75*	*1.00*	5.00	10.00	24.00	100.00	500.00
1907D	2,484,000	*.75*	*1.00*	5.00	10.00	24.00	165.00	
1907O	4,560,000	*.75*	*1.00*	5.00	10.00	24.00	150.00	
1907S	1,360,000	*.75*	*1.00*	5.00	10.00	24.00	185.00	
1908 .... (545)	4,232,545	*.75*	*1.00*	5.00	10.00	24.00	100.00	500.00
1908D	5,788,000	*.75*	*1.00*	5.00	10.00	24.00	140.00	
1908O	6,244,000	*.75*	*1.00*	5.00	10.00	24.00	140.00	
1908S	784,000	*1.00*	4.00	10.00	20.00	60.00	225.00	
1909 .... (650)	9,268,650	*.75*	*1.00*	5.00	10.00	24.00	100.00	500.00
1909D	5,114,000	*.75*	*1.00*	5.00	10.00	24.00	140.00	
1909O	712,000	4.00	6.00	18.00	25.00	75.00	300.00	
1909S	1,348,000	*.75*	*1.00*	5.00	10.00	24.00	185.00	
1910 .... (551)	2,244,551	*.75*	*1.00*	5.00	10.00	24.00	100.00	500.00
1910D	1,500,000	*.75*	*1.00*	5.00	10.00	24.00	165.00	
1911 .... (543)	3,720,543	*.75*	*1.00*	5.00	10.00	24.00	100.00	500.00
1911D	933,600	*.75*	*1.00*	10.00	20.00	90.00	200.00	
1911S	988,000	*.75*	*1.00*	6.00	12.00	30.00	175.00	
1912 .... (700)	4,400,700	*.75*	*1.00*	5.00	10.00	24.00	100.00	500.00
1912S	708,000	*.75*	*1.00*	6.00	12.00	30.00	175.00	
1913 .... (613)	484,613	5.00	7.00	22.00	60.00	200.00	650.00	600.00
1913D	1,450,800	*.75*	*1.00*	5.00	10.00	24.00	140.00	
1913S	40,000	150.00	200.00	500.00	800.00	1,200	2,000	
1914 .... (380)	6,244,610	*.75*	*1.00*	5.00	10.00	24.00	100.00	500.00
1914D	3,046,000	*.75*	*1.00*	5.00	10.00	24.00	140.00	
1914S	264,000	15.00	30.00	45.00	65.00	150.00	325.00	
1915 .... (450)	3,480,450	*.75*	*1.00*	5.00	10.00	24.00	100.00	500.00
1915D	3,694,000	*.75*	*1.00*	5.00	10.00	24.00	100.00	
1915S	704,000	*.75*	*1.00*	6.00	10.00	30.00	125.00	
1916	1,788,000	*.75*	*1.00*	5.00	10.00	24.00	100.00	
1916D	6,540,800	*.75*	*1.00*	5.00	10.00	24.00	100.00	

Italic prices indicate unsettled values due to fluctuating bullion market. See Bullion Chart.

QUARTER DOLLARS

STANDING LIBERTY TYPE 1916-1930

This design is by Hermon A. MacNeil, whose initial M is above and to the right of the date. Liberty bears a shield of protection in her left arm, while the right hand holds the olive branch of peace. There was a modification in 1917. The reverse has a new arrangement of stars and the eagle is higher. After 1924 the date was "recessed," thereby giving it greater protection from the effects of circulation.

G-4 GOOD—*Date and lettering readable. Top of date worn. Liberty's right leg and toes worn off. Left leg and drapery lines show much wear.*

VG-8 VERY GOOD—*Distinct date. Toes show faintly. Drapery lines visible above her left leg.*

F-12 FINE—*High curve of right leg flat from thigh to ankle. Left leg shows only slight wear. Drapery lines over right thigh seen only at sides of leg.*

VF-20 VERY FINE—*Garment line across right leg will be worn but show at sides.*

EF-40 EXTREMELY FINE—*Flattened only at high spots. Her toes are sharp. Drapery lines across right leg are evident.*

MS-60 UNCIRCULATED—*No trace of wear. Light blemishes.*

No stars below eagle 1916-1917

	Quan. Minted	*G-4*	*VG-8*	*F-12*	*VF-20*	*EF-40*	*MS-60*
1916	52,000	$500.00	$650.00	$750.00	$900.00	$1,200	$1,800
1917	8,740,000	3.00	6.00	7.50	15.00	25.00	90.00
1917D	1,509,200	6.00	9.00	13.00	30.00	60.00	100.00
1917S	1,952,000	5.00	8.00	12.00	30.00	65.00	110.00

Stars below eagle 1917-1930

1918S, 8 over 7

Mint mark position is on obverse at left of date.

1917	13,880,000	5.00	7.00	9.00	12.00	20.00	70.00
1917D	6,224,400	9.00	11.00	20.00	30.00	60.00	85.00
1917S	5,552,000	9.00	11.00	14.00	22.00	40.00	85.00
1918	14,240,000	5.00	7.00	10.00	18.00	30.00	80.00
1918D	7,380,000	13.00	15.00	22.00	30.00	55.00	100.00
1918S Norm. date	11,072,000 (both)	7.00	11.00	12.00	14.00	30.00	80.00
1918S 8 over 7		500.00	700.00	1,000	1,300	2,000	5,000
1919	11,324,000	15.00	18.00	20.00	25.00	35.00	85.00
1919D	1,944,000	25.00	35.00	60.00	80.00	150.00	285.00
1919S	1,836,000	25.00	35.00	50.00	65.00	135.00	240.00
1920	27,860,000	3.00	4.00	5.00	10.00	18.00	75.00
1920D	3,586,400	15.00	20.00	30.00	45.00	60.00	110.00
1920S	6,380,000	6.00	8.00	12.00	15.00	20.00	85.00
1921	1,916,000	35.00	45.00	65.00	85.00	130.00	235.00
1923	9,716,000	3.00	4.00	5.00	10.00	18.00	75.00
1923S	1,360,000	50.00	75.00	100.00	135.00	200.00	315.00
1924	10,920,000	3.00	4.00	5.00	10.00	18.00	80.00
1924D	3,112,000	10.00	15.00	25.00	35.00	50.00	85.00
1924S	2,860,000	8.00	10.00	12.00	15.00	32.00	100.00

QUARTER DOLLARS

Recessed Date 1925-1930

	Quan. Minted	*G-4*	*VG-8*	*F-12*	*VF-20*	*EF-40*	*MS-60*
1925	12,280,000	*$.75*	*$1.00*	$3.00	$7.00	$12.00	$70.00
1926	11,316,000	*.75*	*1.00*	3.00	7.00	12.00	70.00
1926D	1,716,000	*.75*	*1.00*	6.00	10.00	15.00	70.00
1926S	2,700,000	*.75*	*1.00*	4.00	8.00	25.00	100.00
1927	11,912,000	*1.00*	*1.10*	3.00	6.00	12.00	70.00
1927D	976,000	*1.00*	*1.10*	6.00	12.00	20.00	90.00
1927S	396,000	3.00	5.00	20.00	65.00	400.00	1,200
1928	6,336,000	*.75*	*1.00*	3.00	6.00	12.00	70.00
1928D	1,627,600	*.75*	*1.00*	3.00	7.00	13.00	70.00
1928S	2,644,000	*.75*	*1.00*	3.00	7.00	12.00	70.00
1929	11,140,000	*.75*	*1.00*	3.00	6.00	12.00	70.00
1929D	1,358,000	*.75*	*1.00*	3.00	6.00	12.00	70.00
1929S	1,764,000	*.75*	*1.00*	3.00	6.00	12.00	70.00
1930	5,632,000	*.75*	*1.00*	3.00	6.00	12.00	70.00
1930S	1,556,000	*.75*	*1.00*	3.00	6.00	12.00	70.00

WASHINGTON TYPE 1932 to Date

This type was intended to be a commemorative issue marking the two-hundredth anniversary of Washington's birth. John Flanagan, a New York sculptor, was the designer. The initals JF are found at the base of the neck. Mint mark is on reverse below wreath. 1932 to 1964. Starting in 1968 mint mark is on obverse at right of ribbon.

VG-8 VERY GOOD—*Wing tips outlined. Rims are fine and even. Tops of letters at rim are flattened.*
F-12 FINE—*Hairlines about ear are visible. Tiny feathers on eagle's breast are faintly visible.*
VF-20 VERY FINE—*Hair details worn but plain. Feathers at sides of eagle's breast are plain.*
EF-40 EXTREMELY FINE—*Hairlines sharp. Wear spots confined to top of eagle's legs and center of breast.*
MS-60 UNCIRCULATED—*No trace of wear. Light blemishes.*
MS-63 UNCIRCULATED—*No trace of wear. Very few noticeable blemishes.*

1976 Bicentennial reverse design

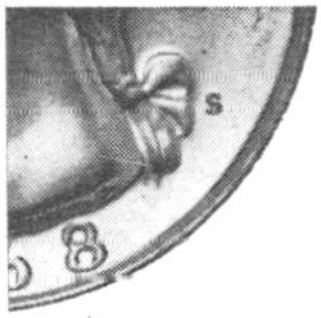

Starting in 1968 mint mark is on obverse at right of ribbon.

Silver Coinage—1932-1964

	Quan. Minted	*VG 8*	*F 12*	*VF 20*	*EF 40*	*MS 60*	*MS 63*	*Proof 63*
1932	5,404,000	*$.75*	*$1.00*	*$1.15*	$3.00	$12.00	$20.00	
1932D	436,800	20.00	25.00	35.00	60.00	225.00	450.00	
1932S	408,000	18.00	20.00	26.00	30.00	100.00	200.00	
1934	31,912,052	*.50*	*1.00*	*1.15*	3.00	10.00	18.00	
1934D	3,527,200	*.75*	*1.00*	*1.15*	5.00	40.00	60.00	
1935	32,484,000	*.50*	*1.00*	*1.15*	3.00	8.00	13.00	
1935D	5,780,000	*.75*	*1.00*	*1.15*	5.00	50.00	60.00	
1935S	5,660,000	*.75*	*1.00*	*1.15*	4.00	25.00	40.00	
1936 . . (3,837)	41,303,837		*.50*	*.60*	*1.00*	10.00	15.00	$250.00
1936D	5,374,000		*.75*	3.00	15.00	110.00	175.00	
1936S	3,828,000		*.50*	*.60*	3.00	22.00	35.00	

Italic prices indicate unsettled values due to fluctuating bullion market. See Bullion Chart.

QUARTER DOLLARS

	Quan. Minted	F-12	VF-20	EF-40	MS-60	MS-63	Proof-63
1937 (5,542)	19,701,542	*$.50*	*$.60*	*$.75*	$10.00	$13.00	$75.00
1937D	7,189,600	*.50*	*.60*	*.75*	15.00	25.00	
1937S	1,652,000	*.50*	*.60*	5.00	45.00	60.00	
1938 (8,045)	9,480,045	*.50*	*.60*	4.00	25.00	30.00	45.00
1938S	2,832,000	*.50*	*.60*	3.00	25.00	30.00	
1939 (8,795)	33,548,795	*.50*	*.60*	*.75*	8.00	10.00	40.00
1939D	7,092,000	*.50*	*.60*	*.75*	15.00	24.00	
1939S	2,628,000	*.50*	*.60*	3.00	25.00	35.00	
1940 (11,246)	35,715,246	*.50*	*.60*	*.75*	5.00	8.00	25.00
1940D	2,797,600	*.50*	*.60*	5.00	25.00	35.00	
1940S	8,244,000	*.50*	*.60*	*.75*	6.00	12.00	
1941 (15,287)	79,047,287	*.50*	*.60*	*.75*	*1.75*	3.00	20.00
1941D	16,714,800	*.50*	*.60*	*.75*	6.00	12.00	
1941S	16,080,000	*.50*	*.60*	*.75*	5.00	10.00	
1942 (21,123)	102,117,123	*.50*	*.60*	*.75*	*1.75*	3.00	20.00
1942D	17,487,200	*.50*	*.60*	*.75*	3.00	6.00	
1942S	19,384,000	*.50*	*.60*	*.75*	20.00	40.00	
1943	99,700,000	*.50*	*.60*	*.75*	*1.75*	3.00	
1943D	16,095,600	*.50*	*.60*	*.75*	4.00	7.00	
1943S	21,700,000	*.50*	*.60*	*.75*	10.00	15.00	
1944	104,956,000	*.50*	*.60*	*.75*	*1.75*	3.00	
1944D	14,600,800	*.50*	*.60*	*.75*	*1.75*	4.00	
1944S	12,560,000	*.50*	*.60*	*.75*	*1.75*	4.00	
1945	74,372,000	*.50*	*.60*	*.75*	*1.75*	3.00	
1945D	12,341,600	*.50*	*.60*	*.75*	*1.75*	3.00	
1945S	17,004,001	*.50*	*.60*	*.75*	*1.75*	3.00	
1946	53,436,000	*.50*	*.60*	*.75*	*1.75*	*2.25*	
1946D	9,072,800	*.50*	*.60*	*.75*	*1.75*	3.00	
1946S	4,204,000	*.50*	*.60*	*.75*	*1.75*	3.00	
1947	22,556,000	*.50*	*.60*	*.75*	*1.75*	*2.50*	
1947D	15,338,400	*.50*	*.60*	*.75*	*1.75*	*2.50*	
1947S	5,532,000	*.50*	*.60*	*.75*	*1.75*	*2.50*	
1948	35,196,000	*.50*	*.60*	*.75*	*1.75*	*2.25*	
1948D	16,766,800	*.50*	*.60*	*.75*	*1.75*	3.00	
1948S	15,960,000	*.50*	*.60*	*.75*	*1.75*	3.00	
1949	9,312,000	*.50*	*.60*	*.75*	6.00	10.00	
1949D	10,068,400	*.50*	*.60*	*.75*	*1.75*	4.00	
1950 (51,386)	24,971,512	*.50*	*.60*	*.75*	*1.75*	*2.25*	18.00
1950D	21,075,600	*.50*	*.60*	*.75*	*1.75*	*2.25*	
1950D, D over S			25.00	60.00	85.00	175.00	
1950S	10,284,004	*.50*	*.60*	*.75*	*2.00*	3.00	
1950S, S over D			30.00	75.00	100.00	200.00	
1951 (57,500)	43,505,602	*.50*	*.60*	*.75*	*1.25*	*2.00*	12.00
1951D	35,354,800	*.50*	*.60*	*.75*	*1.25*	*2.00*	
1951S	9,048,000	*.50*	*.60*	*.75*	*1.25*	4.00	
1952 (81,980)	38,862,073	*.50*	*.60*	*.75*	*1.25*	*2.00*	10.00
1952D	49,795,200	*.50*	*.60*	*.75*	*1.25*	*2.00*	
1952S	13,707,800	*.50*	*.60*	*.75*	*1.25*	3.00	
1953 (122,800)	18,664,920	*.50*	*.60*	*.75*	*1.25*	*2.00*	7.00
1953D	56,112,400	*.50*	*.60*	*.75*	*1.25*	*2.00*	
1953S	14,016,000	*.50*	*.60*	*.75*	*1.25*	*2.00*	
1954 (233,300)	54,645,503	*.50*	*.60*	*.75*	*1.25*	*2.00*	3.50
1954D	42,305,500	*.50*	*.60*	*.75*	*1.00*	*1.50*	
1954S	11,834,722	*.50*	*.60*	*.75*	*1.25*	*2.25*	
1955 (378,200)	18,558,381	*.50*	*.60*	*.75*	*1.25*	*2.00*	3.00
1955D	3,182,400	*.50*	*.60*	*.75*	*1.25*	*2.25*	
1956 (669,384)	44,813,384	*.50*	*.50*	*.50*	*.75*	*.90*	2.25
1956D	32,334,500	*.50*	*.50*	*.50*	*.75*	*.90*	
1957 (1,247,952)	47,779,952	*.50*	*.50*	*.50*	*.75*	*.90*	1.50

Italic prices indicate unsettled values due to fluctuating bullion market. See Bullion Chart.

QUARTER DOLLARS

		Quan. Minted	F-12	EF-40	MS-63	Proof-63
1957D		77,924,160	*$.50*	*$.50*	*$.90*	
1958	(875,652)	7,235,652	*.50*	*.50*	*1.25*	$1.50
1958D		78,124,900	*.50*	*.50*	*.90*	
1959	(1,149,291)	25,533,291	*.50*	*.50*	*.90*	1.50
1959D		62,054,232	*.50*	*.50*	*.90*	
1960	(1,691,602)	30,855,602	*.50*	*.50*	*.90*	1.50
1960D		63,000,324	*.50*	*.50*	*.90*	
1961	(3,028,244)	40,064,244	*.50*	*.50*	*.90*	1.25
1961D		83,656,928	*.50*	*.50*	*.90*	
1962	(3,218,019)	39,374,019	*.50*	*.50*	*.90*	1.25
1962D		127,554,756	*.50*	*.50*	*.90*	
1963	(3,075,645)	77,391,645	*.50*	*.50*	*.90*	1.25
1963D		135,288,184	*.50*	*.50*	*.90*	
1964	(3,950,762)	564,341,347	*.50*	*.50*	*.90*	1.25
1964D		704,135,528	*.50*	*.50*	*.90*	

Clad Coinage—1965 to Date

	Quan. Minted	MS-63	Proof-63
1965	1,819,717,540	$.27	
1966	821,101,500	.27	
1967	1,524,031,848	.27	
1968	220,731,500	.30	
1968D	101,534,000	.27	
1968S Proof	(3,041,506)		$.30
1969	176,212,000	.27	
1969D	114,372,000	.30	
1969S Proof	(2,934,631)		.30
1970	136,420,000	.27	
1970D	417,341,364	.27	
1970S Proof	(2,632,810)		.30
1971	109,284,000	$.28	
1971D	258,634,428	.27	
1971S Proof	(3,220,733)		$.30
1972	215,048,000	.27	
1972D	311,067,732	.27	
1972S Proof	(3,260,996)		.30
1973	346,924,000	.27	
1973D	232,977,400	.27	
1973S Proof	(2,760,339)		.30
1974	801,456,000	.27	
1974D	353,160,300	.27	
1974S Proof	(2,612,568)		.30

BICENTENNIAL COINAGE DATED 1776-1976

	Quan. Minted	MS-63	Proof-63
1776-1976 Copper-nickel clad	809,784,016	$.28	
1776-1976D Copper-nickel clad	860,118,839	.29	
1776-1976S Copper-nickel clad	(7,059,099)		$.40
1776-1976S Silver clad	**11,000,000*	*.80*	
1776-1976S Silver clad	*(*4,000,000)*		1.35

*Approximate mintage.

Eagle Reverse Resumed (Dies slightly modified to lower relief)

	Quan. Minted	MS-63	Proof-63
1977	468,556,000	$.27	
1977D	256,524,978	.27	
1977S Proof	(3,251,152)		$.30
1978	521,452,000	.27	
1978D	287,373,152	.27	
1978S Proof	(3,127,781)		.30
1979	515,708,000	.28	
1979D	489,789,780	.27	
1979S Proof	(3,677,175)		
Filled S			.30
Clear S			.60
1980P	635,832,000	.27	
1980D	518,327,487	.27	
1980S Proof	(3,554,806)		.30
1981P	601,716,000	.27	
1981D	575,722,833	.27	
1981S Proof	(4,063,083)		$.30
1982P	500,931,000	$1.50	
1982D	480,042,788	1.25	
1982S Proof	(3,857,479)		.60
1983P	673,535,000	1.75	
1983D	617,806,446	2.00	
1983S Proof	(3,279,126)		.60
1984P	676,545,000	.27	
1984D	546,483,064	.35	
1984S Proof	(3,065,110)		1.00
1985P	775,818,962	.30	
1985D	519,962,888	1.25	
1985S Proof	(3,362,821)		.60
1986P	551,199,333	.50	
1986D	504,298,660	.50	
1986S Proof	(3,010,497)		1.00

Italic prices indicate unsettled values due to fluctuating bullion market. See Bullion Chart.

QUARTER DOLLARS

	Quan. Minted	MS-63	Proof-63
1987P	582,499,481	$.27	
1987D	655,594,696	.27	
1987S Proof	(4,227,728)		$.60
1988P	562,052,000	.28	
1988D	596,810,688	.27	
1988S Proof	(3,262,948)		.75
1989P	512,868,000	.25	
1989D	896,535,597	.25	
1989S Proof	(3,220,194)		.65
1990P	613,792,000	$.25	
1990D	927,638,181	.25	
1990S Proof	(3,299,559)		$.35
1991P	570,968,000	.25	
1991D	630,966,693	.25	
1991S Proof			.35
1992P		.25	
1992D		.25	
1992S Proof			.35

HALF DOLLARS — 1794 to Date

The half dollar, authorized by the Act of April 2, 1792, was not minted until December, 1794.

The weight of the half dollar was 208 grains and its fineness .8924 when first issued. This standard was not changed until 1837 when the law of January 18, 1837 specified 206¼ grains, .900 fine, which continued in use until 1965.

Arrows at the date in 1853 indicate the reduction of weight to 192 grains. During that year only, rays were added to the field on the reverse side. Arrows remained in 1854 and 1855.

In 1873 the weight was raised to 192.9 grains and arrows were again placed at the date.

FLOWING HAIR TYPE 1794-1795

AG-3 ABOUT GOOD—*Clear enough to identify.*

G-4 GOOD—*Date and letters sufficient to be readable. Main devices outlined, but lack details.*

VG-8 VERY GOOD—*Major details discernible. Letters well formed but worn.*

F-12 FINE—*Hair ends distinguishable. Top hairlines show, but otherwise worn smooth.*

VF-20 VERY FINE—*Hair in center shows some detail. Other details more bold.*

EF-40 EXTREMELY FINE—*Hair above head and down neck detailed with slight wear.*

2 Leaves under wings

3 Leaves under wings

	Quan. Minted	AG-3	G-4	VG-8	F-12	VF-20	EF-40
1794	23,464	$210.00	$525.00	$900.00	$1,400	$2,500	$3,500
1795 All kinds	299,680	125.00	250.00	325.00	425.00	675.00	1,500
1795 Recut date		125.00	275.00	350.00	475.00	725.00	1,600
1795 3 leaves under each wing		175.00	350.00	600.00	1,200	2,000	3,500

DRAPED BUST TYPE, SMALL EAGLE REVERSE 1796-1797

Grading same as above for About Good to Fine.

VF-20 VERY FINE—*Right side of drapery slightly worn. Left side to curls is smooth.*

EF-40 EXTREMELY FINE—*All lines in drapery on bust will show distinctly around to hair curls.*

MS-60 UNCIRCULATED—*No trace of wear. Light blemishes.*

HALF DOLLARS

1796, 15 Stars

1796, 16 Stars

	Quan. Minted	AG-3	G-4	VG-8	F-12	VF-20	EF-40
1796, 15 Stars		$3,500	$5,500	$8,000	$9,000	$15,000	$22,000
1796, 16 stars............	3,918	3,500	5,500	8,000	9,000	15,000	22,000
1797, 15 stars............		3,500	5,500	8,000	9,000	15,000	22,000

DRAPED BUST TYPE, HERALDIC EAGLE REVERSE 1801-1807

	Quan. Minted	G-4	VG-8	F-12	VF-20	EF-40	MS-60
1801	30,289	$75.00	$100.00	$200.00	$400.00	$725.00	$5,100
1802	29,890	65.00	95.00	175.00	300.00	575.00	4,500
1803	188,234	40.00	60.00	125.00	275.00	500.00	4,100

1805, 5 over 4

1806, 6 over 5

	Quan. Minted	G-4	VG-8	F-12	VF-20	EF-40	MS-60
1805, 5 over 4	211,722	50.00	65.00	130.00	275.00	525.00	4,250
1805 Normal date..........		40.00	50.00	80.00	225.00	350.00	3,000
1806	839,576	40.00	50.00	80.00	225.00	350.00	3,000
1806, 6 over 5		40.00	50.00	90.00	250.00	400.00	3,000
1806, 6 over inverted 6.....		45.00	55.00	100.00	275.00	425.00	3,500
1807	301,076	40.00	50.00	80.00	225.00	350.00	3,000

CAPPED BUST TYPE, Lettered Edge 1807-1836

John Reich designed this Capped Head concept of Liberty. The head of Liberty facing left was used on all U.S. coin denominations for the next thirty years.

HALF DOLLARS

G-4 GOOD—*Date and letters readable. Bust worn smooth with outline distinct.*
VG-8 VERY GOOD—*LIBERTY visible but faint. Legends distinguishable. Clasp at shoulder visible. Curl above it nearly smooth.*
F-12 FINE—*Clasp and adjacent curl clearly outlined with slight details.*
VF-20 VERY FINE—*Clasp at shoulder clear. Curl has wear only on highest point. Hair over brow distinguishable.*
EF-40 EXTREMELY FINE—*Clasp and adjacent curl fairly sharp. Brow and hair above distinct. Curls well defined.*
MS-60 UNCIRCULATED—*No trace of wear. Light blemishes.*

First style 1807-1808

	Quan. Minted	*G-4*	*VG-8*	*F-12*	*VF-20*	*EF-40*	*MS-60*
1807	750,500	$16.00	$21.00	$35.00	$75.00	$150.00	$675.00
1808, 8 over 7	} 1,368,600	16.00	20.00	30.00	50.00	90.00	575.00
1808		16.00	20.00	25.00	40.00	70.00	475.00

Remodeled Portrait and Eagle 1809-1834

1809	1,405,810	14.00	17.00	20.00	30.00	65.00	425.00
1810	1,276,276	13.00	16.00	19.00	25.00	55.00	450.00
1811	1,203,644	13.00	15.00	18.00	25.00	55.00	425.00

1812, 2 over 1

1813, 50 C. over UNI

1814, 4 over 3

1812, 2 over 1	} 1,628,059	14.00	16.00	25.00	50.00	100.00	475.00
1812 Normal		13.00	15.00	18.00	25.00	55.00	425.00
1813	} 1,241,903	13.00	15.00	18.00	25.00	55.00	400.00
1813, 50C over UNI . . .		15.00	18.00	32.00	50.00	90.00	475.00
1814, 4 over 3	} 1,039,075	13.00	16.00	21.00	30.00	65.00	400.00
1814 Normal		13.00	15.00	18.00	25.00	55.00	400.00

HALF DOLLARS

1817, 7 over 3

1817, 7 over 4

1817 Punctuated Date

	Quan. Minted	G-4	VG-8	F-12	VF-20	EF-40	MS-60
1815, 5 over 2	47,150	$200.00	$300.00	$400.00	$600.00	$1,000	$2,500
1817 All kinds	1,215,567						
1817, 7 over 3		14.00	25.00	75.00	125.00	210.00	675.00
1817, 7 over 4				2,500	5,000	——	
1817 dated 181.7		13.00	16.00	22.00	40.00	80.00	450.00
1817 Normal		13.00	15.00	18.00	25.00	55.00	400.00

1818, 2nd 8 over 7

1819, 9 over 8

1820, 20 over 19

1818, 8 over 7	1,960,322	13.00	15.00	18.00	25.00	55.00	450.00
1818 Normal		13.00	15.00	18.00	25.00	55.00	400.00
1819 9 over 8	2,208,00	13.00	15.00	18.00	25.00	55.00	425.00
1819 Normal		13.00	15.00	18.00	25.00	55.00	425.00
1820, 20 over 19	751,122	13.00	15.00	18.00	25.00	55.00	450.00
1820 Normal		12.00	14.00	17.00	24.00	50.00	450.00
1821	1,305,797	12.00	14.00	17.00	24.00	50.00	425.00
1822, 2 over 1	1,559,573	18.00	25.00	40.00	50.00	90.00	475.00
1822 Normal		12.00	14.00	17.00	24.00	50.00	450.00
1823 Normal	1,694,200	12.00	14.00	17.00	24.00	50.00	400.00

"Various Dates"
1828 Square Base 2
(probably 4 over
2 over 0)

1824, 4 over 1

1828 Curl Base, Knob 2

1828 Square Base 2

1824 All kinds	3,504,954						
1824 over various dates		12.00	14.00	17.00	24.00	50.00	400.00
1824, 4 over 1		12.00	14.00	17.00	24.00	50.00	400.00
1824 Normal		12.00	14.00	17.00	24.00	50.00	450.00
1825	2,943,166	12.00	14.00	17.00	24.00	50.00	400.00
1826	4,004,180	12.00	14.00	17.00	24.00	50.00	400.00
1827, 7 over 6	5,493,400	12.00	14.00	17.00	24.00	50.00	450.00
1827 Normal		12.00	14.00	17.00	24.00	50.00	400.00
1828 All kinds	3,075,200						
1828 Curl base no knob 2		12.00	14.00	17.00	24.00	50.00	400.00
1828 Curl base knob 2		16.00	20.00	27.00	40.00	60.00	475.00
1828 Sq. base		12.00	14.00	17.00	24.00	50.00	450.00

HALF DOLLARS

	Quan. Minted	G-4	VG-8	F-12	VF-20	EF-40	MS-60
1829, 9 over 7	3,712,156	$12.00	$14.00	$17.00	$24.00	$50.00	$425.00
1829 Normal		12.00	14.00	17.00	24.00	50.00	425.00
1830	4,764,800	12.00	14.00	17.00	24.00	50.00	400.00
1831	5,873,660	12.00	14.00	17.00	24.00	50.00	400.00
1832	4,797,000	12.00	14.00	17.00	24.00	50.00	400.00
1833	5,206,000	12.00	14.00	17.00	24.00	50.00	400.00
1834	6,412,004	12.00	14.00	17.00	24.00	50.00	425.00
1835	5,352,006	12.00	14.00	17.00	24.00	50.00	400.00
1836	6,545,000	12.00	14.00	17.00	24.00	50.00	400.00
1836, 50 over 00		15.00	20.00	25.00	38.00	70.00	500.00

Reeded Edge, Reverse "50 CENTS" 1836-1837

G-4 GOOD—*LIBERTY discernible on headband.*

VG-8 VERY GOOD—*Minimum of 3 letters in LIBERTY must be clear.*

F-12 FINE—*LIBERTY complete.*

VF-20 VERY FINE—*LIBERTY is sharp. Shoulder clasp is clear.*

EF-40 EXTREMELY FINE—*LIBERTY sharp and strong. Hair details show.*

MS-60 UNCIRCULATED—*No trace of wear. Light blemishes.*

1836	1,200	200.00	300.00	400.00	550.00	1,000	2,750
1837	3,629,820	18.00	20.00	25.00	40.00	70.00	500.00

Reeded Edge, Reverse "HALF DOL." 1838-1839

In 1838-39 the mint mark appears on the obverse; thereafter it is on the reverse below the eagle.

1838	3,546,000	18.00	20.00	25.00	40.00	70.00	500.00
1838O	(20)						35,000
1839	1,392,976	18.00	20.00	25.00	38.00	70.00	500.00
1839O	178,976	55.00	80.00	125.00	185.00	275.00	1,800

LIBERTY SEATED TYPE 1839-1891

No Motto Above Eagle 1839-1853

G-4 GOOD—*Scant rim. LIBERTY on shield worn off. Date and letters readable.*

VG-8 VERY GOOD—*Rim fairly defined. At least 3 letters in LIBERTY are evident.*

F-12 FINE—*LIBERTY complete, but weak.*

VF-20 VERY FINE—*LIBERTY mostly sharp.*

EF-40 EXTREMELY FINE—*LIBERTY entirely sharp. Scroll edges and clasp distinct.*

MS-60 UNCIRCULATED—*No trace of wear. Light blemishes.*

HALF DOLLARS

	Quan. Minted	G-4	VG-8	F-12	VF-20	EF-40	MS-60
1839 No drapery from elbow.......		$17.00	$25.00	$40.00	$100.00	$300.00	$2,750

Drapery from Elbow starting 1839

1842 Small Date

	Quan. Minted	G-4	VG-8	F-12	VF-20	EF-40	MS-60
1839	1,972,400	9.00	11.00	16.00	22.00	40.00	250.00
1840	1,435,008	8.00	10.00	15.00	20.00	37.00	250.00
1840O	855,100	8.00	10.00	15.00	20.00	37.00	250.00
1841	310,000	8.00	10.00	15.00	20.00	45.00	275.00
1841O	401,000	8.00	10.00	15.00	20.00	37.00	250.00
1842 Sm. date	} 2,012,764	8.00	10.00	15.00	21.00	37.00	250.00
1842 Med. date		8.00	10.00	15.00	21.00	37.00	250.00
1842O Small date	203,000	150.00	275.00	475.00	950.00	1,750	——
1842O Med. date	754,000	8.00	9.00	13.00	20.00	35.00	250.00
1843	3,844,000	8.00	9.00	13.00	20.00	35.00	250.00
1843O	2,268,000	8.00	9.00	13.00	20.00	35.00	250.00
1844	1,766,000	8.00	9.00	13.00	20.00	35.00	250.00
1844O	2,005,000	8.00	9.00	13.00	20.00	35.00	250.00
1845	589,000	8.00	9.00	13.00	20.00	35.00	250.00
1845O	2,094,000	8.00	9.00	13.00	20.00	35.00	250.00
1846 All kinds	2,210,000	8.00	9.00	13.00	18.00	35.00	250.00
1846 over horizontal 6 (error)......		15.00	30.00	45.00	75.00	110.00	550.00
1846O	2,304,000	8.00	9.00	13.00	18.00	35.00	250.00
1847	1,156,000	8.00	9.00	13.00	18.00	35.00	250.00
1847O	2,584,000	8.00	9.00	13.00	18.00	35.00	250.00
1848	580,000	12.00	17.00	25.00	35.00	60.00	400.00
1848O	3,180,000	8.00	9.00	13.00	18.00	35.00	250.00
1849	1,252,000	8.00	9.00	13.00	18.00	35.00	250.00
1849O	2,310,000	8.00	9.00	13.00	18.00	35.00	250.00
1850	227,000	15.00	21.00	35.00	45.00	125.00	600.00
1850O	2,456,000	8.00	9.00	13.00	18.00	35.00	250.00
1851	200,750	15.00	21.00	35.00	45.00	125.00	600.00
1851O	402,000	8.00	9.00	13.00	18.00	35.00	250.00
1852	77,130	35.00	60.00	100.00	150.00	250.00	700.00
1852O	144,000	15.00	21.00	35.00	45.00	125.00	600.00
1853O		2,500	8,000	15,000	20,000		

HALF DOLLARS

Arrows at Date, Rays Around Eagle 1853 Only

	Quan. Minted	G-4	VG-8	F-12	VF-20	EF-40	MS-60
1853	3,532,708	$7.00	$9.00	$15.00	$45.00	$100.00	$900.00
1853O All kinds	1,328,000	7.00	9.00	15.00	45.00	110.00	1,200

Arrows at Date, No Rays 1854-1855

	Quan. Minted	G-4	VG-8	F-12	VF-20	EF-40	MS-60
1854	2,982,000	6.00	8.00	12.00	21.00	50.00	400.00
1854O	5,240,000	6.00	8.00	12.00	21.00	50.00	400.00
1855 over 1854	759,500		25.00	50.00	100.00	200.00	700.00
1855 Normal date		6.00	8.00	12.00	21.00	50.00	400.00
1855O	3,688,000	6.00	8.00	12.00	21.00	50.00	400.00
1855S	129,950	125.00	175.00	250.00	500.00	1,000	——

No Arrows at Date 1856-1866

	Quan. Minted	G-4	VG-8	F-12	VF-20	EF-40	MS-60
1856	938,000	7.00	8.00	12.00	17.00	35.00	235.00
1856O	2,658,000	7.00	8.00	12.00	17.00	35.00	235.00
1856S	211,000	9.00	11.00	17.00	40.00	80.00	500.00
1857	1,988,000	7.00	8.00	12.00	17.00	35.00	235.00
1857O	818,000	7.00	8.00	12.00	17.00	35.00	235.00
1857S	158,000	11.00	16.00	20.00	45.00	100.00	650.00

	Quan. Minted	G-4	VG-8	F-12	VF-20	EF-40	MS-60	Proof-63
1858	4,226,000	$7.00	$8.00	$12.00	$17.00	$35.00	$235.00	$1,300
1858O	7,294,000	7.00	8.00	12.00	17.00	35.00	235.00	
1858S	476,000	9.00	11.00	15.00	24.00	45.00	500.00	
1859 (800)	748,000	7.00	8.00	12.00	17.00	35.00	235.00	800.00
1859O	2,834,000	7.00	8.00	12.00	17.00	35.00	235.00	
1859S	566,000	9.00	11.00	15.00	25.00	70.00	450.00	
1860 (1,000)	303,700	9.00	11.00	14.00	22.00	40.00	235.00	650.00
1860O	1,290,000	7.00	8.00	12.00	17.00	35.00	235.00	
1860S	472,000	9.00	11.00	14.00	20.00	35.00	275.00	
1861 (1,000)	2,888,400	7.00	8.00	12.00	17.00	35.00	235.00	650.00
1861O	2,532,633	7.00	8.00	12.00	17.00	35.00	235.00	
1861S	939,500	7.00	8.00	12.00	17.00	35.00	250.00	
1862 (550)	253,550	10.00	14.00	18.00	35.00	50.00	400.00	650.00
1862S	1,352,000	7.00	8.00	12.00	17.00	35.00	250.00	
1863 (460)	503,660	9.00	11.00	14.00	22.00	40.00	275.00	650.00
1863S	916,000	7.00	8.00	12.00	17.00	35.00	250.00	
1864 (470)	379,570	9.00	11.00	14.00	22.00	40.00	275.00	650.00
1864S	658,000	7.00	8.00	12.00	17.00	35.00	250.00	
1865 (500)	511,900	9.00	11.00	14.00	22.00	40.00	275.00	650.00
1865S	675,000	7.00	8.00	12.00	17.00	35.00	250.00	
1866S No motto	60,000	23.00	39.00	70.00	120.00	175.00	2,000	

HALF DOLLARS

Motto "In God We Trust" Added Above Eagle 1866-1873

	Quan. Minted	G-4	VG-8	F-12	VF-20	EF-40	MS-60	Proof-63
1866 .... (725)	745,625	$4.00	$5.00	$10.00	$15.00	$30.00	$225.00	$650.00
1866S	994,000	4.00	5.00	10.00	15.00	30.00	275.00	
1867 .... (625)	449,925	5.00	6.00	11.00	16.00	35.00	325.00	650.00
1867S	1,196,000	4.00	5.00	10.00	15.00	30.00	275.00	
1868 .... (600)	418,200	4.00	5.00	10.00	15.00	30.00	250.00	650.00
1868S	1,160,000	4.00	5.00	10.00	15.00	30.00	275.00	
1869 .... (600)	795,900	4.00	5.00	10.00	15.00	30.00	250.00	650.00
1869S	656,000	4.00	5.00	10.00	15.00	30.00	275.00	
1870 .... (1,000)	634,900	4.00	5.00	10.00	15.00	30.00	250.00	650.00
1870CC	54,617	135.00	275.00	500.00	800.00	1,500	——	
1870S	1,004,000	4.00	5.00	10.00	15.00	30.00	275.00	
1871 .... (960)	1,204,560	4.00	5.00	10.00	15.00	30.00	250.00	650.00
1871CC	153,950	24.00	40.00	75.00	150.00	325.00	1,700	
1871S	2,178,000	4.00	5.00	10.00	15.00	30.00	275.00	
1872 .... (950)	881,550	4.00	5.00	10.00	15.00	30.00	225.00	650.00
1872CC	257,000	15.00	25.00	45.00	100.00	170.00	1,200	
1872S	580,000	5.00	6.00	11.00	15.00	30.00	325.00	
1873 .... (600)	801,800	4.00	5.00	10.00	15.00	30.00	325.00	650.00
1873CC	122,500	23.00	37.00	80.00	135.00	200.00	1,500	

Arrows at Date 1873-1874

1873 .... (550)	1,815,700	10.00	14.00	18.00	45.00	125.00	525.00	1,100
1873CC	214,560	16.00	25.00	50.00	90.00	150.00	1,000	
1873S	228,000	14.00	20.00	30.00	50.00	125.00	525.00	
1874 .... (700)	2,360,300	10.00	14.00	18.00	45.00	125.00	525.00	1,100
1874CC	59,000	45.00	75.00	150.00	225.00	500.00	2,000	
1874S	394,000	14.00	20.00	30.00	50.00	125.00	750.00	

No Arrows at Date 1875-1891

1875 .... (700)	6,027,500	4.00	5.00	10.00	15.00	27.00	225.00	600.00
1875CC	1,008,000	4.00	6.00	11.00	20.00	35.00	250.00	

HALF DOLLARS

	Quan. Minted	G-4	VG-8	F-12	VF-20	EF-40	MS-60	Proof-63
1875S	3,200,000	$4.00	$5.00	$10.00	$15.00	$27.00	$225.00	
1876 (1,150)	8,419,150	4.00	5.00	10.00	15.00	27.00	225.00	$600.00
1876CC	1,956,000	4.00	5.00	10.00	16.00	30.00	350.00	
1876S	4,528,000	4.00	5.00	10.00	15.00	27.00	225.00	
1877 (510)	8,304,510	4.00	5.00	10.00	15.00	27.00	225.00	600.00
1877CC	1,420,000	4.00	5.00	10.00	16.00	32.00	250.00	
1877S	5,356,000	4.00	5.00	10.00	15.00	27.00	225.00	
1878 (800)	1,378,400	4.00	5.00	10.00	15.00	27.00	225.00	600.00
1878CC	62,000	60.00	120.00	175.00	270.00	450.00	1,800	
1878S	12,000	1,500	2,500	3,500	6,000	8,000	12,000	
1879 (1,100)	5,900	60.00	75.00	100.00	125.00	180.00	500.00	700.00
1880 (1,355)	9,755	50.00	65.00	90.00	110.00	150.00	450.00	700.00
1881 (975)	10,975	50.00	65.00	90.00	110.00	150.00	450.00	700.00
1882 (1,100)	5,500	60.00	75.00	100.00	125.00	180.00	500.00	700.00
1883 (1,039)	9,039	50.00	65.00	90.00	110.00	150.00	450.00	700.00
1884 (875)	5,275	60.00	75.00	100.00	125.00	180.00	550.00	700.00
1885 (930)	6,130	50.00	65.00	90.00	110.00	150.00	550.00	700.00
1886 (886)	5,886	50.00	65.00	90.00	110.00	150.00	550.00	700.00
1887 (710)	5,710	50.00	65.00	90.00	110.00	150.00	550.00	700.00
1888 (832)	12,833	45.00	60.00	75.00	100.00	140.00	450.00	700.00
1889 (711)	12,711	45.00	60.00	75.00	100.00	140.00	450.00	700.00
1890 (590)	12,590	45.00	60.00	75.00	100.00	140.00	450.00	700.00
1891 (600)	200,600	6.00	10.00	13.00	22.00	40.00	275.00	700.00

BARBER or LIBERTY HEAD TYPE 1892-1915

Like the dime and quarter dollar, this type was designed by Charles E. Barber, whose initial B is on the truncation of the neck.

G-4 GOOD—*Date and legends readable. LIBERTY worn off headband.*
VG-8 VERY GOOD—*Minimum of 3 letters readable in LIBERTY.*
F-12 FINE—*LIBERTY completely readable, but not sharp.*
VF-20 VERY FINE—*All letters in LIBERTY evenly plain.*
EF-40 EXTREMELY FINE—*LIBERTY bold, and its ribbon distinct.*
MS-60 UNCIRCULATED—*No trace of wear. Light blemishes.*

Mint mark location on reverse below eagle.

	Quan. Minted	G-4	VG-8	F-12	VF-20	EF-40	MS-60	Proof-63
1892 (1,245)	935,245	$6.50	$9.50	$15.00	$30.00	$100.00	$300.00	$700.00
1892O	390,000	40.00	55.00	85.00	145.00	240.00	550.00	
1892S	1,029,028	50.00	60.00	85.00	145.00	240.00	500.00	
1893 (792)	1,826,792	4.00	6.00	15.00	30.00	100.00	275.00	700.00
1893O	1,389,000	8.00	12.00	25.00	50.00	140.00	300.00	
1893S	740,000	25.00	35.00	60.00	150.00	200.00	550.00	
1894 (972)	1,148,972	4.00	6.00	20.00	35.00	100.00	300.00	700.00
1894O	2,138,000	4.00	6.00	20.00	35.00	125.00	300.00	
1894S	4,048,690	4.00	6.00	20.00	30.00	100.00	300.00	

Italic prices indicate unsettled values due to fluctuating bullion market. See Bullion Chart.

HALF DOLLARS

	Quan. Minted	G-4	VG-8	F-12	VF-20	EF-40	MS-60	Proof-63
1895 ...... (880)	1,835,218	$3.00	$5.00	$20.00	$35.00	$100.00	$300.00	$700.00
1895O...........	1,766,000	3.00	5.00	20.00	35.00	100.00	325.00	
1895S...........	1,108,086	7.50	11.00	25.00	50.00	125.00	300.00	
1896 ...... (762)	950,762	4.50	6.50	20.00	35.00	100.00	300.00	700.00
1896O.............	924,000	7.00	12.00	35.00	80.00	175.00	600.00	
1896S...........	1,140,948	30.00	40.00	60.00	100.00	200.00	625.00	
1897 ...... (731)	2,480,731	*1.50*	*2.50*	10.00	25.00	65.00	250.00	700.00
1897O.............	632,000	25.00	30.00	70.00	150.00	350.00	850.00	
1897S.............	933,900	40.00	50.00	100.00	175.00	300.00	750.00	
1898 ...... (735)	2,956,735	*1.50*	*2.50*	10.00	25.00	75.00	250.00	700.00
1898O.............	874,000	6.50	10.00	25.00	60.00	150.00	400.00	
1898S...........	2,358,550	*2.50*	4.50	20.00	35.00	100.00	350.00	
1899 ...... (846)	5,538,846	*1.50*	*2.50*	10.00	25.00	65.00	250.00	700.00
1899O...........	1,724,000	*2.50*	4.50	20.00	35.00	130.00	375.00	
1899S...........	1,686,411	*2.50*	4.50	20.00	35.00	100.00	300.00	
1900 ...... (912)	4,762,912	*1.50*	*2.50*	10.00	25.00	65.00	250.00	700.00
1900O...........	2,744,000	*2.50*	4.50	20.00	35.00	125.00	400.00	
1900S...........	2,560,322	*2.50*	4.50	18.00	35.00	100.00	300.00	
1901 ...... (813)	4,268,813	*1.50*	*2.50*	10.00	25.00	65.00	250.00	700.00
1901O...........	1,124,000	*2.50*	5.00	20.00	50.00	150.00	700.00	
1901S.............	847,044	6.00	9.00	35.00	90.00	275.00	850.00	
1902 ...... (777)	4,922,777	*1.50*	*2.50*	10.00	25.00	65.00	275.00	700.00
1902O...........	2,526,000	*2.50*	4.50	12.00	30.00	90.00	350.00	
1902S...........	1,460,670	*2.50*	4.50	12.00	30.00	90.00	325.00	
1903 ...... (755)	2,278,755	*1.50*	*2.50*	10.00	25.00	65.00	250.00	700.00
1903O...........	2,100,000	*2.25*	4.50	12.00	30.00	95.00	310.00	
1903S...........	1,920,772	*2.25*	4.50	12.00	30.00	95.00	310.00	
1904 ...... (670)	2,992,670	*1.50*	*2.50*	10.00	25.00	65.00	250.00	700.00
1904O...........	1,117,600	4.00	6.50	14.00	30.00	160.00	575.00	
1904S.............	553,038	5.00	8.00	20.00	65.00	175.00	550.00	
1905 ...... (727)	662,727	*1.50*	*2.50*	10.00	25.00	65.00	250.00	700.00
1905O.............	505,000	5.00	6.50	16.00	40.00	135.00	375.00	
1905S...........	2,494,000	*2.00*	4.50	12.00	30.00	85.00	325.00	
1906 ...... (675)	2,638,675	*1.50*	*2.50*	10.00	25.00	65.00	250.00	700.00
1906D...........	4,028,000	*2.00*	4.50	12.00	35.00	70.00	250.00	
1906O...........	2,446,000	*2.00*	4.25	11.00	30.00	70.00	275.00	
1906S...........	1,740,154	*1.50*	*2.50*	11.00	35.00	85.00	300.00	
1907 ...... (575)	2,598,575	*1.50*	*2.50*	10.00	25.00	65.00	250.00	700.00
1907D...........	3,856,000	*1.50*	*2.50*	11.00	30.00	70.00	250.00	
1907O...........	3,946,600	*1.50*	*2.50*	11.00	30.00	70.00	250.00	
1907S...........	1,250,000	*1.50*	*2.50*	12.00	35.00	100.00	225.00	
1908 ...... (545)	1,354,545	*1.50*	*2.50*	10.00	25.00	65.00	250.00	700.00
1908D...........	3,280,000	*1.50*	*2.50*	10.00	30.00	65.00	250.00	
1908O...........	5,360,000	*1.50*	*2.50*	10.00	30.00	65.00	250.00	
1908S...........	1,644,828	*1.50*	*2.50*	11.00	35.00	90.00	375.00	
1909 ...... (650)	2,368,650	*1.50*	*2.50*	10.00	30.00	65.00	250.00	700.00
1909O.............	925,400	4.50	5.00	14.00	35.00	110.00	350.00	
1909S...........	1,764,000	*1.50*	*2.50*	12.00	30.00	85.00	275.00	
1910 ...... (551)	418,551	4.50	6.00	15.00	40.00	120.00	310.00	700.00
1910S...........	1,948,000	*1.50*	*2.50*	12.00	30.00	85.00	275.00	
1911 ...... (543)	1,406,543	*1.50*	*2.50*	10.00	25.00	65.00	250.00	700.00
1911D.............	695,080	*1.50*	*2.50*	10.00	25.00	70.00	275.00	
1911S...........	1,272,000	*1.50*	*2.50*	10.00	25.00	70.00	275.00	

Italic prices indicate unsettled values due to fluctuating bullion market. See Bullion Chart.

HALF DOLLARS

	Quan. Minted	G-4	VG-8	F-12	VF-20	EF-40	MS-60	Proof-63
1912 ...... (700)	1,550,700	*$1.50*	*$2.50*	$10.00	$20.00	$65.00	$250.00	$700.00
1912D...........	2,300,800	*1.50*	*2.50*	10.00	25.00	70.00	250.00	
1912S...........	1,370,000	*1.50*	*2.50*	10.00	25.00	70.00	250.00	
1913 ...... (627)	188,627	9.00	11.00	18.00	45.00	120.00	425.00	750.00
1913D.............	534,000	*1.50*	2.50	12.00	22.00	80.00	275.00	
1913S.............	604,000	*1.50*	2.50	13.00	35.00	70.00	275.00	
1914 ...... (380)	124,610	11.00	13.50	25.00	70.00	160.00	425.00	850.00
1914S.............	992,000	*1.50*	*2.50*	12.00	22.00	70.00	375.00	
1915 ...... (450)	138,450	10.00	12.50	22.50	50.00	125.00	425.00	850.00
1915D...........	1,170,400	*1.50*	*2.50*	10.00	20.00	65.00	250.00	
1915S...........	1,604,000	*1.50*	*2.50*	10.00	20.00	65.00	250.00	

LIBERTY WALKING TYPE 1916-1947

This type was designed by A. A. Weinman. The designer's monogram AAW appears under the tip of the wing feathers. On the 1916 coins and some of the 1917 coins the mint mark is located on the obverse below the motto.

G-4 GOOD—*Rims are defined. Motto IN GOD WE TRUST readable.*
VG-8 VERY GOOD—*Motto is distinct. About half of skirt lines at left are clear.*
F-12 FINE—*All skirt lines evident, but worn in spots. Details in sandal below motto are clear.*
VF-20 VERY FINE—*Skirt lines sharp including leg area. Little wear on breast and right arm.*
EF-40 EXTREMELY FINE—*All skirt lines bold.*
MS-60 UNCIRCULATED—*No trace of wear. Light blemishes.*
MS-63 UNCIRCULATED—*No trace of wear. Slight blemishes. Attractive mint luster.*

1916-1917

1917-1947

Mint mark location.

Choice uncirculated well struck specimens are worth more than values listed.

	Quan. Minted	G-4	VG-8	F-12	VF-20	EF-40	MS-60
1916	608,000	$10.00	$12.00	$25.00	$50.00	$85.00	$135.00
1916D............ (Obv.)	1,014,400	7.00	10.00	16.00	35.00	75.00	125.00
1916S............ (Obv.)	508,000	16.00	22.00	55.00	125.00	200.00	425.00
1917	12,292,000	*2.00*	*2.25*	4.00	9.00	18.00	55.00
1917D............ (Obv.)	765,400	5.00	6.50	16.00	45.00	75.00	160.00
1917D............ (Rev.)	1,940,000	*2.00*	*2.25*	10.00	25.00	70.00	275.00
1917S............ (Obv.)	952,000	5.00	7.00	20.00	80.00	225.00	675.00
1917S............ (Rev.)	5,554,000	*2.00*	*2.25*	4.00	14.00	22.00	85.00
1918	6,634,000	*2.00*	*2.25*	4.00	24.00	65.00	190.00
1918D..................	3,853,040	*2.00*	*2.25*	4.00	25.00	70.00	350.00
1918S..................	10,282,000	*2.00*	*2.25*	4.00	15.00	25.00	100.00
1919	962,000	5.00	7.00	10.00	60.00	180.00	550.00

Italic prices indicate unsettled values due to fluctuationg bullion market. See Bullion Chart.

HALF DOLLARS

	Quan. Minted	G-4	VG-8	F-12	VF-20	EF-40	MS-60	Proof-63
1919D	1,165,000	$4.00	$6.00	$9.00	$75.00	$200.00	$950.00	
1919S	1,552,000	*2.00*	5.00	8.00	55.00	190.00	800.00	
1920	6,372,000	*1.25*	*1.35*	*2.00*	12.00	25.00	70.00	
1920D	1,551,000	*1.25*	*1.35*	12.00	60.00	125.00	500.00	
1920S	4,624,000	*1.25*	*1.35*	7.50	20.00	60.00	275.00	
1921	246,000	22.00	38.00	80.00	250.00	700.00	1,000	
1921D	208,000	38.00	52.00	125.00	300.00	750.00	1,250	
1921S	548,000	7.00	10.00	20.00	150.00	900.00	4,200	
1923S	2,178,000	*1.25*	*1.35*	5.00	22.50	70.00	415.00	
1927S	2,392,000	*1.25*	*1.35*	*2.00*	13.00	40.00	325.00	
1928S	1,940,000	*1.25*	*1.35*	*2.00*	15.00	50.00	300.00	
1929D	1,001,200	*1.25*	*1.35*	*2.00*	9.00	30.00	120.00	
1929S	1,902,000	*1.25*	*1.35*	*2.00*	8.50	35.00	125.00	
1933S	1,786,000	*1.25*	*1.35*	*2.00*	6.00	21.00	165.00	
1934	6,964,000	*1.00*	*1.15*	*1.50*	*1.75*	5.00	20.00	
1934D	2,361,400	*1.00*	*1.15*	*1.50*	*2.00*	12.00	50.00	
1934S	3,652,000	*1.00*	*1.15*	*1.50*	*2.00*	12.50	120.00	
1935	9,162,000	*1.00*	*1.15*	*1.50*	*1.75*	4.00	20.00	
1935D	3,003,800	*1.00*	*1.15*	*1.50*	*2.00*	12.00	60.00	
1935S	3,854,000	*1.00*	*1.15*	*1.50*	*2.00*	12.00	65.00	
1936 (3,901)	12,617,901	*1.00*	*1.15*	*1.50*	*1.75*	4.00	20.00	$600.00
1936D	4,252,400	*1.00*	*1.15*	*1.50*	*2.00*	8.00	45.00	
1936S	3,884,000	*1.00*	*1.15*	*1.50*	*2.00*	8.00	65.00	
1937 (5,728)	9,527,728	*1.00*	*1.15*	*1.50*	*1.75*	4.00	25.00	350.00
1937D	1,676,000	*1.00*	*1.15*	*1.50*	*2.00*	12.00	80.00	
1937S	2,090,000	*1.00*	*1.15*	*1.50*	*2.00*	8.00	60.00	
1938 (8,152)	4,118,152	*1.00*	*1.15*	*1.50*	*1.75*	5.00	30.00	300.00
1938D	491,600	10.00	12.00	16.00	20.00	50.00	200.00	
1939 (8,808)	6,820,808	*1.00*	*1.15*	*1.50*	*1.75*	4.00	25.00	290.00
1939D	4,267,800	*1.00*	*1.15*	*1.50*	*1.75*	5.00	30.00	
1939S	2,552,000	*1.00*	*1.15*	*1.50*	*1.75*	7.50	55.00	

	Quan. Minted	VG-8	F-12	VF-20	EF-40	MS-60	MS-63	
1940 (11,279)	9,167,279	*$1.00*	*$1.15*	*$1.50*	*$2.00*	$16.00	$30.00	$250.00
1940S	4,550,000	*1.00*	*1.15*	*1.50*	*2.00*	20.00	32.00	
1941 (15,412)	24,207,412	*1.00*	*1.15*	*1.50*	*2.00*	16.00	30.00	250.00
1941D	11,248,400	*1.00*	*1.15*	*1.50*	*2.00*	22.00	32.00	
1941S	8,098,000	*1.00*	*1.15*	*1.50*	*2.00*	50.00	90.00	
1942 (21,120)	47,839,120	*1.00*	*1.15*	*1.50*	*2.00*	16.00	30.00	250.00
1942D	10,973,800	*1.00*	*1.15*	*1.50*	*2.00*	20.00	40.00	
1942S	12,708,000	*1.00*	*1.15*	*1.50*	*2.00*	30.00	40.00	
1943	53,190,000	*1.00*	*1.15*	*1.50*	*2.00*	16.00	30.00	
1943D	11,346,000	*1.00*	*1.15*	*1.50*	*2.00*	30.00	50.00	
1943S	13,450,000	*1.00*	*1.15*	*1.50*	*2.00*	25.00	40.00	
1944	28,206,000	*1.00*	*1.15*	*1.50*	*2.00*	16.00	30.00	
1944D	9,769,000	*1.00*	*1.15*	*1.50*	*2.00*	16.00	30.00	
1944S	8,904,000	*1.00*	*1.15*	*1.50*	*2.00*	25.00	35.00	
1945	31,502,000	*1.00*	*1.15*	*1.50*	*2.00*	16.00	30.00	
1945D	9,966,800	*1.00*	*1.15*	*1.50*	*2.00*	16.00	30.00	
1945S	10,156,000	*1.00*	*1.15*	*1.50*	*2.00*	18.00	30.00	
1946	12,118,000	*1.00*	*1.15*	*1.50*	*2.00*	16.00	30.00	
1946D	2,151,000	*1.00*	*1.15*	*1.50*	*2.00*	16.00	30.00	
1946S	3,724,000	*1.00*	*1.15*	*1.50*	*2.00*	16.00	30.00	
1947	4,094,000	*1.00*	*1.15*	*1.50*	*2.00*	18.00	30.00	
1947D	3,900,600	*1.00*	*1.15*	*1.50*	*2.00*	18.00	35.00	

Italic prices indicate unsettled values due to fluctuating bullion market. See Bullion Chart.

HALF DOLLARS

FRANKLIN-LIBERTY BELL TYPE 1948-1963

The Benjamin Franklin half dollar and the Roosevelt dime were both designed by John R. Sinnock. His initials appear below the shoulder.

VF-20 VERY FINE—*At least half of the lower and upper incused lines on the rim of the bell must show.*

EF-40 EXTREMELY FINE—*Wear spots appear at top of end curls and hair back of ears. On reverse, Liberty Bell will show wear at top and on lettering.*

MS-60 UNCIRCULATED—*No trace of wear. A few noticeable blemishes.*

MS-63 UNCIRCULATED—*No trace of wear. Light blemishes. Attractive mint luster.*

Mint mark location

Choice, well struck uncirculated halves command higher prices.

	Quan. Minted	VF-20	EF-40	MS-60	MS-63	Proof-63
1948	3,006,814	*$1.00*	*$1.25*	$8.00	$15.00	
1948D	4,028,600	*1.00*	*1.25*	5.00	7.00	
1949	5,614,000	*1.00*	*1.25*	14.00	30.00	
1949D	4,120,600	*1.00*	*1.25*	14.00	28.00	
1949S	3,744,000	*1.00*	*1.25*	25.00	50.00	
1950	(51,386) 7,793,509	*1.00*	*1.25*	10.00	25.00	$175.00
1950D	8,031,600	*1.00*	*1.25*	7.00	15.00	
1951	(57,500) 16,859,602	*1.00*	*1.25*	3.00	8.00	75.00
1951D	9,475,200	*1.00*	*1.25*	10.00	20.00	
1951S	13,696,000	*1.00*	*1.25*	10.00	18.00	
1952	(81,980) 21,274,073	*1.00*	*1.25*	3.00	6.50	50.00
1952D	25,395,600	*1.00*	*1.25*	3.00	6.50	
1952S	5,526,000	*1.00*	*1.25*	10.00	20.00	
1953	(128,800) 2,796,920	*1.00*	*1.25*	8.00	15.00	35.00
1953D	20,900,400	*1.00*	*1.25*	3.00	5.50	
1953S	4,148,000	*1.00*	*1.25*	5.00	13.00	
1954	(233,300) 13,421,503	*1.00*	*1.25*	2.50	4.00	20.00
1954D	25,445,580	*1.00*	*1.25*	2.50	3.00	
1954S	4,993,400	*1.00*	*1.25*	4.00	8.00	
1955	(378,200) 2,876,381	*1.00*	*1.25*	4.00	6.25	15.00
1956	(669,384) 4,701,384	*1.00*	*1.25*	3.00	6.00	10.00
1957	(1,247,952) 6,361,952	*1.00*	*1.25*	2.00	6.00	7.00
1957D	19,966,850	*1.00*	*1.25*	2.00	4.00	
1958	(875,652) 4,917,652	*1.00*	*1.25*	2.00	4.00	9.00
1958D	23,962,412	*1.00*	*1.25*	2.00	3.50	
1959	(1,149,291) 7,349,291	*1.00*	*1.25*	2.00	3.50	6.00
1959D	13,053,750	*1.00*	*1.25*	2.00	3.50	
1960	(1,691,602) 7,715,602	*1.00*	*1.25*	*1.50*	3.00	5.00
1960D	18,215,812	*1.00*	*1.25*	*1.50*	3.00	
1961	(3,028,244) 11,318,244	*1.00*	*1.25*	*1.50*	3.00	4.00
1961D	20,276,442	*1.00*	*1.25*	*1.50*	3.00	
1962	(3,218,019) 12,932,019	*1.00*	*1.25*	*1.50*	2.00	4.00
1962D	35,473,281	*1.00*	*1.25*	*1.50*	2.00	
1963	(3,075,645) 25,239,645	*1.00*	*1.25*	*1.50*	2.50	4.00
1963D	67,069,292	*1.00*	*1.25*	*1.50*	2.50	

Italic prices indicate unsettled values due to fluctuating bullion market. See Bullion Chart.

HALF DOLLARS

KENNEDY TYPE 1964 to Date

Gilroy Roberts, former Chief Engraver of the Mint, designed the obverse of this coin. His stylized initials are on the truncation of the forceful bust of President John F. Kennedy. The reverse, which uses the presidential coat of arms for the motif, is the work of Chief Engraver Frank Gasparro.

1964 Mint mark location

1968 Mint mark location

Silver Coinage 1964

		Quan. Minted	MS-63	Proof-63
1964	(3,950,762)	277,254,766	*$1.25*	$5.00
1964D		156,205,446	*1.25*	

Silver Clad Coinage 1965-1970

	Quan. Minted	MS-63	Proof-63
1965	65,879,366	*.60*	
1966	108,984,932	*.60*	
1967	295,046,978	*.60*	
1968D	246,951,930	*.60*	
1968S Proof	(3,041,506)		1.50
1969D	129,881,800	*.60*	
1969S Proof	(2,934,631)		1.50
1970D (Issued only in mint sets)	2,150,000	7.00	
1970S Proof	(2,632,810)		4.00

Copper-Nickel Clad Coinage 1971-

	Quan. Minted	MS-63	Proof-63
1971	155,164,000	$.55	
1971D	302,097,424	.55	
1971S Proof	(3,220,733)		$1.00
1972	153,180,000	.60	
1972D	141,890,000	.60	
1972S Proof	(3,260,996)		1.00
1973	64,964,000	$.55	
1973D	83,171,400	.55	
1973S Proof	(2,760,339)		$1.00
1974	201,596,000	.55	
1974D	79,066,300	.55	
1974S Proof	(2,612,568)		1.00

BICENTENNIAL COINAGE DATED 1776—1976

	Quan. Minted	MS-63	Proof-63
1776-1976 Copper-nickel clad	234,308,000	$.55	
1776-1976D Copper-nickel clad	287,565,248	.55	

Italic prices indicate unsettled values due to fluctuating bullion market. See Bullion Chart.

HALF DOLLARS

	Quan. Minted	MS-63	Proof-63
1776-1976S Copper-nickel clad	(7,059,099)		$.75
1776-1976S Silver clad	*11,000,000	$2.00	
1776-1976S Silver clad	*(4,000,000)		3.00

*Approximate mintage.

Eagle Reverse Resumed

	Quan. Minted	MS-63	Proof-63
1977	43,598,000	$.55	
1977D	31,449,106	.55	
1977S Proof	(3,251,152)		$1.00
1978	14,350,000	.55	
1978D	13,765,799	.65	
1978S Proof	(3,127,781)		1.00
1979	68,312,000	.53	
1979D	15,815,422	.53	
1979S Proof	(3,677,175)		
Filled S			1.00
Clear S			6.00
1980P	44,134,000	.52	
1980D	33,456,449	.52	
1980S Proof	(3,554,806)		.85
1981P	29,544,000	.52	
1981D	27,839,533	.52	
1981S Proof	(4,063,083)		.85
1982P	10,819,000	.52	
1982D	13,140,102	.52	
1982S Proof	(3,857,479)		1.50
1983P	34,139,000	.53	
1983D	32,472,244	.53	
1983S Proof	(3,279,126)		2.00
1984P	26,029,000	.53	
1984D	26,262,158	.52	
1984S Proof	(3,065,110)		5.00
1985P	18,706,962	$.52	
1985D	19,814,034	.52	
1985S Proof	(3,362,821)		$3.00
1986P	13,107,633	.53	
1986D	15,336,145	.53	
1986S Proof	(3,010,497)		8.00
1987P	*2,890,758	1.50	
1987D	*2,890,758	1.50	
1987S Proof	(4,227,728)		2.50
1988P	13,626,000	.52	
1988D	12,000,096	.52	
1988S Proof	(3,262,948)		4.00
1989P	24,542,000	.50	
1989D	23,000,216	.50	
1989S Proof	(3,220,194)		1.50
1990P	22,278,000	.50	
1990D	20,096,242	.50	
1990S Proof	(3,299,559)		1.50
1991P	14,874,000	.50	
1991D	15,054,678	.50	
1991S Proof			2.00
1992P		.50	
1992D		.50	
1992S Proof			2.00

*Not issued for circulation; included with uncirculated and souvenir sets.

SILVER DOLLARS — 1794 to Date

The silver dollar was authorized by Congress April 2, 1792. Weight and fineness were specified at 416 grains and 892.4 fine. The first issues appeared in 1794 and until 1804 all silver dollars had the value stamped on the edge: HUNDRED CENTS, ONE DOLLAR OR UNIT. After a lapse in coinage of the silver dollar during the period 1804 to 1835, coins were made with either plain or reeded edges and the value was placed on the reverse side.

The weight was changed by the law of January 18, 1837 to 412½ grains, fineness .900. The coinage was discontinued by the Act of February 12, 1873 and reauthorized by the Act of February 28, 1878. The dollar was again discontinued after 1935, and since then only the copper-nickel pieces first authorized in 1971 have been coined for circulation.

FLOWING HAIR TYPE 1794-1795

AG-3 ABOUT GOOD—*Clear enough to identify.*

G-4 GOOD—*Date and letters readable. Main devices outlined, but lack details.*

VG-8 VERY GOOD—*Major details discernible. Letters well formed but worn.*

F-12 FINE—*Hair ends distinguishable. Top hairlines show, but otherwise worn smooth.*

VF-20 VERY FINE—*Hair in center shows some detail. Other details more bold.*

EF-40 EXTREMELY FINE—*Hair well defined but will show some wear.*

MS-60 UNCIRCULATED—*No trace of wear. Light blemishes.*

	Quan. Minted	AG-3	G-4	VG-8	F-12	VF-20	EF-40	MS-60
1794	1,758	$1,700	$3,300	$5,500	$8,250	$14,000	$23,000	——
1795	160,295	250.00	500.00	650.00	800.00	1,200	2,200	$11,000

DRAPED BUST TYPE, SMALL EAGLE REVERSE 1795-1798

AG-3 ABOUT GOOD—*Clear enough to identify.*
G-4 GOOD—*Bust outlined, no detail. Date readable, some leaves evident.*
VG-8 VERY GOOD—*Drapery worn except deepest folds. Hairlines smooth.*
F-12 FINE—*All drapery lines distinguishable. Hairlines near cheek and neck show some detail.*
VF-20 VERY FINE—*Left side of drapery worn smooth.*
EF-40 EXTREMELY FINE—*Drapery shows distinctly. Hair well outlined and detailed.*
MS-60 UNCIRCULATED—*No trace of wear. Light blemishes.*

1795 Bust Type	42,738	$185.00	$375.00	$475.00	$650.00	$950.00	$2,000	$8,500
1796	72,920	150.00	325.00	450.00	600.00	800.00	1,900	7,500
1797	7,776	150.00	325.00	450.00	600.00	800.00	1,900	7,500
1798 All kinds	327,536	150.00	325.00	450.00	600.00	800.00	1,900	7,500

HERALDIC EAGLE REVERSE 1798-1804

G-4 GOOD—*Letters and date readable. E PLURIBUS UNUM obliterated.*
VG-8 VERY GOOD—*Motto partially readable. Only deepest drapery details visible. All other lines smooth.*
F-12 FINE—*All drapery lines distinguishable. Hairlines near cheek and neck show some detail.*
VF-20 VERY FINE—*Left side of drapery worn smooth.*
EF-40 EXTREMELY FINE—*Drapery is distinct. Hair well detailed.*
MS-60 UNCIRCULATED—*No trace of wear. Light blemishes.*

SILVER DOLLARS

	Quan. Minted	G-4	VG-8	F-12	VF-20	EF-40	MS-60
1798 Heraldic eagle		$175.00	$225.00	$275.00	$400.00	$750.00	$5,000
1799	423,515	175.00	225.00	275.00	400.00	750.00	5,000
1800	220,920	175.00	225.00	275.00	400.00	750.00	5,000
1801	54,454	175.00	225.00	275.00	400.00	800.00	5,000
1802	41,650	175.00	225.00	275.00	400.00	800.00	5,000
1803	85,634	175.00	225.00	275.00	400.00	800.00	5,000
1804 Variety 2, letter O above space between clouds							Proof $400,000
1804 Variety 1, letter O in "OF" above cloud							Proof $200,000

GOBRECHT SILVER DOLLARS

Silver dollars of 1836, 1838 and 1839 were mostly made as trial pieces, but some were made in quantities for general circulation. There was no regular issue of dollars 1805 to 1835 inclusive.

	VF-20	EF-40	Proof-60
1836 C. GOBRECHT F. on base. Rev. Eagle flying left amid stars. Plain edge. Although scarce, this is the most common variety and was issued for circulation as regular coinage	$1,800	$2,300	$4,750
1838 Similar obv., designer's name omitted, stars added around border. Rev. Eagle flying left in plain field. Reeded edge	1,900	2,700	5,000
1839 Obv. as above. Rev. Eagle in plain field. Reeded edge. Issued for circulation as regular coinage	2,100	3,000	5,750

SILVER DOLLARS

LIBERTY SEATED TYPE — REGULAR ISSUES 1840-1873

In 1840 silver dollars were again issued for general circulation, and the seated figure of Liberty device was adopted for the obverse, and a heraldic eagle on the reverse.

VG-8 VERY GOOD—*Any 3 letters of LIBERTY at least two-thirds complete.*
F-12 FINE—*All 7 letters of LIBERTY visible though weak.*
VF-20 VERY FINE—*LIBERTY is strong but its ribbon shows slight wear.*
EF-40 EXTREMELY FINE—*Horizontal lines of shield complete. Eagle's eye plain.*
MS-60 UNCIRCULATED—*No trace of wear. Light marks or blemishes.*

Mint mark location is on the reverse below eagle.

	Quan. Minted	*VG-8*	*F-12*	*VF-20*	*EF-40*	*MS-60*	*Proof-63*
1840	61,005	$50.00	$85.00	$125.00	$210.00	$800.00	$2,000
1841	173,000	50.00	80.00	120.00	200.00	700.00	2,000
1842	184,618	50.00	80.00	120.00	200.00	700.00	2,000
1843	165,100	50.00	80.00	120.00	200.00	700.00	2,000
1844	20,000	60.00	90.00	135.00	225.00	950.00	2,000
1845	24,500	60.00	90.00	135.00	225.00	950.00	2,000
1846	110,600	50.00	80.00	120.00	200.00	700.00	2,000
1846O	59,000	65.00	100.00	135.00	250.00	1,400	
1847	140,750	50.00	80.00	120.00	200.00	700.00	2,000
1848	15,000	100.00	200.00	275.00	375.00	950.00	2,000
1849	62,600	50.00	80.00	120.00	200.00	700.00	2,000
1850	7,500	60.00	90.00	135.00	225.00	1,750	3,000
1850O	40,000	65.00	100.00	160.00	300.00	1,400	
1851	1,300	450.00	600.00	1,000	2,000	6,750	7,000
1852	1,100					7,000	5,500
1853	46,110	50.00	80.00	120.00	200.00	825.00	2,400
1854	33,140	55.00	100.00	150.00	275.00	1,000	5,000
1855	26,000	95.00	125.00	175.00	325.00	1,000	3,300
1856	63,500	60.00	100.00	140.00	225.00	950.00	3,200
1857	94,000	55.00	90.00	135.00	210.00	950.00	2,100
1858	Est. (300+)						3,400
1859 (800)	256,500	90.00	125.00	175.00	250.00	1,000	2,100
1859O	360,000	50.00	80.00	120.00	200.00	700.00	
1859S	20,000	100.00	150.00	200.00	375.00	1,750	
1860 (1,330)	218,930	55.00	90.00	150.00	225.00	800.00	2,100
1860O	515,000	50.00	80.00	120.00	200.00	700.00	
1861 (1,000)	78,500	100.00	200.00	300.00	400.00	1,000	2,100
1862 (550)	12,090	95.00	125.00	225.00	350.00	1,100	2,100
1863 (460)	27,660	60.00	100.00	140.00	250.00	900.00	2,000
1864 (470)	31,170	60.00	100.00	140.00	250.00	950.00	2,000
1865 (500)	47,000	60.00	100.00	140.00	250.00	900.00	2,000

SILVER DOLLARS

Motto "In God We Trust" Added to Reverse

	Quan. Minted	VG-8	F-12	VF-20	EF-40	MS-60	Proof-63
1866 .... (725)	49,625	$50.00	$80.00	$120.00	$200.00	$625.00	$1,800
1867 .... (625)	47,525	50.00	80.00	120.00	200.00	625.00	1,800
1868 .... (600)	162,700	50.00	80.00	120.00	200.00	600.00	1,800
1869 .... (600)	424,300	50.00	80.00	120.00	200.00	600.00	1,800
1870 ...... (1,000)	416,000	50.00	80.00	120.00	200.00	600.00	1,800
1870CC	12,462	100.00	150.00	250.00	350.00	2,000	
1870S....................				25,000	35,000	50,000	
1871 .... (960)	1,074,760	50.00	80.00	120.00	200.00	600.00	1,800
1871CC	1,376	900.00	1,500	2,250	3,500	6,500	
1872 .... (950)	1,106,450	50.00	80.00	120.00	200.00	600.00	1,800
1872CC	3,150	300.00	600.00	850.00	1,250	4,500	
1872S................	9,000	100.00	150.00	250.00	400.00	2,500	
1873 .... (600)	293,600	50.00	80.00	120.00	200.00	600.00	1,800
1873CC	2,300	1,000	1,750	3,000	4,000	8,500	

TRADE DOLLARS 1873-1885

This coin was issued for circulation in the Orient to compete with dollar-size coins of other countries. It weighed 420 grains compared to 412½ grains, the weight of the regular silver dollar.

VG-8 VERY GOOD—*About half of mottoes IN GOD WE TRUST and E PLURIBUS UNUM will show. Rim on both sides well defined.*

F-12 FINE—*Mottoes and LIBERTY readable but worn.*

EF-40 EXTREMELY FINE—*Mottoes and LIBERTY are sharp. Only slight wear on rims.*

MS-60 UNCIRCULATED—*No trace of wear. Light blemishes.*

1875S
S over CC

TRADE DOLLARS 1873 - 1885

	Quan. Minted	VG-8	F-12	EF-40	MS-60	Proof-63
1873 (865)	397,500	$30.00	$40.00	$75.00	$325.00	$1,200
1873CC	124,500	35.00	45.00	80.00	500.00	
1873S	703,000	30.00	40.00	75.00	325.00	
1874 (700)	987,800	30.00	40.00	75.00	300.00	1,200
1874CC	1,373,200	35.00	45.00	75.00	425.00	
1874S	2,549,000	30.00	40.00	75.00	300.00	
1875 (700)	218,900	60.00	90.00	200.00	600.00	1,200
1875CC	1,573,700	35.00	45.00	80.00	350.00	
1875S	4,487,000	30.00	40.00	75.00	300.00	
1875S, S over CC		75.00	100.00	200.00	650.00	
1876 (1,150)	456,150	30.00	40.00	75.00	300.00	1,200
1876CC	509,000	35.00	45.00	80.00	350.00	
1876S	5,227,000	30.00	40.00	75.00	300.00	
1877 (510)	3,039,710	30.00	40.00	75.00	300.00	1,200
1877CC	534,000	35.00	50.00	100.00	500.00	
1877S	9,519,000	30.00	40.00	75.00	300.00	
1878 (900)	900					1,200
1878CC	97,000	100.00	175.00	400.00	2,500	
1878S	4,162,000	30.00	40.00	75.00	300.00	
1879 (1,541)	1,541					1,200
1880 (1,987)	1,987					1,200
1881 (960)	960					1,200
1882 (1,097)	1,097					1,200
1883 (979)	979					1,200
1884 (10)	10					20,000
1885 (5)	5					50,000

LIBERTY HEAD OR MORGAN TYPE 1878-1921

George T. Morgan, formerly a pupil of Wyon in the Royal Mint in London, designed the new dollar. His initial M is found at the truncation of the neck, at the last tress. It also appears on the reverse on the left-hand loop of the ribbon.

Sharply struck "proof-like" coins have a highly reflective surface and usually command substantial premiums.

VF-20 VERY FINE—*Two-thirds of hairlines from top of forehead to ear must show. Ear well defined. Feathers on eagle's breast worn.*

EF-40 EXTREMELY FINE—*All hairlines strong and ear bold. Eagle's feathers all plain but slight wear on breast and wing tips.*

AU-50 ABOUT UNCIRCULATED—*Slight trace of wear. Most of mint luster is present although marred by bag marks.*

MS-60 UNCIRCULATED—*No trace of wear. Has full mint luster, but may be noticeably marred by scuff marks or bag abrasions.*

MS-63 UNCIRCULATED—*No trace of wear, full mint luster, few noticeable surface marks.*

Most uncirculated silver dollars have scratches or nicks because of handling of mint bags. Choice sharply struck coins with full brilliance and without blemishes are worth more than listed values.

8 Tail Feathers, 1878 Philadelphia Only
Mint mark location on the reverse below wreath

SILVER DOLLARS

	Quan. Minted	VF-20	EF-40	AU-50	MS-60	MS-63
1878, 8 tail feathers. (500)	750,000	$10.00	$12.00	$18.00	$27.00	$55.00
1878, 7 tail feathers. (500)	9,759,550	*6.00*	*7.00*	*9.00*	20.00	40.00
1878, 7 over 8 feathers..		15.00	18.00	25.00	35.00	85.00
1878CC	2,212,000	17.00	20.00	30.00	50.00	90.00
1878S	9,774,000	*6.00*	*7.00*	11.00	16.00	25.00
1879 (1,100)	14,807,100	*6.00*	*7.00*	*9.00*	15.00	35.00
1879CC	756,000	38.00	100.00	200.00	650.00	1,400
1879O	2,887,000	*6.00*	*7.00*	11.00	20.00	90.00
1879S	9,110,000	*6.00*	*7.00*	10.00	12.00	20.00
1880 (1,355)	12,601,355	*6.00*	*7.00*	*9.00*	13.00	25.00
1880CC	591,000	30.00	50.00	60.00	80.00	115.00
1880O	5,305,000	*6.00*	*7.00*	*9.00*	25.00	225.00
1880S	8,900,000	*6.00*	*7.00*	*9.00*	12.00	18.00
1881 (975)	9,163,975	*6.00*	*7.00*	*9.00*	13.00	22.00
1881CC	296,000	50.00	65.00	80.00	100.00	125.00
1881O	5,708,000	*6.00*	*7.00*	*9.00*	13.00	30.00
1881S	11,760,000	*6.00*	*7.00*	*9.00*	12.00	17.00
1882 (1,100)	11,101,100	*6.00*	*7.00*	*9.00*	13.00	20.00
1882CC	1,133,000	22.00	27.00	34.00	40.00	55.00
1882O	6,090,000	*6.00*	*7.00*	*9.00*	12.00	22.00
1882S	9,250,000	*6.00*	*7.00*	*9.00*	13.00	20.00
1883 (1,039)	12,291,039	*6.00*	*7.00*	*9.00*	13.00	20.00
1883CC	1,204,000	20.00	26.00	35.00	40.00	50.00
1883O	8,725,000	*6.00*	*7.00*	*9.00*	10.00	20.00
1883S	6,250,000	12.00	15.00	55.00	200.00	800.00
1884 (875)	14,070,875	*6.00*	*7.00*	*9.00*	12.00	20.00
1884CC	1,136,000	24.00	30.00	35.00	40.00	50.00
1884O	9,730,000	*6.00*	*7.00*	*9.00*	10.00	16.00
1884S	3,200,000	13.00	18.00	100.00	2,200	8,000
1885 (930)	17,787,767	*6.00*	*7.00*	*9.00*	10.00	20.00
1885CC	228,000	80.00	100.00	110.00	150.00	175.00
1885O	9,185,000	*6.00*	*7.00*	*9.00*	10.00	18.00
1885S	1,497,000	*6.00*	*12.00*	20.00	45.00	135.00
1886 (886)	19,963,886	*6.00*	*7.00*	*9.00*	10.00	20.00
1886O	10,710,000	*6.00*	13.00	28.00	135.00	900.00
1886S	750,000	14.00	18.00	27.00	50.00	135.00
1887 (710)	20,290,710	*6.00*	*7.00*	*9.00*	10.00	20.00
1887O	11,550,000	*6.00*	*7.00*	*9.00*	20.00	110.00
1887S	1,771,000	*6.00*	*7.00*	*9.00*	40.00	150.00
1888 (832)	19,183,832	*6.00*	*7.00*	*9.00*	12.00	21.00
1888O	12,150,000	*6.00*	*7.00*	*9.00*	13.00	22.00
1888S	657,000	15.00	20.00	30.00	60.00	150.00
1889 (811)	21,726,811	*6.00*	*7.00*	*9.00*	10.00	20.00
1889CC	350,000	150.00	350.00	1,300	4,500	8,000
1889O	11,875,000	*6.00*	*7.00*	13.00	40.00	125.00
1889S	700,000	18.00	22.00	30.00	45.00	100.00
1890 (590)	16,802,590	*6.00*	*7.00*	*9.00*	13.00	27.50
1890CC	2,309,041	20.00	25.00	45.00	120.00	235.00
1890O	10,701,000	*6.00*	*7.00*	*9.00*	17.00	50.00

Proof Morgan Dollars where indicated in mintage record (quantity shown in parentheses) are valued approximately as follows:

Proof-60 $450.00 Proof-63 $1,000 Proof-65 $3,000

Italic prices indicate unsettled values due to fluctuating bullion market. See Bullion Chart.

SILVER DOLLARS

	Quan. Minted	VF-20	EF-40	AU-50	MS-60	MS-63
1890S	8,230,373	*$6.00*	*$8.00*	$13.00	$22.00	$35.00
1891 (650)	8,694,206	*6.00*	11.00	15.00	23.00	85.00
1891CC	1,618,000	19.00	24.00	40.00	70.00	125.00
1891O	7,954,529	*6.00*	11.00	18.00	30.00	110.00
1891S	5,296,000	*6.00*	*8.00*	12.00	20.00	60.00
1892 (1,245)	1,037,245	*6.00*	13.00	22.00	45.00	135.00
1892CC	1,352,000	27.50	42.00	105.00	175.00	475.00
1892O	2,744,000	10.00	12.00	26.00	50.00	120.00
1892S	1,200,000	27.50	70.00	450.00	5,500	11,000
1893 (792)	389,792	32.00	52.00	85.00	130.00	285.00
1893CC	677,000	70.00	160.00	275.00	550.00	1,650
1893O	300,000	40.00	100.00	165.00	675.00	2,500
1893S	100,000	800.00	1,800	5,500	12,000	25,000
1894 (972)	110,972	150.00	190.00	315.00	450.00	1,100
1894O	1,723,000	11.00	16.00	42.00	300.00	1,000
1894S	1,260,000	20.00	42.00	85.00	175.00	350.00
1895 (880)	12,880				†8,500	†11,500
1895O	450,000	45.00	90.00	225.00	2,000	8,000
1895S	400,000	80.00	175.00	310.00	525.00	1,400
1896 (762)	9,976,762	*6.00*	*7.00*	*9.00*	10.00	17.00
1896O	4,900,000	*6.00*	12.00	40.00	375.00	2,750
1896S	5,000,000	18.00	45.00	110.00	300.00	675.00
1897 (731)	2,822,731	*6.00*	*7.00*	*9.00*	10.00	17.00
1897O	4,004,000	*6.00*	*7.00*	25.00	250.00	2,100
1897S	5,825,000	*7.00*	10.00	12.00	21.00	37.00
1898 (735)	5,884,735	*6.00*	*7.00*	*9.00*	10.00	18.00
1898O	4,440,000	*6.00*	*7.00*	*9.00*	10.00	17.00
1898S	4,102,000	*7.00*	12.00	32.00	60.00	150.00
1899 (846)	330,846	20.00	28.00	35.00	42.00	60.00
1899O	12,290,000	*7.00*	*8.00*	*9.00*	10.00	17.00
1899S	2,562,000	*7.00*	15.00	30.00	50.00	150.00
1900 (912)	8,830,912	*6.00*	*7.00*	*9.00*	10.00	17.00
1900O	12,590,000	*7.00*	*8.00*	*9.00*	11.00	18.00
1900S	3,540,000	*6.00*	14.00	28.00	50.00	120.00
1901 (813)	6,962,813	15.00	30.00	90.00	600.00	4,000
1901O	13,320,000	*7.00*	*8.00*	*9.00*	11.00	18.00
1901S	2,284,000	11.00	17.50	37.00	120.00	175.00
1902 (777)	7,994,777	*6.00*	10.00	13.00	16.00	28.00
1902O	8,636,000	*6.00*	*7.00*	*9.00*	10.00	17.00
1902S	1,530,000	30.00	40.00	50.00	70.00	125.00
1903 (755)	4,652,755	*6.00*	10.00	13.00	16.00	28.00
1903O	4,450,000	90.00	100.00	110.00	115.00	125.00
1903S	1,241,000	27.00	100.00	350.00	1,000	1,800
1904 (650)	2,788,650	*6.00*	*8.00*	15.00	26.00	80.00
1904O	3,720,000	*6.00*	*7.00*	*9.00*	10.00	17.00
1904S	2,304,000	30.00	60.00	240.00	500.00	900.00
1921	44,690,000	*5.00*	*5.50*	*6.00*	7.00	12.00
1921D	20,345,000	*5.00*	*5.50*	*6.00*	13.00	18.00
1921S	21,695,000	*5.00*	*5.50*	*6.00*	13.00	23.00

†Values are for proofs.

Proof Morgan Dollars where indicated in mintage record (quantity shown in parenthesis) are valued approximately as follows:

Proof-60 $450.00 Proof-63 $1,000 Proof-65 $3,000

Italic prices indicate unsettled values due to fluctuating bullion market. See Bullion Chart.

SILVER DOLLARS

PEACE TYPE 1921-1935

Anthony De Francisci, a medalist, designed this dollar. His monogram is located in the field of the coin under the neck of Liberty.

VF-20 VERY FINE—*Hair over eye well worn. Some strands over ear well defined. Some eagle feathers on top and outside edge of right wing will show.*

EF-40 EXTREMELY FINE—*Hairlines over brow and ear are strong though slightly worn. Outside wing feathers at right and those at top are visible but faint.*

AU-50 ABOUT UNCIRCULATED—*Slight trace of wear. Most of mint luster is present although marred by contact marks.*

MS-60 UNCIRCULATED—*No trace of wear. Has full mint luster but may be noticeably marred by stains, surface marks or bag abrasions.*

MS-63 UNCIRCULATED—*No trace of wear, full mint luster, few noticeable surface marks.*

Most uncirculated silver dollars have scratches or nicks because of handling of mint bags. Choice sharply struck coins with full brilliance and without blemishes are worth more than listed values.

Mint mark location is on reverse below one.

	Quan. Minted	VF-20	EF-40	AU-50	MS-60	MS-63
1921	1,006,473	$15.00	$22.00	$30.00	$75.00	$160.00
1922	51,737,000	*5.00*	*5.50*	*6.00*	7.00	12.00
1922D	15,063,000	*5.00*	*5.50*	*6.50*	10.00	25.00
1922S	17,475,000	*5.00*	*5.50*	*6.50*	12.00	30.00
1923	30,800,000	*5.00*	*5.50*	*6.00*	7.00	12.00
1923D	6,811,000	*5.00*	*5.50*	*6.50*	12.00	30.00
1923S	19,020,000	*5.00*	*5.50*	*6.50*	12.00	30.00
1924	11,811,000	*5.00*	*5.50*	*6.50*	7.00	14.00
1924S	1,728,000	*5.00*	*6.00*	23.00	55.00	260.00
1925	10,198,000	*5.00*	*5.50*	*6.50*	7.00	13.00
1925S	1,610,000	*5.00*	*6.00*	13.00	30.00	100.00
1926	1,939,000	*5.00*	*5.50*	10.00	13.00	27.50
1926D	2,348,700	*5.00*	*5.50*	12.00	25.00	60.00
1926S	6,980,000	*5.00*	*5.50*	11.00	15.00	37.50
1927	848,000	*5.00*	11.00	16.00	30.00	85.00
1927D	1,268,900	*5.00*	*6.00*	37.50	75.00	275.00
1927S	866,000	*5.00*	*6.00*	25.00	50.00	125.00
1928	360,649	60.00	75.00	85.00	115.00	200.00
1928S	1,632,000	*5.00*	10.00	22.00	45.00	225.00
1934	954,057	10.00	11.00	17.00	40.00	75.00
1934D	1,569,500	*5.00*	12.00	20.00	50.00	140.00
1934S	1,011,000	18.00	60.00	250.00	650.00	1,500
1935	1,576,000	*5.00*	*5.50*	12.00	20.00	45.00
1935S	1,964,000	*5.00*	*5.50*	24.00	50.00	135.00

Italic prices indicate unsettled values due to fluctuating bullion market. See Bullion Chart.

EISENHOWER DOLLARS 1971-1978

Honoring both President Dwight D. Eisenhower and the first landing of man on the moon, this design is the work of Chief Engraver Frank Gasparro, whose initials are on the truncation and below the eagle. The reverse is an adaptation of the official Apollo 11 insignia.

Mint mark location is above the date.

	Quan. Minted Proof	Quan. Minted Regular	MS-63	Proof-63
1971 Copper-nickel clad		47,799,000	$1.25	
1971D Copper-nickel clad		68,587,424	1.25	
1971S Silver clad	(4,265,234)	6,868,530	2.00	$2.50
1972 Copper-nickel clad		75,890,000	1.20	
1972D Copper-nickel clad		92,548,511	1.25	
1972S Silver clad	(1,811,631)	2,193,056	2.00	2.50
1973 Copper-nickel clad		*2,000,056	2.50	
1973D Copper-nickel clad		*2,000,000	2.50	
1973S Copper-nickel clad	(2,760,339)			3.25
1973S Silver clad	(1,013,646)	1,883,140	3.00	15.00
1974 Copper-nickel clad		27,366,000	1.20	
1974D Copper-nickel clad		45,517,000	1.20	
1974S Copper-nickel clad	(2,612,568)			2.50
1974S Silver clad	(1,306,579)	1,900,156	2.50	3.00

*1,760,258 of each sold only in sets and not released for circulation. Unissued coins destroyed at mint.

BICENTENNIAL COINAGE DATED 1776-1976

Obverse and Reverse Variety II — Reverse Var. I

Variety I: Design in low relief, bold lettering on reverse. Variety II: Sharp design, delicate lettering on reverse.

BICENTENNIAL DOLLARS

	Quan. Minted	*MS-63*	*Proof-63*
1776-1976 Copper-nickel clad, variety I	4,019,000	$1.25	
1776-1976 Copper-nickel clad, variety II	113,318,000	1.20	
1776-1976D Copper-nickel clad, variety I	21,048,710	1.25	
1776-1976D Copper-nickel clad, variety II	82,179,564	1.20	
1776-1976S Copper-nickel clad, variety I	(2,845,450)		$3.50
1776-1976S Copper-nickel clad, variety II	(4,149,730)		3.50
1776-1976S Silver clad, variety I	* 11,000,000	3.00	
1776-1976S Silver clad, variety I	*(4,000,000)		4.00

*Approximate mintage.

EAGLE REVERSE RESUMED

1977 Copper-nickel clad	12,596,000	1.20	
1977D Copper-nickel clad	32,983,006	1.20	
1977S Copper-nickel clad	(3,251,152)		3.50
1978 Copper-nickel clad	25,702,000	1.20	
1978D Copper-nickel clad	23,012,890	1.20	
1978S Copper-nickel clad	(3,127,781)		4.00

SUSAN B. ANTHONY DOLLARS 1979-1981

Clear S

Filled S

	Quan. minted	*MS-63*	*Proof-63*
1979P	360,222,000	$1.00	
1979D	288,015,744	1.00	
1979S	109,576,000	1.05	
1979S Proof	(3,677,175)		
Filled S			$3.50
Clear S			35.00
1980P	27,610,000	1.00	

	Quan. minted	*MS-63*	*Proof-63*
1980D	41,628,708	$1.00	
1980S	20,422,000	1.10	
1980S Proof	(3,554,806)		$4.50
1981P	3,000,000	1.50	
1981D	3,250,000	1.50	
1981S	3,492,000	1.50	
1981S Proof	(4,063,083)		4.00

GOLD

GOLD DOLLARS 1849-1889

Coinage of the gold dollar was authorized by the Act of March 3, 1849. The weight was 25.8 grains, fineness .900. The first type, struck until 1854, is known as the Liberty Head or small-sized type.

In 1854 the piece was made larger in diameter and thinner. The design was changed to a feather headdress on a female, generally referred to as the Indian Head or large-sized type. In 1856 the type was changed slightly by enlarging the size of the head.

LIBERTY HEAD TYPE 1849-1854

VF-20 VERY FINE—*LIBERTY on headband complete and readable. Knobs on coronet are defined.*

EF-40 EXTREMELY FINE—*Slight wear on Liberty's hair. Knobs on coronet sharp.*

AU-50 ABOUT UNCIRCULATED—*Trace of wear over eye and on coronet.*

MS-60 UNCIRCULATED—*No trace of wear. Light marks and blemishes.*

Mint mark is below wreath.

	Quan. Minted	*VF-20*	*EF-40*	*AU-50*	*MS-60*
1849	688,567	$80.00	$115.00	$125.00	$250.00
1849C	11,634	200.00	400.00	700.00	2,000
1849D	21,588	200.00	400.00	625.00	1,600
1849O	215,000	100.00	140.00	175.00	500.00
1850	481,953	80.00	115.00	125.00	250.00
1850C	6,966	225.00	350.00	600.00	2,000
1850D	8,382	200.00	325.00	575.00	1,750
1850O	14,000	120.00	140.00	300.00	775.00
1851	3,317,671	80.00	115.00	125.00	250.00
1851C	41,267	150.00	225.00	400.00	1,000
1851D	9,882	175.00	275.00	450.00	1,200
1851O	290,000	100.00	150.00	200.00	550.00
1852	2,045,351	80.00	115.00	125.00	250.00
1852C	9,434	200.00	350.00	500.00	1,400
1852D	6,360	200.00	350.00	550.00	1,900
1852O	140,000	100.00	125.00	150.00	525.00
1853	4,076,051	80.00	115.00	125.00	250.00
1853C	11,515	175.00	250.00	400.00	1,700
1853D	6,583	175.00	250.00	450.00	1,800
1853O	290,000	100.00	125.00	150.00	375.00
1854	855,502	80.00	115.00	125.00	250.00
1854D	2,935	250.00	325.00	700.00	1,750
1854S	14,632	150.00	250.00	400.00	900.00

INDIAN HEAD TYPE, Small Head 1854-1856

VF-20 VERY FINE—*Feather curl tips outlined but details worn.*

EF-40 EXTREMELY FINE—*Slight wear on tips of feather curls on headdress.*

AU-50 ABOUT UNCIRCULATED—*Trace of wear on headdress.*

MS-60 UNCIRCULATED—*No trace of wear. Light marks and blemishes.*

	Quan. Minted	*VF-20*	*EF-40*	*AU-50*	*MS-60*
1854	783,943	$125.00	$250.00	$550.00	$1,600
1855	758,269	125.00	250.00	550.00	1,600
1855C	9,803	400.00	700.00	1,400	4,500
1855D	1,811	1,600	2,700	3,200	8,500
1855O	55,000	250.00	375.00	800.00	3,500
1856S	24,600	250.00	375.00	800.00	3,500

GOLD DOLLARS

INDIAN HEAD TYPE, Large Head 1856-1889

VF-20 VERY FINE—*Curled feathers have slight detail. Details worn smooth at eyebrow, hair below headdress and behind ear and bottom curl.*

EF-40 EXTREMELY FINE—*Slight wear above and to right of eye and on top of curled feathers.*

AU-50 ABOUT UNCIRCULATED—*Trace of wear on headdress.*

MS-60 UNCIRCULATED—*No trace of wear. Light marks and blemishes.*

		Quan. Minted	*VF-20*	*EF-40*	*AU-50*	*MS-60*	*Proof-63*
1856		1,762,936	$75.00	$110.00	$120.00	$250.00	$3,500
1856D		1,460	1,200	2,200	3,200	7,500	
1857		774,789	75.00	110.00	120.00	250.00	3,500
1857C		13,280	250.00	400.00	700.00	900.00	
1857D		3,533	300.00	500.00	750.00	2,500	
1857S		10,000	150.00	225.00	300.00	700.00	
1858		117,995	75.00	110.00	120.00	250.00	3,500
1858D		3,477	325.00	500.00	800.00	2,500	
1858S		10,000	150.00	200.00	500.00	1,200	
1859	(80)	168,324	75.00	110.00	120.00	250.00	3,500
1859C		5,235	200.00	400.00	700.00	1,500	
1859D		4,952	350.00	500.00	900.00	2,000	
1859S		15,000	125.00	175.00	400.00	900.00	
1860	(154)	36,668	75.00	110.00	120.00	250.00	3,000
1860D		1,566	1,250	2,500	4,500	7,000	
1860S		13,000	125.00	200.00	350.00	900.00	
1861	(349)	527,499	75.00	110.00	120.00	250.00	3,000
1861D			3,500	5,500	9,000	1,800	
1862	(35)	1,361,390	75.00	110.00	120.00	250.00	3,500
1863	(50)	6,250	200.00	300.00	450.00	1,700	4,500
1864	(50)	5,950	200.00	300.00	400.00	1,400	4,500
1865	(25)	3,725	140.00	300.00	400.00	1,400	4,500
1866	(30)	7,130	125.00	160.00	300.00	650.00	4,000
1867	(50)	5,250	125.00	180.00	325.00	750.00	4,000
1868	(25)	10,525	100.00	150.00	250.00	550.00	4,000
1869	(25)	5,925	125.00	165.00	300.00	650.00	4,000
1870	(35)	6,335	115.00	160.00	275.00	625.00	4,000
1870S		3,000	250.00	375.00	600.00	1,800	
1871	(30)	3,930	115.00	160.00	225.00	500.00	4,000
1872	(30)	3,530	115.00	160.00	225.00	500.00	4,000
1873 Closed 3	(25)	1,825	125.00	175.00	275.00	775.00	4,500
1873 Open 3		123,300	75.00	110.00	120.00	250.00	
1874	(20)	198,820	75.00	110.00	120.00	250.00	4,000
1875	(20)	420	1,000	1,500	2,500	4,800	12,500
1876	(45)	3,245	100.00	135.00	185.00	500.00	3,000
1877	(20)	3,920	100.00	135.00	185.00	500.00	3,000
1878	(20)	3,020	100.00	135.00	185.00	500.00	3,000
1879	(30)	3,030	100.00	135.00	185.00	500.00	3,000
1880	(36)	1,636	100.00	135.00	185.00	500.00	3,000
1881	(87)	7,707	75.00	110.00	120.00	250.00	2,750
1882	(125)	5,125	75.00	110.00	120.00	250.00	2,750
1883	(207)	11,007	75.00	110.00	120.00	250.00	2,750
1884	(1,006)	6,236	75.00	110.00	120.00	250.00	2,500
1885	(1,105)	12,261	75.00	110.00	120.00	250.00	2,500
1886	(1,016)	6,016	75.00	110.00	120.00	250.00	2,500
1887	(1,043)	8,543	75.00	110.00	120.00	250.00	2,500
1888	(1,079)	16,580	75.00	110.00	120.00	250.00	2,500
1889	(1,779)	30,729	75.00	110.00	120.00	250.00	2,500

QUARTER EAGLES—1796-1929
($2.50 GOLD PIECES)

Although authorized by the Act of April 2, 1792, coinage of quarter eagles was not begun until 1796.

CAPPED BUST TO RIGHT 1796-1807

No Stars on Obverse 1796 Only

F-12 FINE—*Hair worn smooth on high spots. E PLURIBUS UNUM weak but readable.*

VF-20 VERY FINE—*Some wear on high spots.*

EF-40 EXTREMELY FINE—*Only slight wear on hair and cheek.*

MS-60 UNCIRCULATED—*No trace of wear. Light blemishes.*

Stars on Obverse 1796-1807

	Quan. Minted	*F-12*	*VF-20*	*EF-40*	*MS-60*
1796 No stars on obverse	963	$5,200	$9,000	$14,000	$30,000
1796 Stars on obverse	432	4,000	6,750	9,000	19,000
1797	427	3,000	5,000	7,500	14,000
1798	1,094	2,000	2,800	3,750	10,000
1802, 2 over 1	3,035	1,250	1,800	2,750	8,500
1804, 13-Star reverse	} 3,327	2,500	4,500	7,000	13,000
1804, 14-Star reverse		1,250	1,800	3,000	8,500
1805	1,781	1,250	1,800	3,000	8,500
1806, 6 over 4, stars 8+5	1,136	1,250	1,800	3,000	8,500
1806, 6 over 5, stars 7+6	480	1,800	3,000	4,500	11,000
1807	6,812	1,250	1,800	3,000	8,500

CAPPED BUST TO LEFT, Large Size 1808

F-12 FINE—*E PLURIBUS UNUM and LIBERTY on headband readable but weak.*

VF-20 VERY FINE—*Motto and LIBERTY clear.*

EF-40 EXTREMELY FINE—*All details of hair are plain.*

MS-60 UNCIRCULATED—*No trace of wear. Light blemishes.*

1808	2,710	5,500	8,000	12,000	35,000

CAPPED HEAD TO LEFT 1821-1834

Those dated 1829-1834 are smaller in diameter than the 1821-1827 pieces.

1821	6,448	1,200	2,500	3,500	9,000
1824, 4 over 1	2,600	1,200	2,500	3,500	9,000
1825	4,434	1,200	2,500	3,500	9,000
1826	760	2,200	3,300	5,000	17,000
1827	2,800	1,200	2,500	3,750	9,500
1829	3,403	1,200	2,500	3,500	8,000
1830	4,540	1,000	2,000	3,000	8,000

QUARTER EAGLES

	Quan. Minted	F-12	VF-20	EF-40	MS-60
1831	4,520	$1,000	$2,000	$3,000	$8,000
1832	4,400	1,000	2,000	3,000	8,000
1833	4,160	1,000	2,000	3,000	8,000
1834 (Motto)	4,000	2,750	5,000	7,500	17,000

CLASSIC HEAD TYPE, No Motto on Reverse 1834-1839

In 1834 the quarter eagle was redesigned. A ribbon binding the hair, bearing the word LIBERTY, replaces the Liberty cap. The motto was omitted from the reverse.

F-12 FINE—*LIBERTY readable and complete. Curl under ear oulined but no detail.*

VF-20 VERY FINE—*LIBERTY plain. Hair curl has detail.*

EF-40 EXTREMELY FINE—*Small amount of wear on top of hair and below L in LIBERTY. Wear evident on wing.*

AU-50 ABOUT UNCIRCULATED—*Trace of wear on coronet and hair above ear.*

MS-60 UNCIRCULATED—*No trace of wear. Light blemishes.*

Mint mark location.

	Quan. Minted	F-12	VF-20	EF-40	AU-50	MS-60
1834 No motto	112,234	$110.00	$150.00	$275.00	$425.00	$900.00
1835	131,402	110.00	150.00	275.00	425.00	900.00
1836	547,986	110.00	150.00	275.00	425.00	900.00
1837	45,080	110.00	150.00	275.00	450.00	1,200
1838	47,030	110.00	150.00	275.00	450.00	1,200
1838C	7,880	200.00	300.00	600.00	900.00	2,750
1839	27,021	100.00	150.00	275.00	450.00	1,200
1839C	18,140	180.00	275.00	575.00	800.00	2,500
1839D	13,674	180.00	275.00	575.00	800.00	2,750
1839O	17,781	150.00	175.00	300.00	600.00	1,800

CORONET TYPE 1840-1907

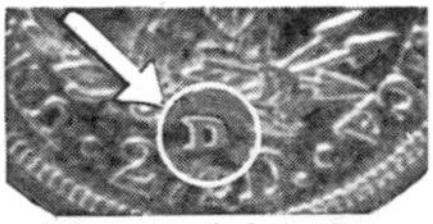

Mint mark location.

4 Plain 4

4 Crosslet 4

	Quan. Minted	VF-20	EF-40	AU-50	MS-60
1840	18,859	$125.00	$175.00	$225.00	$600.00
1840C	12,822	200.00	325.00	500.00	1,300
1840D	3,532	400.00	700.00	1,400	3,000
1840O	33,580	125.00	175.00	225.00	700.00
1841 Proofs only		6,000	12,500	17,500	32,500
1841C	10,281	275.00	450.00	550.00	1,000
1841D	4,164	325.00	575.00	900.00	2,500
1842	2,823	275.00	500.00	600.00	1,400
1842C	6,729	300.00	475.00	550.00	1,000
1842D	4,643	325.00	500.00	900.00	2,000
1842O	19,800	125.00	175.00	225.00	800.00
1843	100,546	125.00	175.00	200.00	550.00
1843D	36,209	275.00	450.00	550.00	1,200
1843O	364,002	125.00	175.00	225.00	675.00
1844	6,784	160.00	200.00	350.00	850.00
1844C	11,622	200.00	250.00	425.00	1,250
1844D	17,332	200.00	300.00	500.00	1,400
1845	91,051	115.00	150.00	175.00	600.00

QUARTER EAGLES

	Quan. Minted	*VF-20*	*EF-40*	*AU-50*	*MS-60*	*Proof-63*
1845D	19,460	$200.00	$275.00	$450.00	$1,300	
1845O	4,000	500.00	800.00	1,200	5,000	
1846	21,598	125.00	175.00	200.00	700.00	
1846C	4,808	325.00	550.00	850.00	2,000	
1846D	19,303	225.00	300.00	600.00	1,400	
1846O	62,000	125.00	175.00	200.00	800.00	
1847	29,814	125.00	175.00	200.00	625.00	
1847C	23,226	200.00	225.00	400.00	1,100	
1847D	15,784	200.00	225.00	475.00	1,200	
1847O	124,000	125.00	175.00	200.00	600.00	
1848	7,497	250.00	400.00	600.00	1,300	

CAL. Above Eagle on Reverse

California Gold Quarter Eagle

In 1848 about two hundred and thirty ounces of gold were sent to Secretary of War Marcy by Col. R. B. Mason, Military Governor of California. The gold was turned over to the mint and made into quarter eagles. The distinguishing mark "CAL." was punched above the eagle on the reverse side, while the coins were in the die.

	Quan. Minted	*VF-20*	*EF-40*	*AU-50*	*MS-60*	*Proof-63*
1848 CAL. above eagle	1,389	3,500	5,500	8,000	16,000	
1848C	16,788	200.00	300.00	500.00	1,100	
1848D	13,771	250.00	375.00	600.00	1,200	
1849	23,294	125.00	165.00	200.00	700.00	
1849C	10,220	250.00	400.00	700.00	1,400	
1849D	10,945	250.00	425.00	750.00	1,700	
1850	252,923	100.00	125.00	150.00	400.00	
1850C	9,148	250.00	400.00	700.00	1,400	
1850D	12,148	250.00	425.00	800.00	1,700	
1850O	84,000	100.00	125.00	150.00	500.00	
1851	1,372,748	100.00	125.00	150.00	275.00	
1851C	14,923	200.00	300.00	500.00	1,200	
1851D	11,264	200.00	300.00	500.00	1,200	
1851O	148,000	100.00	125.00	150.00	400.00	
1852	1,159,681	100.00	125.00	150.00	275.00	
1852C	9,772	225.00	350.00	500.00	1,200	
1852D	4,078	325.00	500.00	800.00	2,200	
1852O	140,000	100.00	125.00	175.00	600.00	
1853	1,404,668	100.00	125.00	150.00	275.00	
1853D	3,178	375.00	625.00	900.00	2,500	
1854	596,258	100.00	125.00	150.00	275.00	
1854C	7,295	275.00	425.00	650.00	1,400	
1854D	1,760	1,250	1,800	2,750	5,500	
1854O	153,000	100.00	125.00	150.00	400.00	
1854S	246		14,000	23,000	—	
1855	235,480	100.00	125.00	150.00	275.00	
1855C	3,677	375.00	625.00	900.00	2,500	
1855D	1,123	1,300	2,200	3,300	8,100	
1856	384,240	100.00	125.00	150.00	275.00	
1856C	7,913	225.00	325.00	475.00	1,500	
1856D	874	1,700	4,250	6,750	13,000	
1856O	21,100	125.00	165.00	250.00	700.00	
1856S	72,120	125.00	165.00	250.00	700.00	
1857	214,130	100.00	125.00	150.00	275.00	$8,000
1857D	2,364	300.00	475.00	850.00	2,200	
1857O	34,000	110.00	135.00	150.00	650.00	
1857S	69,200	110.00	135.00	200.00	550.00	

QUARTER EAGLES

	Quan. Minted	VF-20	EF-40	AU-50	MS-60	Proof-63
1858	47,377	$100.00	$125.00	$150.00	$600.00	$8,000
1858C	9,056	200.00	275.00	450.00	1,200	
1859 (80)	39,444	100.00	125.00	150.00	600.00	6,500
1859D	2,244	275.00	600.00	900.00	2,200	
1859S	15,200	150.00	170.00	225.00	600.00	
1860 (112)	22,675	100.00	125.00	175.00	550.00	4,500
1860C	7,469	200.00	375.00	500.00	1,400	
1860S	35,600	140.00	165.00	225.00	625.00	
1861 (90)	1,283,878	100.00	125.00	150.00	265.00	4,500
1861S	24,000	140.00	165.00	225.00	650.00	
1862, 2 over 1	98,543 (both varieties)		650.00	1,000	——	
1862 (35)		100.00	125.00	150.00	400.00	4,750
1862S	8,000	210.00	400.00	600.00	1,200	
1863 Proofs only (30)	30					——
1863S	10,800	150.00	175.00	250.00	1,100	
1864 (50)	2,874	450.00	900.00	1,800	3,200	7,500
1865 (25)	1,545	450.00	900.00	1,800	3,200	7,500
1865S	23,376	125.00	175.00	275.00	650.00	
1866 (30)	3,110	175.00	225.00	400.00	950.00	4,750
1866S	38,960	125.00	160.00	225.00	800.00	
1867 (50)	3,250	165.00	200.00	400.00	900.00	4,000
1867S	28,000	125.00	165.00	225.00	700.00	
1868 (25)	3,625	150.00	200.00	375.00	750.00	4,000
1868S	34,000	135.00	165.00	225.00	650.00	
1869 (25)	4,345	175.00	200.00	350.00	725.00	4,000
1869S	29,500	150.00	165.00	200.00	550.00	
1870 (35)	4,555	150.00	165.00	225.00	625.00	4,000
1870S	16,000	150.00	165.00	200.00	575.00	
1871 (30)	5,350	150.00	165.00	250.00	650.00	4,000
1871S	22,000	100.00	125.00	150.00	550.00	
1872 (30)	3,030	150.00	175.00	275.00	650.00	4,000
1872S	18,000	100.00	125.00	150.00	550.00	
1873 (25)	178,025	100.00	125.00	150.00	265.00	4,000
1873S	27,000	115.00	135.00	175.00	600.00	
1874 (20)	3,940	175.00	200.00	300.00	650.00	5,250
1875 (20)	420	1,000	2,000	3,000	6,000	16,000
1875S	11,600	115.00	135.00	200.00	750.00	
1876 (45)	4,221	175.00	200.00	325.00	750.00	4,000
1876S	5,000	150.00	165.00	225.00	800.00	
1877 (20)	1,652	250.00	325.00	425.00	1,100	5,000
1877S	35,400	100.00	125.00	150.00	425.00	
1878 (20)	286,260	100.00	125.00	150.00	265.00	4,000
1878S	178,000	100.00	125.00	150.00	265.00	
1879 (30)	88,990	100.00	125.00	150.00	375.00	4,000
1879S	43,500	100.00	125.00	150.00	375.00	
1880 (36)	2,996	125.00	165.00	225.00	650.00	4,000
1881 (51)	691	500.00	750.00	1,500	3,000	5,750
1882 (67)	4,067	115.00	165.00	200.00	600.00	4,000
1883 (82)	2,002	125.00	175.00	225.00	625.00	4,000
1884 (73)	2,023	125.00	175.00	225.00	625.00	4,000
1885 (87)	887	350.00	700.00	1,200	2,500	5,000
1886 (88)	4,088	125.00	175.00	225.00	600.00	4,500
1887 (122)	6,282	115.00	150.00	200.00	600.00	3,500
1888 (97)	16,098	100.00	125.00	150.00	400.00	3,500
1889 (48)	17,648	100.00	125.00	150.00	400.00	3,500
1890 (93)	8,813	100.00	125.00	150.00	400.00	3,500
1891 (80)	11,040	100.00	125.00	150.00	425.00	3,500
1892 (105)	2,545	150.00	175.00	225.00	550.00	3,500
1893 (106)	30,106	100.00	125.00	150.00	250.00	3,500
1894 (122)	4,122	125.00	140.00	185.00	500.00	3,500
1895 (119)	6,119	100.00	125.00	150.00	400.00	3,500

QUARTER EAGLES

		Quan. Minted	VF-20	EF-40	AU-50	MS-60	Proof-63
1896	(132)	19,202	$100.00	$125.00	$150.00	$250.00	$3,500
1897	(136)	29,904	100.00	125.00	150.00	250.00	3,500
1898	(165)	24,165	100.00	125.00	150.00	210.00	3,200
1899	(150)	27,350	100.00	125.00	150.00	210.00	3,200
1900	(205)	67,205	100.00	125.00	150.00	200.00	3,200
1901	(223)	91,323	100.00	125.00	150.00	200.00	3,200
1902	(193)	133,733	100.00	125.00	150.00	200.00	3,200
1903	(197)	201,257	100.00	125.00	150.00	200.00	3,200
1904	(170)	160,960	100.00	125.00	150.00	200.00	3,200
1905	(144)	217,944	100.00	125.00	150.00	200.00	3,200
1906	(160)	176,490	100.00	125.00	150.00	200.00	3,200
1907	(154)	336,448	100.00	125.00	150.00	200.00	3,200

INDIAN HEAD TYPE 1908-1929

Bela Lyon Pratt was the designer of this and the half eagle piece. The coin has no raised milling and the main devices and legends are incuse.

VF-20 VERY FINE—*Hair cord knot distinct. Feathers at top of head clear. Cheekbone worn.*

EF-40 EXTREMELY FINE—*Cheekbone, war bonnet and headband feathers slightly worn.*

AU-50 ABOUT UNCIRCULATED—*Trace of wear on cheekbone and headdress.*

MS-60 UNCIRCULATED—*No trace of wear. Light blemishes.*

Mint mark location is on reverse left of fasces.

		Quan. Minted	VF-20	EF-40	AU-50	MS-60	Matte Proof-63
1908	(236)	565,057	$100.00	$110.00	$130.00	$185.00	$4,200
1909	(139)	441,899	100.00	110.00	130.00	185.00	4,200
1910	(682)	492,682	100.00	110.00	130.00	185.00	4,200
1911	(191)	704,191	100.00	110.00	130.00	185.00	4,200
1911D		55,680	350.00	500.00	750.00	2,100	
1912	(197)	616,197	100.00	110.00	130.00	185.00	4,200
1913	(165)	722,165	100.00	110.00	130.00	185.00	4,500
1914	(117)	240,117	100.00	110.00	130.00	250.00	4,500
1914D		448,000	100.00	110.00	130.00	185.00	
1915	(100)	606,100	100.00	110.00	130.00	185.00	4,500
1925D		578,000	100.00	110.00	130.00	185.00	
1926		446,000	100.00	110.00	130.00	185.00	
1927		388,000	100.00	110.00	130.00	185.00	
1928		416,000	100.00	110.00	130.00	185.00	
1929		532,000	100.00	110.00	130.00	185.00	

THREE DOLLAR GOLD PIECES—1854-1889

The three dollar gold piece was authorized by the Act of February 21, 1853. The coin was first struck in 1854. It was never popular and saw very little circulation.

VF-20 VERY FINE—*Eyebrow, hair about forehead and ear and bottom curl are worn smooth. Curled feather-ends have faint details showing.*

EF-40 EXTREMELY FINE—*Light wear above and to right of eye and on top of curled feathers.*

AU-50 ABOUT UNCIRCULATED—*Trace of wear on top of curled feathers and in hair above and to right of eye.*

MS-60 UNCIRCULATED—*No trace of wear. Light blemishes.*

Mint mark location is on reverse below wreath

	Quan. Minted	VF-20	EF-40	AU-50	MS-60	Proof-63
1854	138,618	$350.00	$450.00	$550.00	$1,250	$15,000
1854D	1,120	3,000	6,000	11,000	16,000	
1854O	24,000	350.00	450.00	600.00	1,500	
1855	50,555	350.00	450.00	550.00	1,250	16,000
1855S	6,600	375.00	475.00	700.00	2,300	

THREE DOLLAR GOLD PIECES

	Quan Minted	VF-20	EF-40	AU-50	MS-60	Proof-63
1856	26,010	$350.00	$450.00	$600.00	$1,500	$12,000
1856S	34,500	350.00	450.00	600.00	1,750	
1857	20,891	350.00	450.00	600.00	1,750	9,000
1857S	14,000	350.00	450.00	600.00	1,900	
1858	2,133	400.00	600.00	850.00	2,200	10,000
1859 (80)	15,638	350.00	450.00	600.00	1,500	8,000
1860 (119)	7,155	350.00	450.00	600.00	1,500	6,500
1860S (2,592 melted at Mint)	7,000	400.00	650.00	800.00	2,300	
1861 (113)	6,072	350.00	450.00	600.00	1,750	6,500
1862 (35)	5,785	350.00	450.00	600.00	1,750	6,500
1863 (39)	5,039	375.00	475.00	650.00	1,850	6,500
1864 (50)	2,680	375.00	475.00	650.00	1,850	6,500
1865 (25)	1,165	450.00	700.00	1,000	3,750	8,000
1866 (30)	4,030	375.00	475.00	650.00	1,850	6,500
1867 (50)	2,650	375.00	475.00	650.00	1,850	6,500
1868 (25)	4,875	375.00	475.00	650.00	1,850	6,500
1869 (25)	2,525	375.00	475.00	650.00	1,850	6,500
1870 (35)	3,535	375.00	475.00	650.00	1,850	6,500
1870S	1		(Unique)			
1871 (30)	1,330	400.00	500.00	700.00	1,850	6,500
1872 (30)	2,030	375.00	475.00	650.00	1,850	6,500
1873 Open 3 (original) (25)	25					16,000
1873 Closed 3		1,200	2,000	2,500	4,500	9,000
1874 (20)	41,820	350.00	400.00	550.00	1,250	8,000
1875 Proofs only (20)	20					——
1876 Proofs only (45)	45					——
1877 (20)	1,488	400.00	700.00	1,250	2,500	9,000
1878 (20)	82,324	350.00	450.00	550.00	1,250	6,000
1879 (30)	3,030	350.00	450.00	600.00	1,500	7,000
1880 (36)	1,036	375.00	475.00	650.00	1,500	7,000
1881 (54)	554	500.00	700.00	1,300	2,500	7,500
1882 (76)	1,576	350.00	450.00	600.00	1,500	5,500
1883 (89)	989	375.00	475.00	650.00	1,750	5,500
1884 (106)	1,106	375.00	475.00	650.00	1,500	5,500
1885 (109)	910	500.00	700.00	900.00	2,300	5,500
1886 (142)	1,142	375.00	475.00	650.00	1,500	5,500
1887 (160)	6,160	375.00	450.00	650.00	1,500	5,500
1888 (291)	5,291	375.00	450.00	650.00	1,500	5,500
1889 (129)	2,429	375.00	450.00	650.00	1,500	5,500

FOUR DOLLAR GOLD OR "STELLA"

These pattern coins were first suggested by the Hon. John A. Kasson, then U.S. Minister to Austria; and it was through the efforts of Dr. W. W. Hubbell, who patented the goloid metal used in making the goloid metric dollars, that we have these beautiful and interesting pieces. Only those struck in gold are listed.

	Quan. Minted	VF-20	EF-40	Proof-60
1879 Flowing hair	425	$7,500	$12,500	$17,500
1879 Coiled hair	10	17,500	25,000	42,000
1880 Flowing hair	15	11,000	15,000	27,000
1880 Coiled hair	10	20,000	30,000	50,000

HALF EAGLES — 1795-1929

($5.00 GOLD PIECES)

The half eagle was the first gold coin struck for the United States. The $5.00 piece was authorized to be coined by the Act of April 2, 1792, and the first type weighed 135 grains, 916 2/3 fine. The weight was changed by the Act of June 28, 1834 to 129 grains, 899.225 fine. Fineness became .900 by the Act of January 18, 1837.

CAPPED BUST TO RIGHT, SMALL EAGLE 1795-1798

F-12 FINE—*Hair worn smooth but with distinct outline. For heraldic type, E PLURIBUS UNUM is faint but readable.*
VF-20 VERY FINE—*Slight to noticeable wear on high spots such as hair, turban, eagle's head and wings.*
EF-40 EXTREMELY FINE—*Slight wear on hair and highest part of cheek.*
MS-60 UNCIRCULATED—*No trace of wear. Light blemishes.*

	Quan. Minted	*F-12*	*VF-20*	*EF-40*	*MS-60*
1795 Small eagle	8,707	$2,500	$4,000	$6,000	$12,000

1796, 6 over 5

1797, 15 Stars

1797, 16 Stars

1796, 6 over 5	6,196	2,500	4,000	5,500	14,000
1797, 15 stars		3,500	5,000	7,500	18,000
1797, 16 stars All kinds	3,609	3,750	5,500	8,200	17,000
1798 Small eagle (7 known)		—	—	—	—

CAPPED BUST TO RIGHT, HERALDIC EAGLE 1795-1807

1795 Heraldic eagle		3,750	5,500	8,500	18,000
1797, 7 over 5		3,500	5,250	8,000	14,000
1798 13 star reverse	24,867	650.00	900.00	1,400	4,000
1798 14 star reverse		1,000	1,800	2,500	5,500
1799	7,451	650.00	900.00	1,400	4,500
1800	37,628	650.00	900.00	1,400	4,000
1802, 2 over 1	53,176	650.00	900.00	1,400	4,000
1803, 3 over 2	33,506	650.00	900.00	1,400	4,000

HALF EAGLES

	Quan. Minted	F-12	VF-20	EF-40	MS-60
1804	30,475	$650.00	$900.00	$1,400	$4,200
1805	33,183	650.00	900.00	1,400	4,200
1806	64,093	650.00	900.00	1,400	4,200
1807	32,488	650.00	900.00	1,400	4,200

CAPPED DRAPED BUST TO LEFT 1807-1812

F-12 FINE—*LIBERTY readable but partly weak.*

VF-20 VERY FINE—*Headband edges slightly worn. LIBERTY is bold.*

EF-40 EXTREMELY FINE—*Slight wear on highest portions of hair. 80% of major curls are plain.*

MS-60 UNCIRCULATED—*No trace of wear. Light blemishes.*

	Quan. Minted	F-12	VF-20	EF-40	MS-60
1807	51,605	650.00	900.00	1,600	4,500
1808, 8 over 7	55,578 (1808, 8 over 7 and 1808)	600.00	850.00	1,100	3,500
1808		600.00	850.00	1,100	3,200
1809, 9 over 8	33,875	600.00	850.00	1,100	3,500
1810	100,287	600.00	850.00	1,100	3,500
1811	99,581	600.00	850.00	1,100	3,500
1812	58,087	600.00	850.00	1,100	3,500

CAPPED HEAD TO LEFT 1813-1829

	Quan. Minted	F-12	VF-20	EF-40	MS-60
1813	95,428	650.00	950.00	1,600	4,000
1814, 4 over 3	15,454	700.00	1,200	1,800	6,500
1815	635			25,000	75,000
1818	48,588	650.00	950.00	1,600	4,000
1819	51,723			20,000	30,000
1820	263,806	650.00	1,000	1,750	4,500
1821	34,641	1,400	3,200	4,750	14,000
1822	17,796	—	—	—	—
1823	14,485	1,100	1,750	2,250	8,000
1824	17,340	3,000	4,500	9,000	15,000
1825, 5 over 1	29,060 (1825, 5 over 1 and 1825, 5 over 4)	1,650	2,500	4,250	11,000
1825, 5 over 4				—	
1826	18,069	1,800	3,250	4,500	12,000
1827	24,913	3,000	5,000	12,000	18,000
1828, 8 over 7	28,029 (1828, 8 over 7 and 1828)	2,700	4,000	8,000	14,000
1828		3,000	4,500	9,000	18,000
1829 Large date	57,442	—	—	—	—

CAPPED HEAD TO LEFT (reduced diameter) 1829-1834

	Quan. Minted	F-12	VF-20	EF-40	MS-60
1829 Small date	inc. above		11,000	17,000	35,000
1830	126,351	1,300	2,250	3,500	7,500
1831	140,594	1,300	2,250	3,500	7,000
1832 Curved-base 2, 12 stars (4 known)	157,487	—	—	—	—
1832 Square-base 2, 13 stars		2,000	4,000	6,000	9,000
1833	193,630	1,300	2,500	3,500	7,000
1834	50,141	1,300	2,500	3,500	7,500

HALF EAGLES

CLASSIC HEAD TYPE 1834-1838

	Quan. Minted	F-12	VF-20	EF-40	MS-60
1834	657,460	$135.00	$175.00	$300.00	$1,000
1835	371,534	135.00	175.00	300.00	1,000
1836	553,147	135.00	175.00	300.00	1,000
1837	207,121	135.00	175.00	300.00	1,000
1838	286,588	135.00	175.00	300.00	1,000
1838C	17,179	400.00	500.00	1,000	3,500
1838D	20,583	400.00	500.00	1,000	3,500

CORONET TYPE, No Motto Above Eagle 1839-1866

VF-20 VERY FINE—*LIBERTY bold. Major lines show in neck hair.*

EF-40 EXTREMELY FINE—*Neck hair details clear. Slight wear on top and lower part of coronet, and hair.*

AU-50 ABOUT UNCIRCULATED—*Trace of wear on coronet and hair above eye.*

MS-60 UNCIRCULATED—*No trace of wear. Light blemishes.*

Mint mark above date 1839 only, below eagle 1840-1908.

	Quan. Minted	VF-20	EF-40	AU-50	MS-60
1839	118,143	$100.00	$125.00	$275.00	$1,000
1839C	17,205	150.00	300.00	600.00	1,400
1839D	18,939	150.00	300.00	600.00	1,400
1840	137,382	100.00	120.00	250.00	850.00
1840C	18,992	150.00	300.00	600.00	1,400
1840D	22,896	150.00	300.00	600.00	1,400
1840O	40,120	125.00	200.00	500.00	1,000
1841	15,833	125.00	200.00	500.00	1,000
1841C	21,467	150.00	300.00	600.00	1,400
1841D	29,392	150.00	300.00	600.00	1,400

1842 Large Date — Large letters — Small Letters

	Quan. Minted	VF-20	EF-40	AU-50	MS-60
1842 Small Letters	27,578	100.00	120.00	200.00	900.00
1842 Large letters		100.00	120.00	200.00	900.00
1842C Small date	27,432	375.00	600.00	900.00	1,800
1842C Large date		125.00	200.00	500.00	1,200
1842D Small date	59,608	125.00	200.00	500.00	1,300
1842D Large date		150.00	350.00	700.00	1,800
1842O	16,400	110.00	150.00	400.00	1,200
1843	611,205	100.00	120.00	175.00	700.00
1843C	44,277	125.00	200.00	400.00	1,300

HALF EAGLES

	Quan. Minted	VF-20	EF-40	AU-50	MS-60
1843D	98,452	$125.00	$200.00	$450.00	$1,200
1843O Small letters	19,075	110.00	150.00	350.00	900.00
1843O Large letters	82,000	110.00	120.00	300.00	1,000
1844	340,330	100.00	120.00	175.00	800.00
1844C	23,631	135.00	275.00	600.00	1,600
1844D	88,982	125.00	200.00	450.00	1,200
1844O	364,600	100.00	120.00	200.00	800.00
1845	417,099	100.00	120.00	175.00	700.00
1845D	90,629	125.00	200.00	300.00	1,000
1845O	41,000	110.00	120.00	200.00	800.00
1846	395,942	100.00	120.00	175.00	700.00
1846C	12,995	150.00	300.00	700.00	1,500
1846D	80,294	125.00	200.00	450.00	1,200
1846O	58,000	110.00	120.00	200.00	1,000
1847	915,981	100.00	120.00	175.00	700.00
1847C	84,151	125.00	200.00	450.00	1,200
1847D	64,405	125.00	200.00	450.00	1,200
1847O	12,000	125.00	225.00	500.00	1,300
1848	260,775	100.00	120.00	175.00	700.00
1848C	64,472	125.00	200.00	450.00	1,200
1848D	47,465	125.00	200.00	450.00	1,200
1849	133,070	100.00	120.00	175.00	800.00
1849C	64,823	125.00	200.00	450.00	1,200
1849D	39,036	125.00	200.00	450.00	1,200
1850	64,491	100.00	120.00	175.00	700.00
1850C	63,591	125.00	200.00	450.00	1,200
1850D	43,984	125.00	200.00	450.00	1,200
1851	377,505	100.00	120.00	175.00	700.00
1851C	49,176	125.00	200.00	450.00	1,200
1851D	62,710	125.00	200.00	450.00	1,200
1851O	41,000	110.00	125.00	250.00	1,000
1852	573,901	100.00	120.00	175.00	700.00
1852C	72,574	125.00	200.00	450.00	1,200
1852D	91,584	125.00	200.00	450.00	1,200
1853	305,770	100.00	120.00	175.00	700.00
1853C	65,571	125.00	200.00	450.00	1,200
1853D	89,678	125.00	200.00	450.00	1,200
1854	160,675	100.00	120.00	175.00	700.00
1854C	39,283	125.00	200.00	450.00	1,200
1854D	56,413	125.00	200.00	450.00	1,200
1854O	46,000	110.00	125.00	275.00	900.00
1854S	268	—	—	—	—
1855	117,098	100.00	120.00	175.00	700.00
1855C	39,788	125.00	200.00	450.00	1,200
1855D	22,432	125.00	200.00	450.00	1,200
1855O	11,100	125.00	200.00	450.00	1,200
1855S	61,000	110.00	120.00	200.00	900.00
1856	197,990	100.00	120.00	175.00	700.00
1856C	28,457	125.00	200.00	450.00	1,200
1856D	19,786	125.00	200.00	450.00	1,200
1856O	10,000	150.00	300.00	500.00	1,300
1856S	105,100	110.00	125.00	200.00	900.00
1857	98,188	100.00	120.00	175.00	700.00
1857C	31,360	125.00	200.00	450.00	1,200
1857D	17,046	125.00	200.00	450.00	1,200
1857O	13,000	125.00	200.00	500.00	1,300
1857S	87,000	110.00	125.00	250.00	900.00
1858	15,136	110.00	125.00	250.00	800.00

Values of common gold coins are based on the prevailing price of gold bullion, and will vary according to current market price. See Bullion Chart.

HALF EAGLES

		Quan. Minted	VF-20	EF-40	AU-50	MS-60	Proof-63
1858C		38,856	$125.00	$200.00	$450.00	$1,200	
1858D		15,362	125.00	200.00	450.00	1,200	
1858S		18,600	110.00	125.00	275.00	900.00	
1859	(80)	16,814	110.00	125.00	250.00	900.00	$9,000
1859C		31,847	125.00	200.00	450.00	1,200	
1859D		10,366	150.00	300.00	600.00	1,400	
1859S		13,220	110.00	150.00	400.00	1,000	
1860	(62)	19,825	110.00	125.00	250.00	800.00	8,000
1860C		14,813	125.00	200.00	450.00	1,200	
1860D		14,635	125.00	200.00	450.00	1,400	
1860S		21,200	150.00	250.00	500.00	—	
1861	(66)	688,150	100.00	120.00	175.00	700.00	8,000
1861C		6,879	750.00	1,100	1,900	3,500	
1861D		1,597	2,000	4,000	6,000	15,000	
1861S		18,000	150.00	300.00	650.00	—	
1862	(35)	4,465	125.00	200.00	450.00	—	8,000
1862S		9,500	150.00	300.00	700.00	—	
1863	(30)	2,472	150.00	350.00	800.00	1,300	8,000
1863S		17,000	110.00	150.00	350.00	950.00	
1864	(50)	4,220	125.00	200.00	450.00	1,400	8,000
1864S		3,888	400.00	800.00	1,500	—	
1865	(25)	1,295	325.00	425.00	800.00	2,100	8,000
1865S		27,612	125.00	175.00	400.00	—	
1866S		9,000	125.00	200.00	600.00	—	

Motto Above Eagle 1866-1908

VF-20 VERY FINE—*Half of hairlines above coronet missing. Hair curls under ear evident, but worn. Motto and its ribbon sharp.*

EF-40 EXTREMELY FINE—*Small amount of wear on top of hair and below L in LIBERTY. Wear evident on wing tips and neck of eagle.*

AU-50 ABOUT UNCIRCULATED—*Trace of wear on tip of coronet and hair above eye.*

MS-60 UNCIRCULATED—*No trace of wear. Light blemishes.*

		Quan. Minted	VF-20	EF-40	AU-50	MS-60	Proof-63
1866	(30)	6,730	125.00	200.00	350.00	1,000	7,200
1866S		34,920	110.00	150.00	300.00	600.00	
1867	(50)	6,920	120.00	170.00	300.00	850.00	6,500
1867S		29,000	125.00	200.00	350.00	—	
1868	(25)	5,725	125.00	200.00	350.00	900.00	7,200
1868S		52,000	110.00	175.00	300.00	—	
1869	(25)	1,785	150.00	275.00	450.00	1,200	7,200
1869S		31,000	110.00	120.00	200.00	600.00	
1870	(35)	4,035	110.00	150.00	275.00	700.00	7,200
1870CC		7,675	700.00	1,400	2,500		
1870S		17,000	125.00	150.00	300.00	—	
1871	(30)	3,230	125.00	175.00	400.00	—	7,200
1871CC		20,770	150.00	275.00	500.00	1,300	
1871S		25,000	110.00	120.00	200.00	700.00	
1872	(30)	1,690	200.00	275.00	500.00	1,300	7,200
1872CC		16,980	200.00	275.00	500.00	1,200	
1872S		36,400	100.00	120.00	200.00	500.00	
1873	(25)	112,505	90.00	100.00	125.00	150.00	7,200
1873CC		7,416	200.00	400.00	800.00	1,600	
1873S		31,000	110.00	120.00	250.00	600.00	
1874	(20)	3,508	120.00	170.00	300.00	800.00	7,500

Values of common gold coins are based on the prevailing price of gold bullion, and will vary according to current market price. See Bullion Chart.

		Quan Minted	VF-20	EF-40	AU-50	MS-60	Proof-63
1874CC		21,198	$120.00	$170.00	$300.00	$900.00	
1874S		16,000	110.00	150.00	300.00	——	
1875	(20)	220		——	——	——	——
1875CC		11,828	150.00	350.00	550.00	1,200	
1875S		9,000	125.00	275.00	425.00	1,000	
1876	(45)	1,477	200.00	350.00	650.00	1,400	$7,200
1876CC		6,887	150.00	275.00	550.00	1,200	
1876S		4,000	150.00	275.00	550.00	1,200	
1877	(20)	1,152	200.00	350.00	700.00	1,700	7,500
1877CC		8,680	150.00	275.00	550.00	1,200	
1877S		26,700	90.00	100.00	125.00	200.00	
1878	(20)	131,740	90.00	100.00	125.00	150.00	7,000
1878CC		9,054	400.00	900.00	1,600		
1878S		144,700	90.00	100.00	125.00	150.00	
1879	(30)	301,950	90.00	100.00	125.00	150.00	7,000
1879CC		17,281	125.00	150.00	300.00	650.00	
1879S		426,200	90.00	110.00	125.00	150.00	
1880	(36)	3,166,436	90.00	110.00	125.00	150.00	6,500
1880CC		51,017	120.00	170.00	225.00	500.00	
1880S		1,348,900	90.00	110.00	125.00	150.00	
1881	(42)	5,708,802	90.00	110.00	125.00	150.00	6,500
1881CC		13,886	125.00	150.00	300.00	650.00	
1881S		969,000	90.00	110.00	125.00	150.00	
1882	(48)	2,514,568	90.00	110.00	125.00	150.00	6,500
1882CC		82,817	110.00	120.00	175.00	400.00	
1882S		969,000	90.00	110.00	125.00	150.00	
1883	(61)	233,461	90.00	100.00	125.00	150.00	6,500
1883CC		12,958	125.00	150.00	300.00	475.00	
1883S		83,200	90.00	100.00	125.00	150.00	
1884	(48)	191,078	90.00	100.00	125.00	150.00	6,000
1884CC		16,402	125.00	150.00	300.00	475.00	
1884S		177,000	90.00	100.00	125.00	150.00	
1885	(66)	601,506	90.00	100.00	125.00	150.00	6,000
1885S		1,211,500	90.00	100.00	125.00	150.00	
1886	(72)	388,432	90.00	100.00	125.00	150.00	6,000
1886S		3,268,000	90.00	100.00	125.00	150.00	
1887 Proofs only	(87)	87					13,000
1887S		1,912,000	90.00	100.00	125.00	150.00	
1888	(95)	18,296	110.00	130.00	140.00	250.00	6,000
1888S		293,900	90.00	100.00	125.00	150.00	
1889	(45)	7,565	110.00	125.00	200.00	500.00	6,000
1890	(88)	4,328	110.00	200.00	300.00	600.00	6,000
1890CC		53,800	90.00	110.00	175.00	250.00	
1891	(53)	61,413	90.00	100.00	125.00	150.00	6,000
1891CC		208,000	90.00	110.00	150.00	200.00	
1892	(92)	753,572	90.00	100.00	125.00	150.00	6,000
1892CC		82,968	90.00	110.00	150.00	200.00	
1892O		10,000	200.00	350.00	600.00	1,200	
1892S		298,400	90.00	100.00	125.00	150.00	
1893	(77)	1,528,197	90.00	100.00	125.00	150.00	6,000
1893CC		60,000	90.00	100.00	150.00	300.00	
1893O		110,000	90.00	100.00	175.00	325.00	
1893S		224,000	90.00	100.00	125.00	150.00	
1894	(75)	957,955	90.00	100.00	125.00	150.00	6,000
1894O		16,600	110.00	115.00	175.00	350.00	
1894S		55,900	100.00	115.00	125.00	150.00	
1895	(81)	1,345,936	90.00	100.00	125.00	150.00	5,500
1895S		112,000	90.00	100.00	125.00	150.00	
1896	(103)	59,063	90.00	100.00	125.00	150.00	5,500

Values of common gold coins are based on the prevailing price of gold bullion, and will vary according to current market price. See Bullion Chart.

HALF EAGLES

		Quan. Minted	VF-20	EF-40	AU-50	MS-60	Proof-63
1896S		155,400	$90.00	$100.00	$125.00	$150.00	
1897	(83)	867,883	90.00	100.00	125.00	150.00	$5,500
1897S		354,000	90.00	100.00	125.00	150.00	
1898	(75)	633,495	90.00	100.00	125.00	150.00	5,500
1898S		1,397,400	90.00	100.00	125.00	150.00	
1899	(99)	1,710,729	90.00	100.00	125.00	150.00	5,500
1899S		1,545,000	90.00	100.00	125.00	150.00	
1900	(230)	1,405,730	90.00	100.00	125.00	150.00	5,500
1900S		329,000	90.00	100.00	125.00	150.00	
1901	(140)	616,040	90.00	100.00	125.00	150.00	5,500
1901S, 1 over 0		3,648,000	90.00	100.00	125.00	150.00	
1901S			90.00	100.00	125.00	150.00	
1902	(162)	172,562	90.00	100.00	125.00	150.00	5,500
1902S		939,000	90.00	100.00	125.00	150.00	
1903	(154)	227,024	90.00	100.00	125.00	150.00	5,500
1903S		1,855,000	90.00	100.00	125.00	150.00	
1904	(136)	392,136	90.00	100.00	125.00	150.00	5,500
1904S		97,000	90.00	100.00	125.00	150.00	
1905	(108)	302,308	90.00	100.00	125.00	150.00	5,500
1905S		880,700	90.00	100.00	125.00	150.00	
1906	(85)	348,820	90.00	100.00	125.00	150.00	5,500
1906D		320,000	90.00	100.00	125.00	150.00	
1906S		598,000	90.00	100.00	125.00	150.00	
1907	(92)	626,192	90.00	100.00	125.00	150.00	5,500
1907D		888,000	90.00	100.00	125.00	150.00	
1908		421,874	90.00	100.00	125.00	150.00	

INDIAN HEAD TYPE 1908-1929

This type conforms to the quarter eagle of the same date. The incuse designs and lettering make this a unique series, along with the quarter eagle, in United States coinage.

VF-20 VERY FINE—*Noticeable wear on large middle feathers and tip of eagle's wing.*

EF-40 EXTREMELY FINE—*Cheekbone, war bonnet and headband feathers slightly worn. Feathers on eagle's upper wing show considerable wear.*

AU-50 ABOUT UNCIRCULATED—*Trace of wear on cheekbone and headdress.*

MS-60 UNCIRCULATED—*No trace of wear. Light blemishes.*

Scarcer coins with well struck mint marks command higher prices.

Mint mark location

		Quan. Minted	VF-20	EF-40	AU-50	MS-60	Matte Proof-63
1908	(167)	578,012	$135.00	$150.00	$175.00	$300.00	$5,000
1908D		148,000	135.00	150.00	175.00	300.00	
1908S		82,000	150.00	200.00	300.00	1,500	
1909	(78)	627,138	135.00	150.00	175.00	300.00	5,000
1909D		3,423,560	135.00	150.00	175.00	300.00	
1909O		34,200	275.00	500.00	900.00	4,000	
1909S		297,200	135.00	150.00	175.00	900.00	
1910	(250)	604,250	135.00	150.00	175.00	300.00	5,000
1910D		193,600	135.00	150.00	175.00	375.00	

Values of common gold coins are based on the prevailing price of gold bullion, and will vary according to current market price. See Bullion Chart.

HALF EAGLES

	Quan. Minted	VF-20	EF-40	AU-50	MS-60	Matte Proof-63
1910S	770,200	$135.00	$150.00	$175.00	$1,000	
1911 (139)	915,139	135.00	150.00	175.00	300.00	$5,000
1911D	72,500	150.00	200.00	350.00	2,700	
1911S	1,416,000	135.00	150.00	175.00	750.00	
1912 (144)	790,144	135.00	150.00	175.00	300.00	5,000
1912S	392,000	135.00	150.00	175.00	800.00	
1913 (99)	916,000	135.00	150.00	175.00	300.00	5,000
1913S	408,000	135.00	150.00	275.00	1,600	
1914 (125)	247,125	135.00	150.00	175.00	300.00	5,000
1914D	247,000	135.00	150.00	175.00	300.00	
1914S	263,000	135.00	150.00	175.00	400.00	
1915 (75)	588,075	135.00	150.00	175.00	300.00	5,000
1915S	164,000	135.00	150.00	225.00	1,300	
1916S	240,000	135.00	150.00	175.00	600.00	
1929	662,000	1,400	2,000	2,750	4,500	

Values of common gold coins are based on the prevailing price of gold bullion, and will vary according to current market price. See Bullion Chart.

EAGLES ($10.00 Gold Pieces) — 1795-1933

Coinage authority including specified weights and fineness of the eagle conforms to that of the half eagle. The small eagle reverse was used until 1797 when the large, heraldic eagle replaced it.

CAPPED BUST TO RIGHT, SMALL EAGLE 1795-1797

F-12 FINE—*Details on turban and head obliterated.*

VF-20 VERY FINE—*Neck hairlines and details under turban and over forehead are worn but distinguishable.*

EF-40 EXTREMELY FINE—*Definite wear on hair to left of eye and strand of hair across and around turban, also on eagle's wing tips.*

MS-60 UNCIRCULATED—*No trace of wear. Light blemishes.*

	Quan. Minted	F-12	VF-20	EF-40	MS-60
1795	5,583	$3,000	$4,500	$7,000	$16,000
1796	4,146	3,000	4,500	7,000	16,000
1797 Small eagle	3,615	3,000	4,500	7,500	18,000

CAPPED BUST TO RIGHT, HERALDIC EAGLE 1797-1804

	Quan. Minted	F-12	VF-20	EF-40	MS-60
1797 Large eagle	10,940	1,100	1,800	2,000	8,000
1798, 8 over 7, 9 stars left, 4 right	900	2,400	4,250	6,500	13,000
1798, 8 over 7, 7 stars left, 6 right	842	6,000	12,000	—	—

EAGLES

	Quan. Minted	F-12	VF-20	EF-40	MS-60
1799	37,449	$1,000	$1,600	$2,500	$7,000
1800	5,999	1,000	1,600	2,500	7,500

	Quan. Minted	F-12	VF-20	EF-40	MS-60
1801	44,344	1,000	1,600	2,500	7,000
1803	15,017	1,000	1,600	2,500	7,000
1804	3,757	1,750	2,500	4,000	11,000

CORONET TYPE, No Motto Above Eagle 1838-1866

In 1838 the weight and diameter of the eagle were reduced and the obverse and reverse were redesigned. Liberty now faces left and the word LIBERTY is placed on the coronet.

VF-20 VERY FINE—*Hairlines above coronet partly worn. Curls under ear worn but defined.*

EF-40 EXTREMELY FINE—*Small amount of wear on top of hair and below L in LIBERTY. Wear evident on wing tips and neck of eagle.*

AU-50 ABOUT UNCIRCULATED—*Trace of wear on tip of coronet and hair above eye.*

MS-60 UNCIRCULATED—*No trace of wear. Light blemishes.*

Mint mark location on reverse below eagle

	Quan. Minted	VF-20	EF-40	AU-50	MS-60
1838	7,200	$300.00	$600.00	$1,000	$4,000
1839 Large letters	25,801	225.00	400.00	750.00	2,800
1839 Small letters	12,447	275.00	500.00	1,000	3,000
1840	47,338	190.00	225.00	350.00	1,800
1841	63,131	190.00	225.00	350.00	1,600
1841O	2,500	190.00	550.00	700.00	3,200
1842	81,507	190.00	225.00	325.00	1,500
1842O	27,400	190.00	225.00	350.00	2,000
1843	75,462	190.00	225.00	325.00	1,500
1843O	175,162	190.00	225.00	325.00	1,600
1844	6,361	190.00	400.00	550.00	2,000
1844O	118,700	190.00	225.00	325.00	1,600
1845	26,153	190.00	225.00	325.00	1,700
1845O	47,500	190.00	225.00	325.00	1,600
1846	20,095	190.00	225.00	325.00	1,600
1846O	81,780	190.00	225.00	300.00	1,500
1847	862,258	190.00	225.00	300.00	1,500
1847O	571,500	190.00	225.00	325.00	1,700
1848	145,484	190.00	225.00	300.00	1,500
1848O	35,850	190.00	225.00	300.00	1,500
1849	653,618	190.00	225.00	325.00	1,700

EAGLES

	Quan. Minted	VF-20	EF-40	AU-50	MS-60	Proof-63
1849O	23,900	$200.00	$225.00	$300.00	$1,500	
1850	291,451	190.00	225.00	300.00	1,500	
1850O	57,500	190.00	225.00	300.00	1,500	
1851	176,328	190.00	225.00	300.00	1,500	
1851O	263,000	190.00	225.00	300.00	1,500	
1852	263,106	190.00	225.00	300.00	1,500	
1852O	18,000	190.00	250.00	350.00	1,600	
1853, 3 over 2	201,253	225.00	400.00			
1853		190.00	225.00	300.00	1,500	
1853O	51,000	190.00	225.00	300.00	1,500	
1854	54,250	190.00	225.00	300.00	1,500	
1854O	52,500	190.00	225.00	300.00	1,500	
1854S	123,826	190.00	225.00	300.00	1,500	
1855	121,701	190.00	225.00	300.00	1,500	—
1855O	18,000	220.00	250.00	350.00	1,600	
1855S	9,000	250.00	400.00	600.00	2,750	—
1856	60,490	190.00	225.00	300.00	1,500	
1856O	14,500	190.00	250.00	300.00	1,600	
1856S	68,000	190.00	225.00	300.00	1,500	
1857	16,606	190.00	225.00	300.00	1,500	—
1857O	5,500	300.00	600.00	800.00	2,750	
1857S	26,000	190.00	225.00	300.00	1,500	
1858	2,521	2,000	3,000	4,500	14,000	—
1858O	20,000	190.00	225.00	300.00	1,600	
1858S	11,800	210.00	250.00	350.00	1,800	
1859 (80)	16,093	190.00	225.00	300.00	1,500	$5,000
1859O	2,300	550.00	900.00	1,500	3,300	
1859S	7,000	300.00	550.00	700.00	2,200	
1860 (50)	15,105	190.00	225.00	300.00	1,600	4,500
1860O	11,100	210.00	250.00	350.00	1,800	
1860S	5,000	300.00	600.00	750.00	3,000	
1861 (69)	113,233	190.00	225.00	300.00	1,500	4,500
1861S	15,500	210.00	225.00	300.00	1,500	
1862 (35)	10,995	210.00	250.00	300.00	1,500	4,500
1862S	12,500	210.00	225.00	300.00	1,500	
1863 (30)	1,248	1,000	2,200	3,000	4,000	7,200
1863S	10,000	275.00	400.00	550.00	1,600	
1864 (50)	3,580	400.00	650.00	900.00	2,300	6,500
1864S	2,500	900.00	1,600			
1865 (25)	4,005	340.00	550.00	700.00	2,300	5,500
1865S	16,700	340.00	550.00	700.00	2,300	
1866S	8,500	400.00	800.00	1,200	2,600	

Motto Above Eagle 1866-1907

Mint mark location on the reverse below eagle.

VF-20 VERY FINE—*Half of hairlines over coronet visible. Curls under ear worn but defined. IN GOD WE TRUST and its ribbon are sharp.*

EF-40 EXTREMELY FINE—*Small amount of wear on top of hair and below L in LIBERTY. Wear evident on wing tips and neck of eagle.*

AU-50 ABOUT UNCIRCULATED—*Trace of wear on hair above eye and on coronet.*

MS-60 UNCIRCULATED—*No trace of wear. Light blemishes.*

EAGLES

		Quan. Minted	VF-20	EF-40	AU-50	MS-60	Proof-63
1866	(30)	3,780	$225.00	$275.00	$450.00	$1,000	$7,500
1866S		11,500	210.00	250.00	300.00	700.00	
1867	(50)	3,140	225.00	275.00	450.00	1,000	6,500
1867S		9,000	210.00	250.00	300.00	700.00	
1868	(25)	10,655	210.00	250.00	300.00	600.00	6,500
1868S		13,500	190.00	250.00	300.00	600.00	
1869	(25)	1,855	300.00	500.00	800.00	1,200	6,500
1869S		6,430	210.00	250.00	300.00	700.00	
1870	(35)	4,025	225.00	300.00	450.00	750.00	6,500
1870CC		5,908	600.00	1,500	2,500		
1870S		8,000	210.00	250.00	300.00	700.00	
1871	(30)	1,820	300.00	500.00	800.00	2,100	6,500
1871CC		8,085	300.00	600.00	900.00		
1871S		16,500	190.00	250.00	300.00	600.00	
1872	(30)	1,650	400.00	700.00	1,150	2,000	6,500
1872CC		4,600	275.00	475.00	600.00	1,800	
1872S		17,300	200.00	250.00	300.00	550.00	
1873	(25)	825	650.00	1,200	2,100	4,500	14,500
1873CC		4,543	450.00	900.00	1,600	3,300	
1873S		12,000	210.00	250.00	300.00	550.00	
1874	(20)	53,160	180.00	185.00	190.00	225.00	7,000
1874CC		16,767	225.00	220.00	275.00	700.00	
1874S		10,000	210.00	220.00	275.00	550.00	
1875	(20)	120		—	—		—
1875CC		7,715	250.00	275.00	550.00	1,200	
1876	(45)	732	550.00	1,200	1,900	4,200	8,500
1876CC		4,696	300.00	600.00	725.00	1,600	
1876S		5,000	210.00	250.00	425.00	900.00	
1877	(20)	817	600.00	1,100	1,800	4,500	13,000
1877CC		3,332	300.00	550.00	800.00	2,000	
1877S		17,000	175.00	200.00	230.00	350.00	
1878	(20)	73,800	175.00	180.00	190.00	200.00	7,000
1878CC		3,244	300.00	550.00	1,000	2,000	
1878S		26,100	175.00	180.00	190.00	200.00	
1879	(30)	384,770	175.00	180.00	190.00	200.00	6,000
1879CC		1,762	1,100	2,500	3,500	7,250	
1879O		1,500	500.00	900.00	1,600	4,250	
1879S		224,000	175.00	180.00	190.00	200.00	
1880		1,644,876	175.00	180.00	190.00	200.00	6,000
1880CC		11,190	175.00	190.00	275.00	600.00	
1880O		9,200	175.00	190.00	200.00	400.00	
1880S		506,250	175.00	185.00	190.00	200.00	
1881	(40)	3,877,260	175.00	180.00	190.00	200.00	6,000
1881CC		24,015	175.00	190.00	275.00	375.00	
1881O		8,350	175.00	225.00	300.00	550.00	
1881S		970,000	175.00	180.00	190.00	200.00	
1882	(40)	2,324,480	175.00	180.00	190.00	200.00	6,000
1882CC		6,764	175.00	250.00	300.00	600.00	
1882O		10,820	175.00	190.00	250.00	350.00	
1882S		132,000	175.00	180.00	190.00	200.00	
1883	(40)	208,740	175.00	180.00	190.00	200.00	6,000
1883CC		12,000	175.00	250.00	300.00	600.00	
1883O		800	950.00	1,850	3,100	6,500	
1883S		38,000	175.00	180.00	190.00	200.00	
1884	(45)	76,905	175.00	180.00	190.00	200.00	11,000
1884CC		9,925	175.00	250.00	300.00	600.00	
1884S		124,250	175.00	180.00	190.00	200.00	
1885	(65)	253,527	175.00	180.00	190.00	200.00	6,000
1885S		228,000	175.00	180.00	190.00	200.00	

Values of common gold coins are based on the prevailing price of gold bullion, and will vary according to current market price. See Bullion Chart.

EAGLES

	Quan. Minted	VF-20	EF-40	AU-50	MS-60	Proof-63
1886 . . . . . (60)	236,160	$175.00	$180.00	$190.00	$200.00	$6,000
1886S	826,000	175.00	180.00	190.00	200.00	
1887 . . . . . (80)	53,680	175.00	180.00	190.00	200.00	6,000
1887S	817,000	175.00	180.00	190.00	200.00	
1888 . . . . . (75)	132,996	175.00	180.00	190.00	200.00	6,000
1888O	21,335	175.00	180.00	190.00	300.00	
1888S	648,700	175.00	180.00	190.00	200.00	
1889 . . . . . (45)	4,485	175.00	250.00	300.00	550.00	6,000
1889S	425,400	175.00	180.00	190.00	200.00	
1890 . . . . . (63)	58,043	175.00	180.00	190.00	375.00	6,000
1890CC	17,500	175.00	180.00	190.00	300.00	
1891 . . . . . (48)	91,868	175.00	180.00	190.00	200.00	6,000
1891CC	103,732	175.00	180.00	200.00	325.00	
1892 . . . . . (72)	797,552	175.00	180.00	190.00	200.00	6,000
1892CC	40,000	175.00	180.00	190.00	400.00	
1892O	28,688	175.00	180.00	190.00	200.00	
1892S	115,500	175.00	180.00	190.00	200.00	
1893 . . . . . (55)	1,840,895	175.00	180.00	190.00	200.00	5,500
1893CC	14,000	175.00	180.00	300.00	450.00	
1893O	17,000	175.00	180.00	250.00	350.00	
1893S	141,350	175.00	180.00	190.00	200.00	
1894 . . . . . (43)	2,470,778	175.00	180.00	190.00	200.00	5,500
1894O	107,500	175.00	180.00	190.00	200.00	
1894S	25,000	175.00	180.00	190.00	200.00	
1895 . . . . . (56)	567,826	175.00	180.00	190.00	200.00	5,500
1895O	98,000	175.00	180.00	190.00	200.00	
1895S	49,000	175.00	180.00	190.00	200.00	
1896 . . . . . (78)	76,348	175.00	180.00	190.00	200.00	5,500
1896S	123,750	175.00	180.00	190.00	200.00	
1897 . . . . . (69)	1,000,159	175.00	180.00	190.00	200.00	5,500
1897O	42,500	175.00	180.00	190.00	200.00	
1897S	234,750	175.00	180.00	190.00	200.00	
1898 . . . . . (67)	812,197	175.00	180.00	190.00	200.00	5,500
1898S	473,600	175.00	180.00	190.00	200.00	
1899 . . . . . (86)	1,262,305	175.00	180.00	190.00	200.00	5,500
1899O	37,047	175.00	180.00	190.00	200.00	
1899S	841,000	175.00	180.00	190.00	200.00	
1900 . . . . . (120)	293,960	175.00	180.00	190.00	200.00	5,500
1900S	81,000	175.00	180.00	190.00	200.00	
1901 . . . . . (85)	1,718,825	175.00	180.00	190.00	200.00	5,500
1901O	72,041	175.00	180.00	190.00	200.00	
1901S	2,812,750	175.00	180.00	190.00	200.00	
1902 . . . . . (113)	82,513	175.00	180.00	190.00	200.00	5,500
1902S	469,500	175.00	180.00	190.00	200.00	
1903 . . . . . (96)	125,926	175.00	180.00	190.00	200.00	5,500
1903O	112,771	175.00	180.00	190.00	200.00	
1903S	538,000	175.00	180.00	190.00	200.00	
1904 . . . . . (108)	162,038	175.00	180.00	190.00	200.00	5,500
1904O	108,950	175.00	180.00	190.00	200.00	
1905 . . . . . (86)	201,078	175.00	180.00	190.00	200.00	5,500
1905S	369,250	175.00	180.00	190.00	200.00	
1906 . . . . . (77)	165,497	175.00	180.00	190.00	200.00	5,500
1906D	981,000	175.00	180.00	190.00	200.00	
1906O	86,895	175.00	180.00	190.00	200.00	
1906S	457,000	175.00	180.00	190.00	200.00	
1907 . . . . . (74)	1,203,973	175.00	180.00	190.00	200.00	5,500
1907D	1,030,000	175.00	180.00	190.00	200.00	
1907S	210,500	175.00	180.00	190.00	200.00	

Values of common gold coins are based on the prevailing price of gold bullion, and will vary according to current market price. See Bullion Chart.

EAGLES

INDIAN HEAD TYPE 1907-1933

No Motto

With Motto

in god we trust

Mint mark location is above left tip of branch on 1908D no motto, and at left of arrow points thereafter.

VF-20 VERY FINE—*Bonnet feathers worn near band. Hair high points show wear.*

EF-40 EXTREMELY FINE—*Slight wear on cheekbone and headdress feathers. Eagle's eye and left wing will show slight wear.*

AU-50 ABOUT UNCIRCULATED—*Trace of wear on hair above eye and on forehead.*

MS-60 UNCIRCULATED—*No trace of wear. Light blemishes.*

Uncirculated (MS-65) coins are worth substantial premiums.

No Motto on Reverse 1907-1908

	Quan. Minted	*VF-20*	*EF-40*	*AU-50*	*MS-60*	*Proof-63*
1907 Wire rim, periods	500			$2,600	$5,500	$8,000
1907 Rounded rim, periods before and after •E•PLURIBUS•UNUM•	42					15,000
1907 No periods	239,406	$275.00	$325.00	350.00	400.00	
1908 No motto	33,500	275.00	335.00	375.00	600.00	
1908D No motto	210,000	260.00	275.00	325.00	425.00	

Motto on Reverse 1908-1933

		Quan. Minted	*VF-20*	*EF-40*	*AU-50*	*MS-60*	*Matte Proof-63*
1908	(116)	341,486	260.00	275.00	325.00	350.00	7,000
1908D		836,500	260.00	310.00	330.00	425.00	
1908S		59,850	260.00	310.00	330.00	2,000	
1909	(74)	184,863	260.00	310.00	330.00	350.00	7,000
1909D		121,540	260.00	310.00	330.00	450.00	
1909S		292,350	260.00	310.00	330.00	600.00	
1910	(204)	318,704	260.00	310.00	330.00	350.00	7,000
1910D		2,356,640	260.00	310.00	330.00	350.00	
1910S		811,000	260.00	310.00	330.00	600.00	
1911	(95)	505,595	260.00	310.00	330.00	400.00	7,000
1911D		30,100	325.00	400.00	500.00	2,500	
1911S		51,000	260.00	275.00	400.00	1,200	
1912	(83)	405,083	260.00	275.00	330.00	350.00	7,000
1912S		300,000	260.00	275.00	330.00	800.00	
1913	(71)	442,071	260.00	275.00	330.00	350.00	7,000
1913S		66,000	260.00	275.00	400.00	4,500	
1914	(50)	151,050	260.00	275.00	330.00	350.00	8,000
1914D		343,500	260.00	275.00	330.00	350.00	
1914S		208,000	260.00	275.00	330.00	750.00	
1915	(75)	351,075	260.00	275.00	330.00	400.00	8,000
1915S		59,000	260.00	275.00	400.00	1,400	
1916S		138,500	260.00	275.00	350.00	650.00	
1920S		126,500	2,200	3,500	6,000	10,000	
1926		1,014,000	260.00	275.00	330.00	350.00	
1930S		96,000	1,300	1,800	3,250	7,500	
1932		4,463,000	260.00	275.00	330.00	350.00	
1933		312,500				—	

Values of common gold coins are based on the prevailing price of gold bullion, and will vary according to current market price. See Bullion Chart.

DOUBLE EAGLES ($20.00 Gold Pieces) — 1850-1933

This largest denomination of all regular United States issues was authorized to be coined by the Act of March 3, 1849. Its weight was 516 grains, .900 fine.

Mint mark location is below the eagle

VF-20 VERY FINE—*LIBERTY is bold. Jewels on crown defined. Lower half worn flat. Hair worn about ear.*
EF-40 EXTREMELY FINE—*Trace of wear on rounded prongs of crown and down hair curls. Minor bag marks.*
AU-50 ABOUT UNCIRCULATED—*Trace of wear on hair over eye and on coronet.*
MS-60 UNCIRCULATED—*No trace of wear. Light blemishes.*

Without Motto on Reverse 1850-1866

	Quan. Minted	VF-20	EF-40	AU-50	MS-60	Proof-63
1850	1,170,261	$350.00	$375.00	$450.00	$1,300	
1850O	141,000	350.00	375.00	550.00	1,600	
1851	2,087,155	350.00	375.00	450.00	1,200	
1851O	315,000	350.00	375.00	550.00	1,600	
1852	2,053,026	350.00	375.00	450.00	1,200	
1852O	190,000	350.00	375.00	550.00	1,600	
1853	1,261,326	350.00	375.00	450.00	1,100	
1853O	71,000	350.00	375.00	550.00	1,800	
1854	757,899	350.00	375.00	450.00	1,700	
1854O	3,250	12,000	16,000	20,000		
1854S	141,468	350.00	375.00	450.00	2,000	
1855	364,666	350.00	375.00	450.00	1,000	
1855O	8,000	1,000	1,500	2,800	——	
1855S	879,675	350.00	375.00	450.00	1,000	
1856	329,878	350.00	375.00	450.00	1,000	
1856O	2,250	12,000	20,000	30,000		
1856S	1,189,750	350.00	375.00	450.00	1,000	
1857	439,375	350.00	375.00	450.00	1,000	
1857O	30,000	350.00	375.00	500.00	1,750	
1857S	970,500	350.00	375.00	450.00	1,000	
1858	211,714	350.00	375.00	450.00	1,000	
1858O	35,250	350.00	375.00	700.00	2,750	
1858S	846,710	350.00	375.00	500.00	1,000	
1859 (80)	43,677	350.00	410.00	700.00	2,400	
1859O	9,100	800.00	1,200	2,000	4,000	
1859S	636,445	350.00	375.00	450.00	1,000	
1860 (59)	577,729	350.00	375.00	450.00	1,000	
1860O	6,600	800.00	1,500	2,000	3,600	
1860S	544,950	350.00	375.00	450.00	1,000	
1861 (66)	2,976,519	350.00	375.00	450.00	1,000	
1861O	17,741	525.00	1,000	1,600	3,400	
1861S	768,000	350.00	375.00	450.00	1,000	
1862 (35)	92,168	350.00	375.00	450.00	1,600	$15,000
1862S	854,173	350.00	375.00	450.00	1,000	

Values of common gold coins are based on the prevailing price of gold bullion, and will vary according to current market price. See Bullion Chart.

DOUBLE EAGLES

	Quan. Minted	VF-20	EF-40	AU-50	MS-60	Proof-63
1863 (30)	142,820	$350.00	$375.00	$450.00	$1,300	$14,000
1863S	966,570	350.00	375.00	450.00	1,000	
1864 (50)	204,285	350.00	375.00	450.00	1,200	14,000
1864S	793,660	350.00	375.00	450.00	1,000	
1865 (25)	351,200	350.00	375.00	450.00	1,000	14,750
1865S	1,042,500	350.00	375.00	450.00	1,000	
1866S est	*12,000*	500.00	1,200	3,000	—	

Motto Above Eagle, Value TWENTY D. 1866-1876

	Quan. Minted	VF-20	EF-40	AU-50	MS-60	Proof-63
1866 (30)	698,775	325.00	360.00	370.00	900.00	13,000
1866S	842,250	325.00	360.00	370.00	525.00	
1867 (50)	251,065	325.00	360.00	370.00	600.00	13,000
1867S	920,750	325.00	360.00	370.00	600.00	
1868 (25)	98,600	325.00	360.00	370.00	900.00	13,000
1868S	837,500	325.00	360.00	370.00	600.00	
1869 (25)	175,155	325.00	360.00	370.00	600.00	13,000
1869S	686,750	325.00	360.00	370.00	600.00	
1870 (35)	155,185	325.00	360.00	370.00	900.00	13,000
1870CC	3,789	7,500	13,000	—	—	
1870S	982,000	325.00	360.00	370.00	475.00	
1871 (30)	80,150	325.00	360.00	370.00	550.00	13,000
1871CC	17,387	800.00	1,300	2,000		
1871S	928,000	325.00	360.00	450.00	800.00	
1872 (30)	251,880	325.00	360.00	370.00	425.00	13,000
1872CC	26,900	400.00	475.00	675.00	1,400	
1872S	780,000	325.00	360.00	370.00	425.00	
1873 (25)	1,709,825	475.00	525.00	625.00	725.00	13,000
1873CC	22,410	450.00	500.00	650.00	1,600	
1873S	1,040,600	325.00	360.00	370.00	425.00	
1874 (20)	366,800	325.00	360.00	370.00	425.00	14,000
1874CC	115,085	475.00	500.00	550.00	900.00	
1874S	1,214,000	325.00	360.00	370.00	425.00	
1875 (20)	295,740	325.00	360.00	370.00	425.00	—
1875CC	111,151	450.00	475.00	525.00	800.00	
1875S	1,230,000	325.00	360.00	370.00	425.00	
1876 (45)	583,905	325.00	360.00	370.00	425.00	13,000
1876CC	138,441	450.00	475.00	500.00	800.00	
1876S	1,597,000	325.00	360.00	370.00	425.00	

Values of common gold coins are based on the prevailing price of gold bullion, and will vary according to current market price. See Bullion Chart.

DOUBLE EAGLES

TWENTY DOLLARS 1877-1907

		Quan. Minted	VF-20	EF-40	AU-50	MS-60	Proof-63
1877	(20)	397,670	$325.00	$360.00	$370.00	$400.00	$13,000
1877CC		42,565	450.00	500.00	525.00	800.00	
1877S		1,735,000	325.00	360.00	370.00	400.00	
1878	(20)	543,645	325.00	360.00	370.00	400.00	12,000
1878CC		13,180	450.00	500.00	600.00	1,300	
1878S		1,739,000	325.00	360.00	370.00	400.00	
1879	(30)	207,630	325.00	360.00	370.00	400.00	12,000
1879CC		10,708	550.00	650.00	900.00	2,000	
1879O		2,325	1,100	1,500	2,700	6,500	
1879S		1,223,800	325.00	360.00	370.00	400.00	
1880	(36)	51,456	325.00	360.00	370.00	450.00	12,000
1880S		836,000	325.00	360.00	370.00	400.00	
1881	(61)	2,260	1,100	2,250	3,500	6,000	16,000
1881S		727,000	325.00	360.00	370.00	400.00	
1882	(59)	630	1,600	4,200	8,000	16,000	—
1882CC		39,140	425.00	450.00	500.00	800.00	
1882S		1,125,000	325.00	360.00	370.00	400.00	
1883 Proofs only	(92)	92					—
1883CC		59,962	325.00	360.00	500.00	950.00	
1883S		1,189,000	325.00	360.00	370.00	400.00	
1884 Proofs only	(71)	71					—
1884CC		81,139	325.00	360.00	500.00	900.00	
1884S		916,000	325.00	360.00	370.00	400.00	
1885	(77)	828	1,200	3,000	6,000	11,000	—
1885CC		9,450	500.00	700.00	1,000	1,800	
1885S		683,500	325.00	360.00	370.00	400.00	
1886	(106)	1,106	2,500	5,000	9,000	16,000	24,000
1887 Proofs only	(121)	121					28,000
1887S		283,000	325.00	360.00	370.00	400.00	
1888	(105)	226,266	325.00	360.00	370.00	400.00	10,000
1888S		859,600	325.00	360.00	370.00	400.00	
1889	(41)	44,111	325.00	360.00	370.00	400.00	10,000
1889CC		30,945	325.00	360.00	370.00	800.00	
1889S		774,700	325.00	360.00	370.00	400.00	
1890	(55)	75,995	325.00	360.00	370.00	400.00	10,000
1890CC		91,209	325.00	360.00	370.00	900.00	
1890S		802,750	325.00	360.00	370.00	400.00	
1891	(52)	1,442	650.00	1,400	2,100	4,000	12,000
1891CC		5,000	600.00	1,100	1,600	3,500	
1891S		1,288,125	325.00	360.00	370.00	400.00	
1892	(93)	4,523	500.00	650.00	950.00	3,000	10,000
1892CC		27,265	325.00	425.00	550.00	1,200	
1892S		930,150	325.00	360.00	370.00	400.00	
1893	(59)	344,339	325.00	360.00	370.00	400.00	9,000
1893CC		18,402	325.00	360.00	650.00	1,400	

Values of common gold coins are based on the prevailing price of gold bullion, and will vary according to current market price. See Bullion Chart.

DOUBLE EAGLES

		Quan. Minted	VF-20	EF-40	AU-50	MS-60	Proof-63
1893S		996,175	$325.00	$360.00	$370.00	$400.00	
1894	(50)	1,368,990	325.00	360.00	370.00	400.00	$9,000
1894S		1,048,550	325.00	360.00	370.00	400.00	
1895	(51)	1,114,656	325.00	360.00	370.00	400.00	9,000
1895S		1,143,500	325.00	360.00	370.00	400.00	
1896	(128)	792,663	325.00	360.00	370.00	400.00	9,000
1896S		1,403,925	325.00	360.00	370.00	400.00	
1897	(86)	1,383,261	325.00	360.00	370.00	400.00	9,000
1897S		1,470,250	325.00	360.00	370.00	400.00	
1898	(75)	170,470	325.00	360.00	370.00	400.00	9,000
1898S		2,575,175	325.00	360.00	370.00	400.00	
1899	(84)	1,669,384	325.00	360.00	370.00	400.00	9,000
1899S		2,010,300	325.00	360.00	370.00	400.00	
1900	(124)	1,874,584	325.00	360.00	370.00	400.00	9,000
1900S		2,459,500	325.00	360.00	370.00	400.00	
1901	(96)	111,526	325.00	360.00	370.00	400.00	9,000
1901S		1,596,000	325.00	360.00	370.00	400.00	
1902	(114)	31,254	325.00	360.00	370.00	450.00	9,000
1902S		1,753,625	325.00	360.00	370.00	400.00	
1903	(158)	287,428	325.00	360.00	370.00	400.00	9,000
1903S		954,000	325.00	360.00	370.00	400.00	
1904	(98)	6,256,797	325.00	360.00	370.00	400.00	9,000
1904S		5,134,175	325.00	360.00	370.00	400.00	
1905	(92)	59,011	325.00	360.00	370.00	500.00	9,000
1905S		1,813,000	325.00	360.00	370.00	400.00	
1906	(94)	69,690	325.00	360.00	370.00	400.00	9,000
1906D		620,250	325.00	360.00	370.00	400.00	
1906S		2,065,750	325.00	360.00	370.00	400.00	
1907	(78)	1,451,864	325.00	360.00	370.00	400.00	9,000
1907D		842,250	325.00	360.00	370.00	400.00	
1907S		2,165,800	325.00	360.00	370.00	400.00	

SAINT-GAUDENS TYPE 1907-1933

The $20 gold piece designed by Augustus Saint-Gaudens is considered to be the most beautiful United States coin. The first coins issued were 11,250 high relief pieces struck for general circulation. The relief is much higher than later issues and the date 1907 is in Roman numerals. A few of the proof coins were made using the lettered edge collar from the extremely high relief version. These can be distinguished by a pronounced bottom left serif on the N in UNUM, and other minor differences. Flat-relief double eagles were issued later in 1907 with Arabic numerals, and continued through 1933.

The field of the rare extremely high relief experimental pieces is excessively concave and connects directly with the edge without any border, giving it a sharp knifelike appearance; Liberty's skirt shows two folds on the side of her right leg; the Capitol building in the background at left is very small; the sun, on the reverse side, has 14 rays, as opposed to the regular high relief coins that have only 13 rays extending from the sun. High relief proofs are trial or experimental pieces.

DOUBLE EAGLES

VF-20 VERY FINE—*Minor wear on legs and toes. Eagle's left wing and breast feathers worn.*

EF-40 EXTREMELY FINE—*Drapery lines on chest visible. Wear on left breast, knee and below. Eagle's feathers on breast and right wing are bold.*

AU-50 ABOUT UNCIRCULATED—*Trace of wear on nose, breast, and knee. Wear visible on eagle's wings.*

MS-60 UNCIRCULATED—*No trace of wear. Light marks or blemishes.*

	Proof
1907 Ex. high relief, plain edge (Unique)	——
1907 Ex. high relief, lettered edge	——

	Quan. Minted	*VF-20*	*EF-40*	*AU-50*	*MS-60*	*Proof*
1907 high relief, Roman numerals (MCMVII),	11,250	$1,500	$2,200	$3,000	$4,000	——

Arabic Numerals

No Motto — Motto IN GOD WE TRUST. 1908-1933

Mint mark location is on obverse above date.

	Quan. Minted	*VF-20*	*EF-40*	*AU-50*	*MS-60*	*Matte Proof-63*
1907	361,667	$365.00	$370.00	$400.00	$445.00	
1908	4,271,551	365.00	370.00	380.00	410.00	
1908D	663,750	365.00	370.00	380.00	410.00	
1908 (101)	156,359	365.00	370.00	400.00	445.00	$9,000
1908D	349,500	365.00	370.00	380.00	410.00	
1908S	22,000	375.00	500.00	775.00	2,200	

1909, 9 over 8

	Quan. Minted	*VF-20*	*EF-40*	*AU-50*	*MS-60*	*Matte Proof-63*
1909 (67)	161,282	360.00	370.00	380.00	425.00	9,000
1909, 9 over 8		360.00	370.00	380.00	410.00	
1909D	52,500	425.00	500.00	625.00	1,200	
1909S	2,774,925	360.00	370.00	380.00	410.00	
1910 (167)	482,167	360.00	370.00	380.00	410.00	9,000
1910D	429,000	360.00	370.00	380.00	410.00	
1910S	2,128,250	360.00	370.00	380.00	410.00	
1911 (100)	197,350	360.00	370.00	380.00	410.00	9,000
1911D	846,500	360.00	370.00	380.00	410.00	
1911S	775,750	360.00	370.00	380.00	410.00	
1912 (74)	149,824	360.00	370.00	380.00	425.00	9,000
1913 (58)	168,838	360.00	370.00	380.00	425.00	9,000
1913D	393,500	360.00	370.00	380.00	410.00	
1913S	34,000	360.00	370.00	400.00	700.00	
1914 (70)	95,320	360.00	370.00	380.00	425.00	9,000
1914D	453,000	360.00	370.00	380.00	410.00	
1914S	1,498,000	360.00	370.00	380.00	410.00	
1915 (50)	152,050	360.00	370.00	380.00	425.00	9,000

Values of common gold coins are based on the prevailing price of gold bullion, and will vary according to current market price. See Bullion Chart.

DOUBLE EAGLES

	Quan. Minted	VF-20	EF-40	AU-50	MS-60	Matte Proof-63
1915S	567,500	$360.00	$370.00	$380.00	$410.00	
1916S	796,000	360.00	370.00	380.00	410.00	
1920	228,250	360.00	370.00	380.00	410.00	
1920S	558,000	3,000	4,000	5,000	9,000	
1921	528,500	4,500	5,500	7,000	12,000	
1922	1,375,500	360.00	370.00	380.00	410.00	
1922S	2,658,000	400.00	450.00	500.00	600.00	
1923	566,000	360.00	370.00	380.00	410.00	
1923D	1,702,250	360.00	370.00	380.00	410.00	
1924	4,323,500	360.00	370.00	380.00	410.00	
1924D	3,049,500	450.00	475.00	525.00	1,100	
1924S	2,927,500	450.00	475.00	525.00	900.00	
1925	2,831,750	360.00	370.00	380.00	410.00	
1925D	2,938,500	400.00	500.00	700.00	1,200	
1925S	3,776,500	400.00	500.00	700.00	1,200	
1926	816,750	360.00	370.00	380.00	410.00	
1926D	481,000	450.00	650.00	800.00	1,500	
1926S	2,041,500	400.00	475.00	600.00	900.00	
1927	2,946,750	360.00	370.00	380.00	410.00	
1927D	180,000				75,000	
1927S	3,107,000	1,500	2,000	2,750	5,500	
1928	8,816,000	360.00	370.00	380.00	410.00	
1929	1,779,750	1,500	2,000	2,600	4,500	
1930S	74,000	3,000	5,500	6,500	9,000	
1931	2,938,250	2,500	4,500	5,200	8,000	
1931D	106,500	2,500	4,750	5,200	8,000	
1932	1,101,750	2,750	5,200	6,250	8,000	
1933	445,500	None placed in circulation				

COMMEMORATIVE SILVER COINS

Isabella Quarter

In 1892, to commemorate the World's Columbian Exposition in Chicago, Congress authorized the coinage of a special half dollar and quarter dollar, thus starting a long line of United States commemorative coins. Nearly all commemorative coins have been distributed by private individuals or commissions; they paid the mint the face value of the coins and in turn sold the pieces at a premium to collectors. There are a few instances in which some of the very large issues were later released to circulation at face value.

		Quan. Available	AU-50	MS-60
1893	Isabella Quarter (Columbian Exposition)	24,214	$135.00	$325.00

COMMEMORATIVE SILVER

(Half Dollars Listed alphabetically)

Alabama, Albany, Antietam, Arkansas

2x2 in Field

		Quan. Available	AU-50	MS-60
1921	Alabama, "2 x 2" in field	6,006	$80.00	$165.00
1921	Same, no "2 x 2"	59,038	45.00	115.00

1936	Albany, New York	17,671	145.00	175.00

1937	Battle of Antietam 1862-1937	18,028	275.00	300.00

1935	Arkansas Centennial	13,012	Set	150.00
1935D	Same	5,505		
1935S	Same	5,506		

COMMEMORATIVE SILVER

Arkansas, Bay Bridge, Boone

		Quan. Available		*AU-50*	*MS-60*
1936	Arkansas Centennial, same as 1935 — date 1936 on reverse	9,660			
1936D	Same	9,660	Set		$150.00
1936S	Same	9,662			
1937	Arkansas Centennial, same as 1935	5,505			
1937D	Same	5,505	Set		155.00
1937S	Same	5,506			
1938	Arkansas Centennial, same as 1935	3,156			
1938D	Same	3,155	Set		200.00
1938S	Same	3,156			
1939	Arkansas, same as 1935	2,104			
1939D	Same	2,104	Set		500.00
1939S	Same	2,105			
	Single type coin			$38.00	50.00

1936S	San Francisco-Oakland Bay Bridge	71,424		60.00	70.00

1934 added on reverse

1934	Daniel Boone Bicentennial	10,007		50.00	60.00
1935	Same	10,010			
1935D	Same	5,005	Sct		160.00
1935S	Same	5,005			
1935	Daniel Boone Bicentennial, same as 1934 but small 1934 added on reverse	10,008			
1935D	Same	2,003	Set		350.00
1935S	Same	2,004			
1936	D. Boone Bicentennial, same as 1934	12,012			
1936D	Same	5,005	Set		160.00
1936S	Same	5,006			
1937	D. Boone Bicentennial, same as 1934	9,810			
1937D	Same	2,506	Set		400.00
1937S	Same	2,506			
1938	Daniel Boone, same as 1934	2,100			
1938D	Same	2,100	Set		600.00
1938S	Same	2,100			
	Single type coin			50.00	60.00

COMMEMORATIVE SILVER

Bridgeport, California, Carver-Washington, Cincinnati

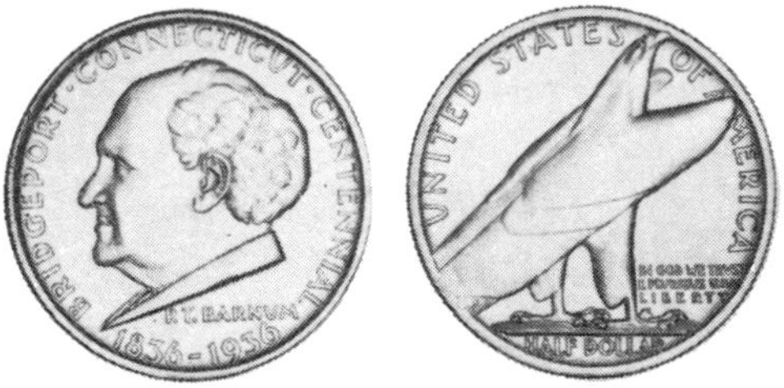

		Quan. Available	*AU-50*	*MS-60*
1936	Bridgeport, Conn., Centennial	25,015	$65.00	$75.00

1925S	California Diamond Jubilee	86,394	60.00	75.00

1951 Carver-Washington	110,018	Set	35.00
1951D	10,004		
1951S	10,004		
1952	2,006,292	Set	40.00
1952D	8,006		
1952S	8,006		
1953	8,003	Set	40.00
1953D	8,003		
1953S	108,020		
1954	12,006	Set	35.00
1954D	12,006		
1954S	122,024		
Single type coin			8.00

1936	Cincinnati Music Center	5,005	Set		500.00
1936D	Same	5,005			
1936S	Same	5,006			
	Single type coin			150.00	175.00

COMMEMORATIVE SILVER

Cleveland, Columbia, S.C., Columbian, Connecticut

		Quan. Available	*AU-50*	*MS-60*
1936	Cleveland, Great Lakes Exposition	50,030	$35.00	$45.00

1936	Columbia, S.C., Sesquicentennial	9,007	Set	430.00
1936D	Same	8,009		
1936S	Same	8,007		
	Single type coin		125.00	140.00

1892	Columbian Exposition	950,000	15.00	45.00
1893	Same	1,550,405	13.00	40.00

1935	Connecticut Tercentenary	25,018	110.00	135.00

Delaware, Elgin, Gettysburg, Grant

		Quan. Available	AU-50	MS-60
1936	Delaware Tercentenary	20,993	$125.00	$150.00

1936	Elgin, Illinois, Centennial	20,015	125.00	140.00

1936	Battle of Gettysburg 1863-1938	26,928	125.00	155.00

1922	Grant Memorial, small star above word "Grant" in obv. field	4,256	240.00	500.00
	(Fake stars have flattened spot on reverse.)			
1922	Same, no star in obverse field	67,405	45.00	55.00

COMMEMORATIVE SILVER
Hawaiian, Hudson, Huguenot, Illinois

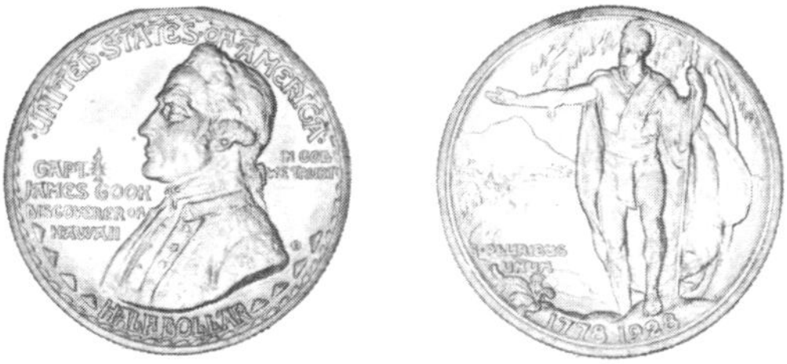

		Quan. Available	AU-50	MS-60
1928	Hawaiian Sesquicentennial........................	10,008	$450.00	$650.00

1935	Hudson N. Y. Sesquicentennial....................	10,008	250.00	275.00

1924	Huguenot-Walloon Tercentenary..................	142,080	40.00	50.00

1918	Illinois Centennial..............................	100,058	40.00	50.00

Iowa, Lexington, Long Island, Lynchburg

		Quan. Available	*AU-50*	*MS-60*
1946	Iowa Centennial	100,057	$40.00	$55.00

1925	Lexington-Concord Sesquicentennial	162,013	40.00	43.00

1936	Long Island Tercentenary	81,826	35.00	45.00

1936	Lynchburg, Va., Sesquicentennial	20,013	100.00	115.00

Maine, Maryland, Missouri, Monroe

		Quan. Available	AU-50	MS-60
1920	Maine Centennial	50,028	$40.00	$65.00

1934	Maryland Tercentenary	25,015	80.00	100.00

2 ★ 4 in field

1921	Missouri Centennial "2 ★ 4" above "1821"	5,000	155.00	250.00
1921	Same, no "2 ★ 4"	15,428	100.00	200.00

1923S	Monroe Doctrine Centennial	274,077	20.00	25.00

New Rochelle, Norfolk, Oregon, Panama-Pacific

		Quan. Available	AU-50	MS-60
1938	New Rochelle, N. Y. 1688-1938	15,266	$200.00	$220.00

		Quan. Available	AU-50	MS-60
1936	Norfolk, Va., Bicentennial	16,936	325.00	340.00

		Quan. Avail.	AU-50	MS-60			Quan. Avail.	AU-50	MS-60
1926	Oregon Trail	47,955	$45.00	$60.00	1938	Oregon	6,006	Set	$390.00
1926S	Same	83,055	45.00	60.00	1938D	Same	6,005		
1928	Same	6,028	90.00	100.00	1938S	Same	6,006		
1933D	Same	5,008	150.00	175.00	1939	Oregon	3,004	Set	850.00
1934D	Same	7,006	80.00	100.00	1939D	Same	3,004		
1936	Same	10,006	65.00	80.00	1939S	Same	3,005		
1936S	Same	5,006	80.00	100.00		Single type coin		$40.00	60.00
1937D	Same	12,008	65.00	75.00					

		Quan. Available	AU-50	MS-60
1915S	Panama-Pacific Exposition	27,134	110.00	185.00

COMMEMORATIVE SILVER

Pilgrim, Rhode Island, Roanoke, Robinson

		Quan. Available	AU-50	MS-60
1920	Pilgrim Tercentenary	152,112	$35.00	$45.00
1921	Same, with 1921 date added in field	20,053	45.00	55.00

		Quan. Available	AU-50	MS-60
1936	Rhode Island Tercentenary	20,013 (Set)		
1936D	Same	15,010 (Set)		180.00
1936S	Same	15,011 (Set)		
	Single type coin		50.00	60.00

		Quan. Available	AU-50	MS-60
1937	Roanoke Island, N. C., 1587-1937	29,030	120.00	135.00

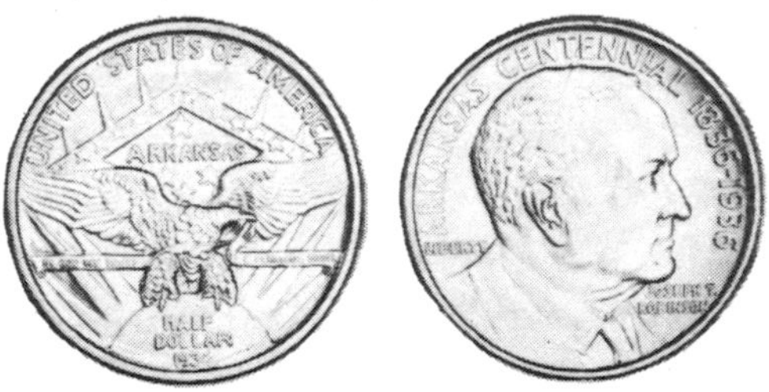

		Quan. Available	AU-50	MS-60
1936	Arkansas Centennial (Robinson)	25,265	50.00	60.00

COMMEMORATIVE SILVER

San Diego, Sesquicentennial, Spanish Trail, Stone Mountain

		Quan. Available	*AU-50*	*MS-60*
1935S	San Diego, California-Pacific Expo.	70,132	$40.00	$45.00
1936D	Same	30,092	45.00	55.00

1926	Sesquicentennial of American Independence	141,120	40.00	50.00

1935	Old Spanish Trail 1535-1935	10,008	450.00	510.00

1925	Stone Mountain Memorial	1,314,709	20.00	25.00

COMMEMORATIVE SILVER

Texas, Vancouver, Vermont

Date	Issue	*Quan. Available*		*AU-50*	*MS-60*
1934	Texas Centennial	61,463		$55.00	$65.00
1935	Texas Centennial, same as 1934	9,996	Set		195.00
1935D	Same	10,007			
1935S	Same	10,008			
1936	Texas Centennial, same as 1934	8,911	Set		195.00
1936D	Same	9,039			
1936S	Same	9,055			
1937	Texas Centennial, same as 1934	6,571	Set		250.00
1937D	Same	6,605			
1937S	Same	6,637			
1938	Texas Centennial, same as 1934	3,780	Set		400.00
1938D	Same	3,775			
1938S	Same	3,814			
	Single type coin			50.00	65.00

Date	Issue	*Quan. Available*	*AU-50*	*MS-60*
1925S	Fort Vancouver Centennial	14,994	135.00	175.00

Date	Issue	*Quan. Available*	*AU-50*	*MS-60*
1927	Vermont Sesquicentennial (Bennington)	28,162	90.00	110.00

Washington, B.T., Wisconsin, York County

	Quan. Available		MS-60
1946 Booker T. Washington Memorial	1,000,546	Set	$25.00
1946D	200,113		
1946S	500,279		
1947	100,017	Set	25.00
1947D	100,017		
1947S	100,017		
1948	8,005	Set	55.00
1948D	8,005		
1948S	8,005		

	Quan. Available		MS-60
1949	6,004	Set	$125.00
1949D	6,004		
1949S	6,004		
1950	6,004	Set	100.00
1950D	6,004		
1950S	512,091		
1951	510,082	Set	80.00
1951D	7,004		
1951S	7,004		
Single type coin			9.00

		Quan. Available	AU-50	MS-60
1936	Wisconsin Centennial	25,015	$120.00	$135.00

1936	York County, Maine Tercentenary	25,015	115.00	130.00

COMMEMORATIVE SILVER

York County, Lafayette

		Quan. Available	AU-50	MS-60
1900	Lafayette Dollar	36,026	$175.00	$425.00

COMMEMORATIVE GOLD

Grant, Lewis & Clark, Louisiana Purchase, McKinley, Panama-Pacific

		Quan. Available	AU-50	MS-60
1922	Grant Memorial Dollar, star above word "Grant"	5,016	$900.00	$1,000
1922	Same, without star	5,000	800.00	900.00

1904	Lewis and Clark Exposition Dollar	10,025	350.00	650.00
1905	Lewis and Clark Exposition Dollar	10,041	350.00	600.00

1903	Louisiana Purchase Jefferson Dollar	17,500	350.00	300.00
1903	Louisiana Purchase McKinley Dollar	17,500	230.00	300.00

1916	McKinley Memorial Dollar	9,977	240.00	300.00
1917	McKinley Memorial Dollar	10,000	245.00	335.00

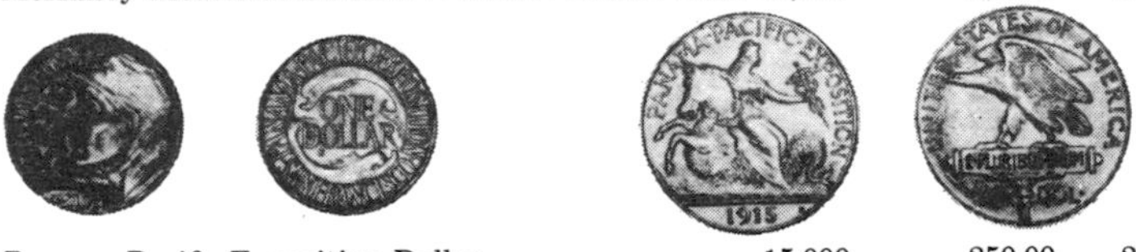

1915S	Panama-Pacific Exposition Dollar	15,000	250.00	275.00
1915S	Panama-Pacific Exposition $2.50	6,749	660.00	1,100

COMMEMORATIVE GOLD

U.S. Sesquicentennial

		Quan. Available	*AU-50*	*MS-60*
1915S	Panama-Pacific $50 Round	483	$15,000	$18,000
1915S	Panama-Pacific $50 Octagonal	645	13,500	15,500

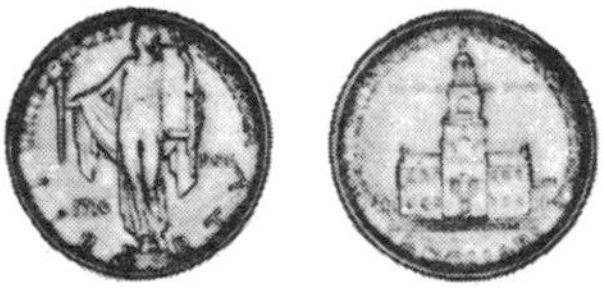

1926	United States Sequicentennial $2.50	46,019	190.00	240.00

MODERN COMMEMORATIVES

Washington

		Quan. Issued	*MS-63*	*Proof-63*
1982D	Geo. Washington-250th Anniversary	2,210,458	$4.00	
1982S	Same, Proof..................................	(4,894,044)		$3.75

MODERN COMMEMORATIVES

Los Angeles, Statue of Liberty

			Quan. Issued	MS-63	Proof-63
1983P	Discus Thrower Silver Dollar		294,543	$12.00	
1983D	Same type D mint		174,014	16.00	
1983S	Same type S mint	(1,577,025)	174,014	11.00	$10.00

1984P	Olympic Coliseum Silver Dollar		217,954	13.00	
1984D	Same type D mint		116,675	20.00	
1984S	Same type S mint	(1,801,210)	116,675	25.00	10.00

1984P	Olympic Gold Eagle	(33,309)			225.00
1984D	Olympic Gold Eagle	(34,533)			190.00
1984S	Olympic Gold Eagle	(48,551)			180.00
1984W	Olympic Gold Eagle	(381,085)	75,886	180.00	175.00

MODERN COMMEMORATIVES

Statue of Liberty, Constitution

		Quan. Issued	MS-63	Proof-63
1986D	Statue of Liberty	928,008	$4.00	
1986S	Same type S mint, Proof	(6,925,627)		$4.25

		Quan. Issued	MS-63	Proof-63
1986P	Statue of Liberty Dollar	723,635	12.00	
1986S	Same type S mint, proof	(6,414,638)		9.00

		Quan. Issued		MS-63	Proof-63
1986W	Statue of Liberty $5.00	(404,013)	95,248	110.00	105.00

		Quan. Issued	MS-63	Proof-63
1987P	Constitution Dollar	451,629	8.00	
1987S	Same type S mint, proof	(2,747,116)		9.00

		Quan. Issued		MS-63	Proof-63
1987W	U.S. Constitution Gold $5.00	(651,659)	214,225	80.00	83.00

MODERN COMMEMORATIVES

Olympics, Congress

		Quan. Issued	MS-63	Proof-63
1988P	Olympic Silver Dollar	191,368	$18.00	
1988S	Same type S mint, proof	(1,354,366)		$9.00

		Quan. Issued	MS-63	Proof-63
1988W	Olympic Gold $5.00	(281,465) 62,913	95.00	85.00

		Quan. Issued	MS-63	Proof-63
1989D	Congress Bicentennial Half Dollar	163,753	6.00	
1989S	Congress Bicentennial Half Dollar	(767,897)		7.00

		Quan. Issued	MS-63	Proof-63
1989D	Congress Silver Dollar	135,203	24.00	
1989S	Congress Silver Dollar	(762,198)		24.00

MODERN COMMEMORATIVES

Congress, Eisenhower, Mt. Rushmore, Korean, U.S.O.

	Quan. Issued	MS-63	Proof-63
1989W Congress Bicentennial Gold $5.00	(164,690) 46,899	125.00	125.00

	Quan. Issued	MS-63	Proof-63
1990W Eisenhower Silver Dollar	(241,669)	20.00	
1990P Same type P mint	(638,335)		18.00
1991D Mount Rushmore Half Dollar		6.00	
1991S Same type S mint			9.00
1991P Mount Rushmore Silver Dollar		25.00	
1991S Same type S mint			27.00
1991W Mount Rushmore Gold $5.00		165.00	165.00
1991D Korean War Silver Dollar		20.00	
1991P Same type S mint			22.00
1991D U.S.O. Silver Dollar		20.00	
1991S Same type S mint			22.00
1992P Olympic Half Dollar		6.00	
1992S Same type S mint			9.00
1992D Olympic Dollar		23.00	
1992S Same type S mint			27.00
1992W Olympic Gold $5.00		180.00	190.00

PRIVATE OR TERRITORIAL GOLD COINS

Private coins were circulated in most instances because of a shortage of regular coinage. The words "Private Gold," used with reference to coins struck outside of the United States Mint, are a general term. In the sense that no state or territory had authority to coin money, private gold simply refers to those interesting necessity pieces of various shapes, denominations and degrees of intrinsic worth which were circulated in isolated areas of our country by individuals, assayers, bankers, etc. Some will use the words "Territorial" and "State" to cover certain issues because they were coined and circulated in a territory or state. While the state of California properly sanctioned the ingots stamped by F. D. Kohler as state assayer, in no instance were any of the gold pieces struck by authority of any of the territorial governments.

The stamped ingots put out by Augustus Humbert, the United States assayer of gold, were not recognized at the United States Mint as an official issue of coins, but simply as ingots, though Humbert placed the value and fineness on the pieces as an official agent of the federal government.

TEMPLETON REID

Georgia 1830

The first private gold coinage under the Constitution was struck by Templeton Reid, a jeweler and gunsmith, in Milledgeville, Georgia in July, 1830. To be closer to the mines, he moved to Gainesville where most of his coins were made. Although weights were accurate, Reid's assays were not and his coins were slightly short of claimed value. Accordingly, he was severely attacked in the newspapers and soon lost the public's confidence.

		V. Fine
1830 $2.50	V.F.	$15,000
1830 $5.00	V.F.	40,000

		V. Good
1830 TEN DOLLARS	V.G.	$22,000
(No date) TEN DOLLARS	V.G.	15,000

TEMPLETON REID

"California Gold 1849"

1849 TEN DOLLAR CALIFORNIA GOLD (Smithsonian Collection) .... Unique

THE BECHTLERS

Rutherford County, N. C. 1830-1852

Two skilled German metallurgists, Christopher Bechtler and his son August, and later Christopher Bechtler, Junior, a nephew of Christopher the elder, operated a "private" mint at Rutherfordton, North Carolina. Rutherford county in which Rutherfordton is located was the principal source of the nation's gold supply from 1790 to 1840.

CHRISTOPHER BECHTLER

	V. Fine	E. Fine	Unc.
ONE DOLLAR CAROLINA, 28 gr. N reversed	$475.00	$700.00	$1,800
ONE DOLLAR N. CAROLINA, 28 gr. no star	1,100	2,100	4,200

ONE DOLLAR N. CAROLINA, 30 gr.	625.00	1,100	2,400
$2.50 CAROLINA, 67 gr. 21 carats	850.00	1,350	3,500

$2.50 CAROLINA, 70 gr. 20 carats	950.00	1,600	3,500
$2.50 GEORGIA, 64 gr. 22 carats.	1,150	1,750	4,000

THE BECHTLERS

	V. Fine	E. Fine	Unc.
$2.50 NORTH CAROLINA, 75 gr. 20 carats. RUTHERFORD in a circle. Border of lg. beads	$2,000	$3,200	$5,500
$2.50 NORTH CAROLINA, without 75 G	1,800	2,600	5,000

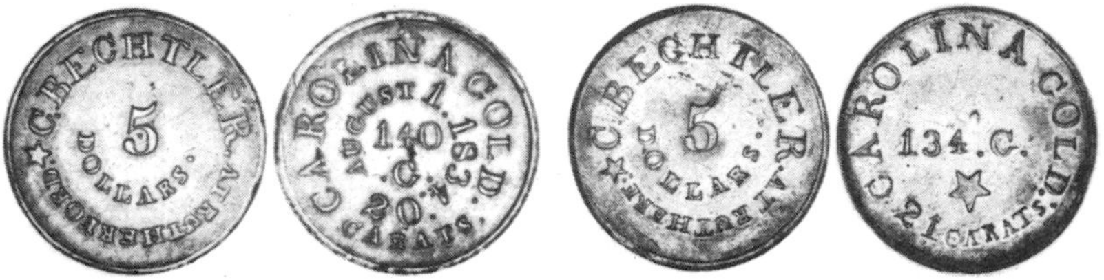

5 DOLLARS CAROLINA, RUTHERFORD, 140 gr. 20 carats. Date August 1, 1834.			
Plain edge	1,250	2,100	4,700
Reeded edge	1,300	2,500	4,000
BECHTLER without star and C	—		
5 DOLLARS CAROLINA, 134 gr. 21 carats, with star	1,300	2,600	5,000

5 DOLLARS GEORGIA, RUTHERF. 128 gr. 22 carats	1,500	2,500	4,500
5 DOLLARS GEORGIA, RTHERF. 128 gr. 22 carats	1,500	2,500	4,500
5 DOLLARS CAROLINA, RUTHERF. 140 gr. 20 carats. Date August 1, 1834 (illustrated)	2,000	3,000	—
Similar. 20 distant from carats	3,000	4,750	—

Without 150 G

5 DOLLARS NORTH CAROLINA, 150 gr. 20 carats	2,500	3,500	7,500
5 DOLLARS. Same as last variety without 150 G	2,500	3,500	7,500

THE BECHTLERS

AUGUST BECHTLER

1842-1852

	V. Fine	E. Fine	Unc.
1 DOLLAR CAROLINA, 27 gr. 21 carats.	$400.00	$525.00	$1,200
5 DOLLARS CAROLINA, 134 gr. 21 carats.	1,000	2,000	3,900

5 DOLLARS CAROLINA, 128 gr. 22 carats.	2,000	3,000	5,750
5 DOLLARS CAROLINA, 141 gr. 20 carats.	2,000	3,000	5,750

NORRIS, GREGG & NORRIS

San Francisco 1849

These pieces are considered the first of the California private gold coins. A newspaper account dated May 31, 1849, described a five-dollar gold coin, struck at Benicia City, though with the imprint San Francisco, and the private stamp of Norris, Gregg and Norris.

	Fine	V. Fine	E. Fine	Unc.
1849 HALF EAGLE — Plain edge	$1,200	$1,700	$3,500	$9,000
1849 HALF EAGLE — Reeded edge	1,200	1,700	3,750	10,000
1850 HALF EAGLE with STOCKTON beneath date				(Unique)

MOFFAT & CO.

San Francisco 1849-1853

The firm of Moffat and Company was perhaps the most important of the California private coiners. The assay office they conducted was semi-official in character, and successors to this firm later established the United States Branch mint of San Francisco.

In June or July, 1849, Moffat & Co. began to issue small rectangular pieces of gold in values from $9.43 to $264. The $9.43, $14.25 and $16.00 varieties are the only types known today.

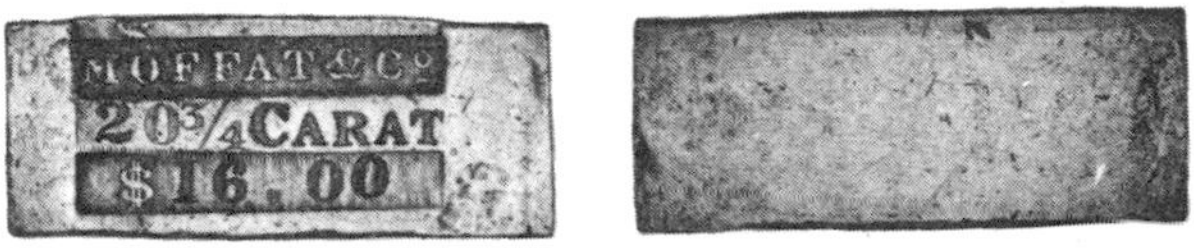

$9.43 Ingot (Unique)		—
$14.25 Ingot (Unique)		—
$16.00 Ingot	E.F.	$16,000

The dies for the $10 piece were cut by Albert Kuner. The words MOFFAT & CO. appear on the coronet of Liberty instead of the word LIBERTY as in regular United States issues.

	Fine	V. Fine	E. Fine	Unc.
1849 FIVE DOL.	$400.00	$700.00	$1,200	$4,500
1850 FIVE DOL.	400.00	700.00	1,200	4,500
1849 TEN DOL.	850.00	1,200	2,750	6,250
1849 TEN D..	850.00	1,200	2,750	6,250

United States Assay Office

AUGUSTUS HUMBERT

U. S. Assayer 1851

When Augustus Humbert was appointed United States Assayer, he placed his name and the government stamp on the ingots of gold issued by Moffat & Co. The assay office, a Provisional Government Mint, was a temporary expedient to accommodate the Californians until the establishment of a permanent branch mint.

The fifty-dollar gold piece was accepted as legal tender on a par with standard U.S. gold coins.

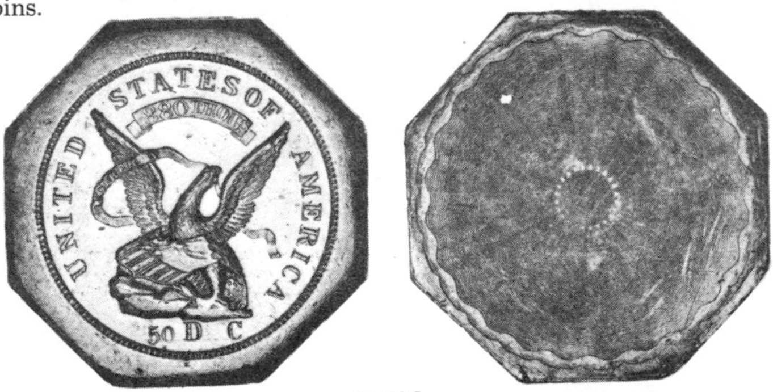

MOFFAT — HUMBERT

LETTERED EDGE VARIETIES

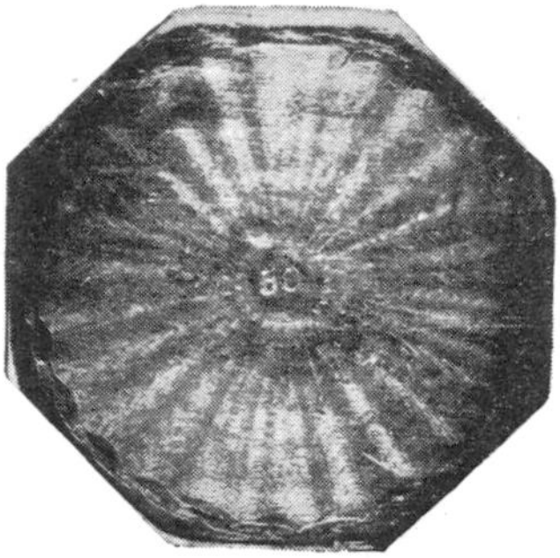

50 on reverse

	Fine	V. Fine	E. Fine	Unc.
1851 50 D C 880 THOUS., no 50 on Reverse. Sunk in edge: AUGUSTUS HUMBERT UNITED STATES ASSAYER OF GOLD CALIFORNIA 1851	$3,500	$5,000	$10,000	—
1851 50 D C Similar to last variety, but 50 on Reverse	4,500	5,500	12,000	—
1851 Similar to last variety, but 887 THOUS	4,250	5,250	11,000	—

REEDED EDGE VARIETIES

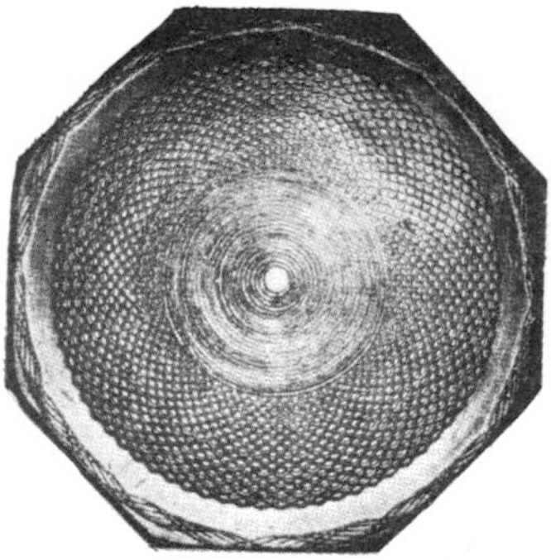

	Fine	V. Fine	E. Fine	Unc.
1851 FIFTY DOLLS 880 THOUS. "Target" Reverse	2,750	4,000	6,500	16,000
1851 FIFTY DOLLS 887 THOUS. "Target" Reverse	2,750	4,000	6,500	16,000
1852 FIFTY DOLLS 887 THOUS.	3,000	4,500	8,000	18,000

Moffat & Co. proceeded in January, 1852 to issue a new ten-dollar piece bearing the stamp MOFFAT & CO.

MOFFAT — HUMBERT

	Fine	V. Fine	E. Fine	Unc.
1852 TEN D. MOFFAT & CO.	$900.00	$1,800	$3,000	—

1852 TWENTY DOLS. 1852, 2 over 1	1,500	2,750	4,000	—

1852 TEN DOLS. 1852, 2 over 1	650.00	900.00	1,800	—
1852 TEN DOLS.	600.00	800.00	1,600	$5,000

UNITED STATES ASSAY OFFICE OF GOLD

1852

The firm of Moffat & Co. dissolved and a new reorganized company known as the United States Assay Office of Gold, composed of Curtis, Perry and Ward took over the contract.

	Fine	V. Fine	E. Fine	Unc.
1852 FIFTY DOLLS. 887 THOUS.	$2,750	$4,500	$8,500	$20,000
1852 FIFTY DOLLS. 900 THOUS.	3,000	4,750	10,000	22,000

1852 TEN DOLS 884 THOUS.	500.00	1,000	1,400	5,000
1853 TEN D. 884 THOUS.	2,000	3,000	6,750	—
1853 TEN D. 900 THOUS.	1,250	1,900	3,000	—
1853 TWENTY D. 884 THOUS.	3,750	6,000	11,000	—
1853 TWENTY D. 900 THOUS.	650.00	1,000	1,500	4,000

The last Moffat issue was the 1853 twenty dollar piece which is very similar to the U.S. double eagle of that period. It was struck after the retirement of Mr. Moffat from the Assay Office.

1853 TWENTY D.	1,000	1,500	2,500	4,500

CINCINNATI MINING & TRADING CO.

The origin and location of this company are unknown.

	E. Fine	Unc.
1849 FIVE DOLLARS	—	—
1849 TEN DOLLARS	—	—

MASSACHUSETTS AND CALIFORNIA COMPANY

San Francisco 1849

This company was believed to have been organized in Northampton, Mass. in May 1849.

	V. Fine
1849 FIVE D.	$25,000

MINERS' BANK

San Francisco 1849

The institution of Wright & Co., exchange brokers located in Portsmouth Square, San Francisco, was known as the Miners' Bank.

A ten dollar piece was issued in the autumn of 1849, but the coins were not readily accepted because they were worth less than face value.

	V. Fine	E. Fine	Unc.
(1849) TEN. D.	$4,000	$7,000	$19,000

J.S. ORMSBY

Sacramento 1849

The initials J. S. O. which appear on certain issues of California privately coined gold pieces represent the firm of J. S. Ormsby & Co. They struck both five and ten dollar denominations, all undated.

J.S. ORMSBY

	V. Fine
(1849) 5 DOLLS. (Unique)	——
(1849) 10 DOLLS.	——

PACIFIC COMPANY

San Francisco 1849

The origin of the Pacific Co. is very uncertain. All data regarding the firm is based on conjecture.

Edgar H. Adams wrote that he believed that the coins bearing the stamp of the Pacific Company were produced by the coining firm of Broderick and Kohler.

	E. Fine
1849 5 DOLLARS	$30,000
1849 10 DOLLARS	50,000

F. D. KOHLER

California State Assayer 1850

The State Assay Office was authorized April 12, 1850. Governor Burnett appointed F. D. Kohler that year who thereupon sold his assaying business to Baldwin & Co. He served at both San Francisco and Sacramento Offices. The State Assay Offices were discontinued at the time the U. S. Assay Office was established Feb. 1, 1851.

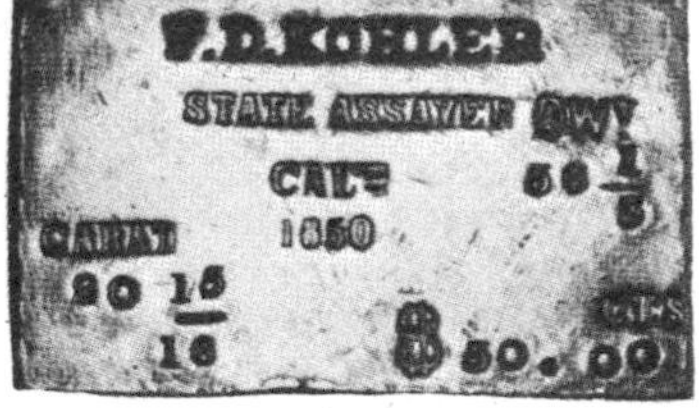

$36.55 Sacramento	——
$47.71 Sacramento	——
$37.31 San Francisco	——
$40.07 San Francisco	——
$41.68 San Francisco	——
$45.34 San Francisco	——
$50.00 San Francisco	——
$54.09 San Francisco	——

DUBOSQ & COMPANY

San Francisco 1850

Theodore Dubosq, a Philadelphia jeweler who took melting and coining machinery to San Francisco in 1849, produced the following pieces.

	V. Fine
1850 FIVE D.	$25,000
1850 TEN D.	30,000

BALDWIN & COMPANY

San Francisco 1850

George C. Baldwin and Thomas S. Holman were in the jewelry business in San Francisco and were known as Baldwin & Co. They were the successors to F. D. Kohler & Co., taking over their machinery and other equipment in May, 1850.

	Fine	V. Fine	E. Fine	Unc.
1850 FIVE DOL.	$1,500	$2,300	$4,250	$8,500
1850 TEN DOLLARS — Horseman type	6,250	11,000	18,000	——

1851 TEN D.	3,000	5,000	10,000	——

1851 TWENTY D.	35,000	——

SHULTZ & COMPANY

San Francisco 1851

The firm located in back of Baldwin's establishment operated a brass foundry beginning in 1851. Judge G. W. Shultz and William T. Garratt were partners in the enterprise.

	Fine	V. Fine
1851 FIVE D.	$7,000	$12,000

DUNBAR & COMPANY

San Francisco 1851

Edward E. Dunbar operated the California Bank in San Francisco. He later returned to New York and organized the famous Continental Bank Note Co.

	E. Fine
1851 FIVE D	$37,000

WASS, MOLITOR & COMPANY

San Francisco 1852-1855

The gold smelting and assaying plant of Wass, Molitor & Co. was operated by Count S. C. Wass and A. P. Molitor. They maintained an excellent laboratory and complete apparatus for analysis and coinage of gold.

Large Head — Small Head

	Fine	V. Fine	E. Fine	Unc.
1852 FIVE DOLLARS	$1,000	$1,750	$3,250	$9,000
1852 TEN D. Large head	800.00	1,500	2,500	—
1852 TEN D. Small head	1,500	2,750	4,500	—
1855 TEN D.	3,500	6,500	10,000	—

Large Head

Small Head

	Fine	V. Fine	E. Fine	Unc.
1855 TWENTY DOL. Large head	——	——	——	——
1855 TWENTY DOL. Small head	$3,000	$7,000	$9,000	——

1855 50 DOLLARS	5,500	8,000	15,000	——

KELLOGG & COMPANY

San Francisco 1854-1855

When the U.S. Assay Office ceased operations a period ensued during which no private firm was striking gold. The new San Francisco branch mint did not produce coins for some months after Curtis & Perry took the contract for the government. The lack of coin was again keenly felt by businessmen who petitioned Kellogg & Richter to "supply the vacuum" by issuing private coin. Their plea was answered on Feb. 9, 1854, when Kellogg & Co. placed their first twenty-dollar piece in circulation.

	Fine	V. Fine	E. Fine	Unc
1854 TWENTY D.	$800.00	$1,250	$1,600	$5,000
1855 TWENTY D.	800.00	1,250	1,600	5,000

KELLOGG & COMPANY

	Proof
1855 FIFTY DOLLS.	—

OREGON EXCHANGE COMPANY

Oregon City, 1849

THE BEAVER COINS OF OREGON

On February 16, 1849, the legislature passed an act providing for a mint and specified five and ten dollar gold coins without alloy. Oregon City, the largest city in the territory with a population of about 1,000, was designated as the location for the mint. At the time this act was passed Oregon had been brought into the United States as a territory by act of Congress. When the new governor arrived March 2, he declared the coinage act unconstitutional.

	Fine	V. Fine	E. Fine	Unc.
1849 5 D	$4,000	$7,500	$9,500	—
1849 TEN D	12,500	20,000	30,000	—

MORMON GOLD PIECES

Salt Lake City, Utah 1849-1860

Brigham Young was the instigator of this coinage system and personally supervised the mint which was housed in a little adobe building in Salt Lake City. The mint was inaugurated late in 1849 as a public convenience.

	Fine	V. Fine	E. Fine	Unc.
1849 TWO AND HALF DO	$1,500	$2,500	$3,750	—
1849 FIVE DOLLARS	1,250	1,750	2,750	$6,500

MORMON GOLD PIECES

	Fine	V. Fine
1849 TEN DOLLARS		$45,000
1849 TWENTY DOLLARS	$13,000	19,000

	Fine	V. Fine	E. Fine	Unc.
1850 FIVE DOLLARS	$1,500	$2,000	$3,250	——
1860 5D	2,750	4,500	7,000	$13,000

COLORADO GOLD PIECES

Clark, Gruber & Co. — Denver 1860-1861

Clark, Gruber and Co. was a well known private minting firm in Denver, Colo. in the early sixties.

	Fine	V. Fine	E. Fine	Unc.
1860 2½ D	$350.00	$600.00	$950.00	$3,750
1860 Five D	400.00	750.00	1,200	4,500

1860 TEN D	1,250	1,900	3,750	7,500
1860 TWENTY D	9,000	15,000	30,000	——

COLORADO GOLD PIECES

	Fine	V. Fine	E. Fine	Unc.
1861 2½ D	$400.00	$600.00	$1,000	$4,250
1861 FIVE D.	550.00	850.00	1,600	5,500
1861 TEN D	700.00	900.00	2,000	6,000

1861 TWENTY D	2,000	3,000	8,000	—

JOHN PARSONS & COMPANY

Tarryall Mines — Colorado 1861

Very little is known about the mint of John Parsons and Co. It probably operated in Colorado, near (the original) Tarryall, in the summer of 1861.

PIKES PEAK GOLD

	V. Fine
(1861) Undated 2½ D	$20,000
(1861) Undated FIVE D	30,000

J. J. CONWAY & COMPANY

Georgia Gulch, Colorado, 1861

The value of gold dust caused disagreement among the merchants and the miners in all gold mining areas. The firm of J. J. Conway & Co. solved this difficulty by bringing out its gold pieces in August, 1861.

J. J. CONWAY & COMPANY

		V. Fine
(1861)	Undated 2½ DOLL'S	$20,000
(1861)	Undated FIVE DOLLARS	35,000
(1861)	Undated FIVE DOLLARS, Similar. Variety without numeral 5 on reverse	25,000

(1861)	Undated TEN DOLLARS	21,000

CALIFORNIA SMALL DENOMINATION GOLD

There was a scarcity of small coins during the Californiagold rush and starting in 1852, quarter, half and dollar pieces were privately minted from native gold to alleviate the shortage. The need and acceptability of these pieces declined after 1856 and they then became popular as souvenirs. Authentic pieces all have CENTS, DOLLAR, or an abbreviation thereof on the reverse. The tokens are much less valuable. Modern restrikes and replicas have no numismatic value.

Values are only for genuine coins with the denomination on the reverse expressed as: CENTS, DOL., DOLL., *or* DOLLAR.

		EF-40	AU-50	MS-60
25c Octagonal:	Liberty head	$35.00	$50.00	$100.00
	Indian head	50.00	75.00	125.00
	Washington head	150.00	250.00	350.00
25c Round:	Liberty head	40.00	55.00	100.00
	Indian head	50.00	80.00	150.00
	Washington head	250.00	350.00	450.00
50c Octagonal:	Liberty head	50.00	80.00	120.00
	Liberty head/Eagle	275.00	400.00	625.00
	Indian head	100.00	150.00	225.00
50c Round:	Liberty head	55.00	85.00	125.00
	Indian head	70.00	110.00	185.00
$1.00 Octagonal:	Liberty head	120.00	200.00	250.00
	Liberty head/Eagle	600.00	850.00	1,300
	Indian head	225.00	275.00	450.00
$1.00 Round:	Liberty head	550.00	800.00	1,200
	Indian head	650.00	950.00	1,500

CIVIL WAR TOKENS — 1861-1864

Civil War Tokens are generally divided into two groups: tradesmen's tokens, and anonymously issued pieces with political or patriotic themes. They came into existence only because of the scarcity of government coins and disappeared as soon as the bronze coins of 1864 met the public demand for small copper change.

These tokens are of great variety in composition and design. A number were more or less faithful imitations of the copper-nickel cent. A few of this type have the word "NOT" in very small letters above the words "ONE CENT."

	Fine	*V. Fine*	*Unc.*
Copper or Brass Tokens	$2.00	$3.00	$14.00
Nickel or German Silver Tokens	10.00	18.00	32.00
White Metal Tokens	10.00	20.00	35.00
Copper-Nickel Tokens	18.00	26.00	60.00
Silver Tokens	35.00	50.00	120.00

BULLION VALUE OF COINS

Common date silver coins are valued according to the price of silver bullion. In recent years the price of silver bullion has been subject to extreme fluctuation. Therefore, when you read this it is highly probable that the current bullion price may differ from the prevailing market price used in tabulating valuations of many 19th and 20th century silver coins (priced in italics) listed in this edition. The following chart will help to determine the approximate bullion value of these coins at various price levels. Or, the approximate value may be calculated by multiplying the current spot price of silver times the content for each coin as indicated below. Dealers generally purchase common silver coins at 15% below bullion value, and sell them at 15% above bullion value.

Silver Bullion	*Wartime Nickel .05626 oz.*	*Dime .07234 oz.*	*Quarter .18084 oz.*	*Half Dollar .36169 oz.*	*Silver Clad Half Dollar .14792 oz.*	*Silver Dollar .77344 oz.*
$3.00	$.17	$.22	$.58	$1.09	$.45	$2.32
3.50	.20	.26	.63	1.26	.52	2.71
4.00	.23	.29	.72	1.45	.59	3.09
4.50	.25	.33	.81	1.63	.67	3.48
5.00	.28	.36	.90	1.81	.74	3.87
5.50	.31	.40	1.00	1.99	.81	4.25
6.00	.34	.44	1.09	2.17	.89	4.64

The value of common date gold coins listed in this book may be affected by the rise or fall in the price of gold bullion. Nearly all U.S. gold coins have an additional premium value beyond their bullion content, and thus are not subject to the minor variations described for silver coins. The premium amount is not necessarily tied to the bullion price of gold, but is usually determined by supply and demand levels for actual gold coins occurring in the numismatic marketplace. Because these factors can vary significantly, there is no reliable formula for calculating "percentage above bullion" prices that would remain accurate over time. For this reason the chart below lists bullion values based on gold content only. Consult your nearest coin dealer to ascertain current premium prices.

Price Per Ounce	*$5.00 Liberty Head 1839-1908 Indian Head 1908-1929*	*$10.00 Liberty Head 1838-1907 Indian Head 1907-1933*	*$20.00 1849-1933*
$300.00	72.56	145.13	290.25
325.00	78.60	157.22	314.44
350.00	84.65	169.31	338.63
375.00	90.70	181.40	362.81
400.00	96.75	193.50	387.00
425.00	102.80	205.60	411.19

UNITED STATES BULLION COINS

Silver

Designers: Adolph A. Weinman (obverse), John Mercanti (reverse); composition 99.93% silver, .07% copper; weight 31.101 grams; diameter 40.6mm; net weight one oz. pure silver; reeded edge; mints: Philadelphia, San Francisco.

	Quan. Issued	*Unc.*	*Proof*
$1 1986	5,393,005	$9.00	
$1 1986S	1,446,778		$15.00
$1 1987	11,442,335	5.00	
$1 1987S	(904,732)		14.00
$1 1988	5,004,500	5.50	
$1 1988S	(557,370)		60.00
$1 1989	5,203,327	5.50	
$1 1989S			$14.00
$1 1990	5,840,210	$5.00	
$1 1990S			20.00
$1 1991		5.00	
$1 1991S			20.00
$1 1992		5.00	
$1 1992S			20.00

Gold

Designers: Augustus Saint-Gaudens (obverse), Miley Busiek (reverse); composition, 91.67% gold, 3% silver, 5.33% copper; reeded edge; mints: Philadelphia, West Point.
$50 diameter 32.7mm; weight 33.931 grams; net weight one oz. pure gold.
$25 diameter 27mm; weight 16.966 grams; net weight ½ oz. pure gold.
$10 diameter 22mm; weight 8.483 grams; net weight ¼ oz. pure gold.
$ 5 diameter 16.5mm; weight 3.393 grams; net weight 1/10 oz. pure gold.

	Quan. Issued	*Unc.*	*Proof*
$ 5(1986)	912,609	$35.00	
$ 5(1987)	580,266	35.00	
$ 5(1988)	159,500	35.00	
$ 5(1988)P	(143,881)		$45.00
$ 5(1989)	264,790	37.00	
$ 5(1989)P			45.00
$ 5(1990)	210,210	36.00	
$ 5(1990)P			45.00
$ 5(1991)		36.00	
$ 5(1991)P			45.00
$ 5(1992)		36.00	
$ 5(1992)P			45.00
$10(1986)	726,031	85.00	
$10(1987)	269,255	$85.00	
$10(1988)	49,000	85.00	
$10(1988)P	(98,028)		$95.00
$10(1989)	81,789	85.00	
$10(1989)P			95.00
$10(1990)	41,000	115.00	
$10(1990)P			100.00
$10(1991)		120.00	
$10(1991)P			100.00
$10(1992)		120.00	
$10(1992)P		100.00	
$25(1986)	599,566	170.00	
$25(1987)	131,255	170.00	

UNITED STATES BULLION COINS

	Quan. Issued	Unc.	Proof		Quan. Issued	Unc.	Proof
$25(1987)P	(143,398)		$175.00	$50(1987)	1,045,500	$345.00	
$25(1988)	45,000	$175.00		$50(1987)W	(147,498)		$360.00
$25(1988)P	(76,528)		175.00	$50(1988)	465,000	345.00	
$25(1989)	44,829	175.00		$50(1988)W	(87,133)		375.00
$25(1989)P			190.00	$50(1989)	415,790	345.00	
$25(1990)	31,000	275.00		$50(1989)W			400.00
$25(1990)P			225.00	$50(1990)	373,210	345.00	
$25(1991)		270.00		$50(1990)W			425.00
$25(1991)P			225.00	$50(1991)		345.00	
$25 1992		175.00		$50(1991)W			425.00
$25 1992P			225.00	$50 1992		345.00	
$50(1986)	1,362,650	345.00		$50 1992W			550.00
$50(1986)W	(446,290)		360.00				

ARE YOUR COINS GENUINE . . .

Coin authentication and certification service is available at a fee through the following associations. Coins must not be submitted without first requesting mailing instructions and a schedule of fees charged for this service. Inquiries about coin authentication should be accompanied by a self-addressed stamped envelope and send to:

American Numismatic Association
Certification Service
818 N. Cascade
Colorado Springs, Colo. 80903

International Numismatic Society
Authentication Bureau
P.O. Box 66555
Washington, D.C. 20035

INDEX

LIMITED EDITION, BLUE BOOK MEDAL

In recognition of the 50th Annual edition of Whitman's *Handbook of United States Coins* ("Blue Book"), Whitman® Coin Products is issuing a limited edition, proof-like, one ounce .999 pure silver medal.

It is complimentary to and forms a beautiful collector's set with the special *A Guide Book of United States Coins* ("Red Book") medal. Both of these outstanding medals are excellent gifts and fine keepsakes.

To order your Blue Book Medal, fill in and mail the order blank below (or a copy of it) with check or money order for $9.95 U.S. (plus sales tax where applicable) plus the proof of purchase label from the front cover of this book. (Only one medal may be ordered per proof of purchase.)

I understand I may return the medal within 14 days and receive a full refund if not completely satisfied.

Mail To:
Whitman Coin Department
Western Publishing Company, Inc.
P.O. Box 700, M.S. #438
Racine, WI 53401

Place Proof of
Purchase Label Here

NAME ______________________________
Please Print

ADDRESS ______________________________

CITY ______________ STATE __________ ZIP __________

PLACE OF PURCHASE ______________________________

Offer expires April 30, 1993. This is a limited offer which may be cancelled at any time without notice subject to availability and dependent on bullion price of silver. Good only in Continental U.S.A., Alaska, Hawaii and Canada. **Allow 6-8 weeks for delivery.**

cut along line